Sport in the City

Sport is seen as an increasingly important aspect of urban and regional planning. Related programmes have moved to the forefront of agendas for cities of the present and future. This has occurred as the barriers between so-called 'high' and 'popular' culture continue to disintegrate. Sport is now a key component within strategies for the cultural regeneration of cities and regions, a tendency with mixed outcomes—at times fostering genuinely democratic arrangements, at others pseudo-democratic arrangements—whereby political, business and cultural elites manipulate a sense of sameness and unity among their fellow citizens to smooth the path for the pursuit of what are actually vested interests. Almost any active enactment of a 'sports city of culture' risks divisiveness. Recognizing controversies, with both potentially positive and negative outcomes, this book examines sport within contexts of urban and regional regeneration, via a number of rather different case studies. Within these studies, the role of sport stadium development, franchise expansion and sports-fan (and anti-sport) activism is addressed and articulated with issues concerning, *inter alia*, public funding, environmental impact, urban infrastructure and citizen identity.

The 'sport in the city' project commenced as a research symposium held at the University of Otago, Dunedin, New Zealand and a number of the essays originate from this occasion.

This book was previously published as a special issue of *Sport in Society*.

Michael P. Sam is Senior Lecturer in Sport Policy and Management at the University of Otago, New Zealand.

John E. Hughson is Professor of Sport and Cultural Studies at the University of Central Lancashire, UK.

Sport in the City
Cultural Connections

Edited by
Michael P. Sam and John E. Hughson

Routledge
Taylor & Francis Group

LONDON AND NEW YORK

First published 2011
by Routledge
2 Park Square, Milton Park, Abingdon, Oxon, OX14 4RN

Simultaneously published in the USA and Canada
by Routledge
711 Third Avenue, New York, NY 10017

Routledge is an imprint of the Taylor & Francis Group, an informa business

British Library Cataloguing in Publication Data
A catalogue record for this book is available from the British Library

ISBN 13: 978-0-415-46656-1

Typeset in Times New Roman
by Taylor & Francis Books

Disclaimer
The publisher would like to make readers aware that the chapters in this book are referred to as articles as they had been in the special issue. The publisher accepts responsibility for any inconsistencies that may have arisen in the course of preparing this volume for print.

Printed and bound in Great Britain by
TJI Digital, Padstow, Cornwall

Contents

SPORT IN THE GLOBAL SOCIETY – CONTEMPORARY PERSPECTIVES

Series Editor: Boria Majumdar

SPORT IN THE CITY

Cultural Connections

Sport in the Global Society – Contemporary Perspectives
Series Editor: Boria Majumdar

The social, cultural (including media) and political study of sport is an expanding area of scholarship and related research. While this area has been well served by the Sport in the Global Society Series, the surge in quality scholarship over the last few years has necessitated the creation of *Sport in the Global Society: Contemporary Perspectives*. The series will publish the work of leading scholars in fields as diverse as sociology, cultural studies, media studies, gender studies, cultural geography and history, political science and political economy. If the social and cultural study of sport is to receive the scholarly attention and readership it warrants, a cross-disciplinary series dedicated to taking sport beyond the narrow confines of physical education and sport science academic domains is necessary. Sport in the Global Society: Contemporary Perspectives will answer this need.

Titles in the Series

Sport in the city: cultural and political connections

Michael P. Sam[a] and John E. Hughson[b]

[a]School of Physical Education, University of Otago, New Zealand; [b]School of Sport, Tourism and the Outdoors, University of Central Lancashire, UK

There is little doubt that sport holds a prominent place within cities. Clearly the most glaring examples of sport's influence on the city are in relation to infrastructure. Facilities such as arenas and Olympic-sized swimming pools are what many now come to expect of a modern city. Stadiums in particular are some of the most striking (though not always aesthetically appealing) structures on urban skylines, and are significant for the simple fact that they generate so many spillover effects including: the need to relocate or displace nature, heritage buildings and even citizens; and the need for added public transport and parking facilities. Beyond these structural effects, contemporary civic connections with sport are also significant because they so often reveal a complex process of constructing a credible (but fragile) sense of identity for local citizens. It is telling, for instance, that when civic elites extol (and conflate) sport's links with 'community', they do so for the simple reason that to speak out against one is to speak out against the other.[1]

Indeed the strong connections between sport and the city arise from the almost infinite claims that can be placed on sport in terms of its benefits. In municipalities the world over, the main justifications and debates when it comes to sport concern its capacity to achieve health benefits, reduce crime, relieve neighbourhood tensions, induce economic regeneration, retain 'human capital' and so on. Regardless of the truth of these claims (and the fact that sport can just as easily exacerbate urban problems as 'fix' them), sport's malleable qualities make it a strategic and resilient instrument for any number of interests to mobilize around.

We are grateful to be given this opportunity to pursue our interests in these connections. The seeds for this volume were planted at the 'Sport in the City' symposium held at the University of Otago, Dunedin, New Zealand, in November 2007. The symposium was generously funded by Otago University's School of Physical Education, owing much to the support of the School's then Acting-Dean Michael Boyes. Three of the papers in the volume were presented in earlier versions at the symposium (others have been published in a special issue of the *International Journal of Cultural Policy* 14, no. 4, 2008), viz., the papers by Davies, Kohe, Sam and Scherer, and Spirou. Other papers have been subsequently commissioned.

It has now been a decade since Chris Gratton and Ian Henry's edited collection entitled *Sport in the City: The Role of Sport in Economic and Social Regeneration*. The book is still relevant today because the issues of urban regeneration, mega-events, sport tourism and sport policy remain as interlinked, perennial concerns for cities, aided in large part by the mandates of city economic development units. 'Sport tourism' is now part of the parlance of 'place positioning' strategies and the competition for corporate investment as a means of increasing a city's tax base, has translated directly into cities competing with each other for prominent (as well as not-so-prominent) sporting events.[2]

Despite Gratton and Henry's concluding hopes, for improved output measures and better monitoring of regeneration projects, we are at something of an impasse when evaluating economic and social impacts. The promise of 'better' decision-making and conflict resolution through econometrics is as elusive today as it was throughout the 1980s and 1990s. Indeed, the contradictory interpretations between those who see higher property prices, for example, as a positive economic indicator versus those would argue this to be evidence of a burden on the poor, are indicative of the ease with which impacts can convey contrasting political stories. Perhaps as a consequence of this impasse, there are detectable signs of convergence in how cities portray the influence of sport. Whereas previously the language of sport-city investments revolved around economic spin-offs, the emphasis tends now to be placed on 'legacies'.

On the surface such evolving discourses appear to be a positive development because it means cities now have to demonstrate and plan for the prospect of longer-term benefits to citizens and communities. It is therefore insufficient to simply say that this event or a new stadium will 'put us on the map' (though of course such rhetoric is as common as ever). Instead, proponents now speak of fostering sustainable economic development or of retaining a pool of social and human 'capital'. One popular legacy claimed of large sport events, for example, is the creation of a massive volunteer workforce whose goodwill and skills can be potentially harnessed in the future. In other cases the legacy is meant to be the fostering of a 'cultural common ground' – though, as Hughson points out, civic attempts to bring the arts and sport communities together are more akin to 'bureaucratically engineered amalgams' than genuine efforts towards building a city's cultural citizenship.[3]

Thus while contemporary assurances of deep-seated societal changes and socio-political reforms may well be prophetic, these are often manifested in unintended or unanticipated ways. Time and again we see sport bids and facilities become a polarizing issue, not only because they involve large capital expenditures but also because they invite the consideration of 'opportunity costs' – that is, debates about what other strategies are being foregone. Indeed, successful bids such as those for London 2012 are just as likely to result in delaying needed infrastructure as they are in inducing it. This is not to say that legacies and their spillover effects are all bad – in some cases one might say the acrimonious debates accompanying bids and stadium proposals create a certain (valuable) public 'restlessness'.[4] Though often painted as the result of oppressive forces from the neoliberal order, we should not overlook that stadium plebiscites tend also to generate a wave of interest in civic affairs.

But in the absence of public revolt, there appears no discernable change in the desire for cities to use sport as a policy instrument for economic stimulus. Indeed what we seem to be witnessing in this subsequent generation of public spending is the 'triumph of hope over experience', where such strategies are arguably not chosen because they work, but rather because they fulfil a 'logic of appropriateness'.[5] Put simply, the imperative to 'market' the city is now taken to be a universal axiom and civic officials see the preservation and growth of sport as part of the roles they are expected to play. But as David Whitson warns, 'we have to recognise that our interests as fans, however powerfully felt, may not coincide with our interests as citizens'.[6] One of the key dimensions of sport and cities is therefore the way in which identities are created, changed, exploited. That civic elites and the media have explicitly used sport as a means of creating a sense of sameness is hardly new, but as experience tells us, moulding identities across neighbourhoods that are ethnically, culturally and linguistically diverse can be problematic. This is a common theme and raises questions regarding the extent to which sport in the city shapes civic aspirations, goals and identities. Event bids and stadium redevelopments have often served as the basis for civic elites to encourage citizens to 'think big' and become 'global leaders'.[7]

Costas Spirou's essay in this collection is instructive in this regard, suggesting that US cities are now akin to corporations in their seeking a competitive edge through 'image building activities'. This paper provides an insightful view of the connections between private interests, civic politics and community resistance. It begins by tracing the historical development of urban renewal paradigms along with the growing influence of professional sport. Spirou's case studies then provide a rare view on the intersection of race, class and political representation in Chicago. More uniquely still, the analysis of multiple stadium projects makes it possible to see the overlapping interests and the 'policy learning' that can take place for both proponents and opponents. Typifying the pluralist nature of American politics, Spirou points to the capacity for community groups to extract benefits, but only after observing the fate of other unsuccessful community resistance groups. Business interests meanwhile are entrenched through the legitimacy of public-private partnerships and their role (and influence) is thus assured for the next era of stadium updates and redevelopments.

To stem the tide of what Schimmel calls the fundamental irrationality of public financing of mega sport projects, there remains a need to develop more sophisticated means of evaluating impacts and legacies or at the very least to discern what other variables might count as evidence.[8] An important consideration is therefore: does sport 'work'? To this end, Larissa E. Davies explores the body of evidence surrounding sport-related regeneration initiatives in the UK. Davies outlines how sport has increasingly become part of urban policy initiatives, while at the same time national-level sport policies have themselves embraced the new rationales of regeneration. Thus at both national and local levels, there is a growing demand for evidence to support the view of sport as an industry worthy of local investment. Based on a synthesis of the most common research themes and instruments, Davies argues for a more comprehensive agenda that would include both quantitative and qualitative measures ultimately used for establishing appropriate baselines for future policy makers. In her view, short-term impacts take precedence over more meaningful evaluations of legacies. As Davies suggests, the 2012 Olympic Games therefore represent a timely opportunity to explore local initiatives and the extent of their regenerative capacities. The question, of course, is whether there can be a genuine political will to understand the consequences of large-scale sport investments, particularly when the stakes and risks are so high.

These tensions are at the heart of Sam and Scherer's essay, which investigates the processes of deliberation on a proposed new sport stadium in Dunedin, New Zealand. There are few studies that take the perspective of local government as a starting point; the authors explore the conundrum for local authorities to be both entrepreneurial and publicly accountable. In their view, a key dilemma for decision-makers is the need to balance two contradictory imperatives: in this case the desire for independent (evidence-based) investigations, while also meeting the expectations for economic development/coopera-tion through a public-private partnership. The city's choice to outsource investigations to a 'pro-stadium' organization (whose membership was self-appointed) undeniably created consequences in terms of public responsiveness. Ultimately, Sam and Scherer argue, this had the effect of replacing the institutionalized planning practice of 'prepare, reveal and defend' with a newer mantra of 'delay, market and sell'.

The elephant in the room in such cases is the power to control the nature of debates. In the essay by Sam and Scherer, the Dunedin stadium debates serve as the backdrop against which we see proponents mobilize their interests through the use of internet technologies. Their case outlines stadium proponents' efforts to carve out 'clean' and uncluttered spaces for their rationales and justifications using new media technologies such as YouTube. These highly orchestrated public relations or 'astroturfing' strategies are testament to the importance of bypassing traditional media in order to disseminate unfiltered messages that support the cause. While this case illustrates the counter-measures of opponents, the deliberately insulated platforms are significant from the standpoint that public legitimacy is often already enjoyed by the proponents who are 'first movers' in cyberspace as elsewhere. Indeed the issues raised here touch upon much broader questions around the capacity for citizens to engage in local, politically charged debates. Sam and Scherer thus ask whether the sheer volume of fluctuating material and the often-mystifying use of economic multipliers, amongst other issues, will paradoxically predispose citizens to uncritically accept what is easily available and, in turn, further decertify traditional media.

David Roberts' essay focuses on one of the major global sporting events, the FIFA World Cup (soccer). Written based on research undertaken prior to the staging of this event in South Africa in June/July 2010, Roberts' essay is particularly concerned with the policing measures put in place in the city of Durban for the ostensible purpose of providing a safe environment for tourists for the duration of the World Cup. Roberts contends that the World Cup is being used by Durban (and other host cities) as an opportunity to overcome a growing reputation for lawlessness and disorder in urban South Africa. The plan for the longer-term is for Durban to be imaged as a safe tourist location beyond 2010. The World Cup is thus being used by civic planners to showcase this desired future. However, Roberts contends that the logistical demands required for the policing and associated control measures during the World Cup period will not be sustainable beyond the specific event. This is not to argue that such measures, which in some ways are draconian, should be ongoing but to highlight how a sports mega-event can be politically manipulated and managed to assuage the fears of global tourists about the dangers of urban crime in an otherwise attractive destination city in a key developing nation.

While much of the work spanning sport, cities and culture examines immovable objects, infrastructure and such, there is much less focus on so-called 'tangible movable sport heritage' such as sport museums and halls of fame.[9] Geoffrey Kohe's work presents a case study of a national sport hall of fame (New Zealand's) that offers an opportunity to view the way in which civic spaces devoted to sport can elicit collective memories and identities. His investigation confirms that sport halls of fame are often explicitly intended to instil a sense of nostalgia, reverence and religiosity for sporting figures and heroes. Whilst appreciative of audiences' needs for 'sensuousness' to connect with artefacts, Kohe points out that halls of fame tend to prioritize form over content, introducing a tension between the academic portrayals of history and the more nostalgic depictions of sporting moments. In this light, Kohe advocates for stronger connections between sport historian academics and the sport halls so that these sites can help citizens to better know sport's connections with national culture.

Along similar lines, Sarah Gee and Steven J. Jackson's work reminds us that the sport-city nexus is where a range of cultural identities are given shape. Their paper focuses on a 'local' brewery and brand of beer – Speight's – along with their wider cultural articulations with what the authors call the 'holy trinity' of sport, masculinity and alcohol. Through their examination of places and ad promotions, we are alerted to a particularly localized representation of hegemonic masculinity, one that is produced, represented and consumed through the creation of a mediated 'Speight's Space'. Gee and Jackson point out that the sense of nostalgia used to stimulate memories, perform histories and symbolize identities effectively defines the inhabitants of this 'holy trinity' space and the city itself. These are important considerations, for while sport's indivisible link with alcohol may be a civic concern in terms of public health and safety, it also has some bearing on what it means to be a diehard fan and by extension, a loyal (masculine) citizen. Thus, as the authors conclude, when civic elites argue for a new sport stadium or franchise amidst fears that their city might become a backwater, perhaps they are also signalling deep-seated anxieties about the potential loss of a spatial 'holy trinity'.

Working from a sport-management perspective, Patrizia Zagnoli and Elena Radicchi present an essay considering the role of a 'football fan community' as a key stakeholder within the overall operational environment of a large professional soccer club, the Florence-based AFC Fiorentina. Their paper presents quite a different approach to that from critical sociology, which tends to observe fan groupings as always in potential opposition to football clubs. From the latter perspective, fan groupings provide an important balance, even a core challenge, against the increasing business orientation of football clubs. Contrarily, Zagnoli and Radicchi's starting point is to consider how a range of supporter types can be considered in regard to the 'value creation' they bring to the club in terms of social viability. Working with both qualitative and quantitative data Zagnoli and Radicchi identity sub-categories existing within what they refer to as the 'Viola fan community'. The quantitative dimension of their study brings forward social demographic information about the fan base that would not be available from a purely qualitative approach. Cutting across the fan categories is a 'strong local identity' that Zagnoli and Radicchi attribute to AFC Fiorentina's civic representational status as *the* football club of that city. As a result, they suggest in conclusion, football clubs with a historically embedded unitary civic status experience a tighter bind with fans as stakeholders, which, while not unproblematic, holds significant possibility for the maintenance of a club's 'social network'.

In a rather novel essay Hughson and Kohe set out their plan for 'Groove' a joined-up tourist experience in southern New Zealand from Dunedin to Queenstown. Drawing on the idea of the 'Supercity', taken from the English architect Will Alsop, the authors propose the idea of a 'super region' that would highlight, develop and add to currently existing tourism possibilities. At present Dunedin and Queenstown are administered and promoted as quite discrete tourism experiences. Hughson and Kohe, in an engagement of 'public intellectualism', via the advocacy of a position they refer to as 'postmodern boosterism', contend that both Dunedin and Queenstown, and the towns along their connecting highway, can benefit from a more coordinated approach to tourism planning and delivery. Success of the plan will require a bolstering of regional identity and sport will play a key role in this regard. Hughson and Kohe argue that Groove can serve as a sporting 'brand' not only to help advance this reconstituted identity but to enhance the image and develop the capability of both Dunedin and Queenstown as locations for international sporting fixtures. To this end, the authors controversially support the building of a large-scale stadium complex in Dunedin. However, such support is given within the context of their 'super region' plan rather than a stand-alone initiative for Dunedin. Hughson and Kohe's essay, fanciful as its actual implementation may appear, should prompt thoughts about the promotional and development possibilities of regionally connected tourism for relatively remote locations, especially those with sporting profiles that can be maximized to the benefit of broad-based interests.

As this volume demonstrates, there are a myriad of approaches to researching sport in the city. Perspectives cut across a wide range of disciplines from sociology, economics and urban studies, to public management, politics and cultural studies. This is undoubtedly a strength, insofar as it provides a rich picture of the complexities of the cultural connections that emerge at the sport-city nexus. By the same token, this expanse poses a challenge since most of our analyses use individual case studies that render comparison relatively difficult. Drawing lessons from different national (and municipal) contexts is challenging enough for academics; however, the collated diversity of findings and critiques pose an even greater barrier within the context of evidence-based policy development and enactment. As a consequence much of this work tends to be ignored or dismissed by the very powers who arguably might most benefit from it.

Notes

[1] Ingham and McDonald, 'Sport and Community/Communitas'.
[2] Whitson and Macintosh, 'The Global Circus'.
[3] Hughson, 'Sport and Cultural Policy'.
[4] Sam and Scherer, 'The Steering Group'.
[5] March and Olsen, 'The Logic of Appropriateness'.
[6] In Silver, *Thin Ice*, 8.
[7] Whitson and Horne, 'Underestimated Costs and Overestimated Benefits?'.
[8] Schimmel, 'Deep Play'.
[9] Ramshaw, 'More Than Just Nostalgia'.

References

Gratton, Chris, and Ian P. Henry. *Sport in the City: The Role of Sport in Economic and Social Regeneration*. London, New York: Routledge, 2001.

Hughson, J. 'Sport and Cultural Policy in the Re-Imagined City'. *International Journal of Cultural Policy* 14, no. 4 (2008): 355–60.

Ingham, A.G., and M.G. McDonald. 'Sport and Community/Communitas'. In *Sporting Dystopias: The Making and Meaning of Urban Sport Cultures*, edited by Ralph C. Wilcox, 17–34. Albany: State University of New York Press, 2003.

March, J.G., and J.P. Olsen. 'The Logic of Appropriateness'. In *The Oxford Handbook of Public Policy*, edited by M. Moran, M. Rein, and R.E. Goodin, 689–708. Oxford: Oxford University Press, 2006.

Ramshaw, Gregory. 'More Than Just Nostalgia? Exploring the Heritage/Sport Tourism Nexus'. In *Heritage, Sport and Tourism: Sporting Pasts – Tourist Futures*, edited by Sean Gammon and Gregory Ramshaw, 9–21. London: Routledge, 2007.

Sam, M.P., and J. Scherer. 'The Steering Group as Policy Advice Instrument: A Case of "Consultocracy" in Stadium Deliberations'. *Policy Sciences* 39, no. 2 (2006): 169–81.

Schimmel, K. 'Deep Play: Sports Mega-Events and Urban Social Conditions in the USA'. *The Sociological Review* 54, no. 2 (2006): 160–74.

Silver, Jim. *Thin Ice: Money, Politics and the Demise of an NHL Franchise*. Halifax, NS: Fernwood Publishing, 1996.

Whitson, D., and J. Horne. 'Underestimated Costs and Overestimated Benefits? Comparing the Outcomes of Sports Mega-Events in Canada and Japan'. *Sociological Review* 54, no. 2 (2006): 71–89.

Whitson, D., and D. Macintosh. 'The Global Circus: International Sport, Tourism, and the Marketing of Cities'. *Journal of Sport and Social Issues* 20 (1996): 278–95.

Cultural policy and the dynamics of stadium development

Costas Spirou

Department of Social and Behavioral Sciences, National-Louis University, Chicago, USA

Cities across the United States increasingly turn to culture industries as a way to revitalize their urban cores and re-image themselves to both residents and prospective visitors. It is expected that this strategy will differentiate cities, bringing about widespread economic benefits at a time of intense inter-city competition. This essay examines how professional sports fit this dynamic and specifically discusses the important role that stadium development plays in advancing a related public-policy agenda. By reviewing the plans for four stadium-development projects in Chicago, this contribution reveals the complexities of these practices, which rarely consider the impact on the neighbourhoods themselves. The unanticipated outcomes of these processes are often shaped by race, class, varying political actors and community organizations.

Introduction

During the last decade, American cities have engaged in a complex process of attempting to remake themselves by utilizing cultural strategies to craft new urban identities and by employing numerous initiatives aimed at reviving and growing their local economies. In response to fiscal pressures and other larger socio-economic structural changes, cities have aggressively embarked on plans to de-emphasize images of their past. In turn, they are endeavouring to replace those identities by constructing new, culturally based representations relying on entertainment, leisure and urban tourism. Museums, festivals, revamped public spaces, tourism bubbles, sports stadiums, theatre districts, ethnic precincts, convention centres and urban beautification programmes are some of the tools utilized to advance a new direction.

This trend is clearly communicated by the results of a national survey of city halls, which found that tourist and entertainment infrastructures have recently emerged as primary forms of public investment in cities across the country.[1] City Hall officials of 458 cities in the United States reported that they either already have in place or are currently developing facilities for the creation of historic districts (76%), museums (69%), performing arts centres (58%), entertainment and restaurant districts (58%), festivals (55%), outdoor concert venues (49%), cultural districts (48%), waterfront development (41%), convention hotels (41%), convention centers (40%), sports stadiums (39%) and recreation facilities (30%).

Culture-driven strategies have also been fuelled by the fact that citizens now have more leisure-expendable income than ever before. This has led city governments to increase expenditure on culture and specialized bureaucracies. Policy-making bodies ventured to enhance their provision of cultural services in order to cater to a growing, more sophisticated and differentiated public demand. The outcome of these trends resulted in the development of an economy of urban tourism. As a result we can observe cities and their governments turning their attention to showcasing their heritage and exporting their cultural identity, hoping to translate these policies into revenue streams capable of social and economic transformation.

This essay focuses on one aspect of this culture-driven regeneration policy, specifically the use of professional sport and its main infrastructure, the stadium. Cities in the United States are rejuvenating their downtowns through massive expenditure in the form of stadium construction. Many of these facilities became part of a publicly funded trend in hopes of economically rescuing and revitalizing ailing neighbourhoods and reversing trends of chronic decline and disinvestment. 'Pumping money' into a downtown is often the driving force behind recent stadium location decisions. Framed within the cultural realm of urban redevelopment, this strategy has increasingly become a central facet of contemporary planning initiatives.

Urban restructuring and the search for new alternatives

The end of World War II signalled extensive structural transformations that came to reshape American cities. The leadership of urban centres in the 1950s and 1960s continued to view fiscal growth opportunities in the same manner as their predecessors approached city building decades earlier. Investment in manufacturing, reliance on the export-base theory as the prominent mode of assessing current and future economic development opportunities and growth outcomes, emphasis on the downtown as the main core for financial activity, and upgrading infrastructure to provide support and help cities respond to the rising use of automobile and air travel via the construction of highways and airports dominated the economic-development thinking at the time.[2] Sport, tourism and related cultural forms did not fit the planning mix and were viewed, at best, as an inconsequential element of financial activity.[3]

Ill-equipped and without a strategy in place to address the significant changes that followed, cities simply proved incapable of providing an effective response to extensive economic restructuring resulting from de-industrialization and decentralization. Population and business flight to the suburbs was more than a statistical reality. Its implications meant massive job losses, significant increases in social problems, a diminishing tax base, reduced city services and rapid urban decay. The mismatched, pro-growth, post-war policies unfortunately also reached into the response cycle. The introduction of urban renewal programmes failed to resurrect these once dominant cities and edge cities began to form, gaining further financial prominence in outlying suburbia.

While urban restructuring was in full force, another set of changes were also in effect. Advances in technology, expanding levels of education, the rapid emergence of the media in mainstream America, swift economic growth and other, related sociological factors gave rise to additional leisure time. These forces, following World War II, altered the nature of leisure from being passive to being active, provided greater discretionary income, eased travel, professionalized tourism, increased business travel and injected strong elements of Fordism into the culture/tourist industry.[4]

It is within this context that the dynamics of local governing becomes altered as a response to the condition of the cities referenced above. The growing economic decline, the impact of globalization which substantially reduced the primacy of US production activities, and the diminished contributions by the federal government to the cities and states, all revealed an unfavourable picture as officials increasingly faced a new fiscal reality of shrinking budgets and services. Cities responded by divorcing themselves from their manufacturing dependency, searching to diversify and strengthen the various sectors of their economy. Urban tourism thus emerges as an appealing alternative, one that slowly has gained favour by local officials and civic boosters.

As cities searched to develop or enhance their spaces and rushed to take advantage of this new growth potential, they faced numerous challenges mainly in the areas of urban identity and urban competition. Specifically, how can a city with a formerly strong and nationally/internationally identifiable manufacturing economy convert itself into a tourist/sports destination? Most importantly, how does it convince potential visitors of its new services and sense of 'attractiveness'? Similarly what are its advantages within this reformulated environment?

The rise of urban tourism injected competition and required cities to be entrepreneurial and business like in their approach. In *Marketing Places: Attracting Investment, Industry, and Tourism to Cities, States and Nations*, international marketing guru Philip Kotler along with Donald H. Haider and Irving Rein definitively make the point that competition is a new inherent reality that cannot be avoided: 'Places have to visualize a clearer sense of the functions they perform and the roles they play....A place that fails to examine its prospects and potential critically is likely to lose out to more attractive competitors.'[5] In that context the city is not different from the corporation which must engage in image building activities, promote its products and be prepared to deal with change if it wants to maintain its competitive edge and grow its market share.

Given this new economic outlook, it is apparent that the financial stakes are very high for cities. According to Kotler, Haider and Rein,

> Tourism and the business hospitality market have emerged as viable place development strategies on a footing equal to business retention, business attraction, grow your own business, and export development/reverse investment. In a service-driven economy of aging population, these two businesses are generally expected to grow at rates ahead of the national economy.[6]

The competition for tourists has had a tremendous impact on cities as spatial transformation, increased commodification, rapid segmentation of urban form and function, and new economic and planning mechanisms became widely introduced. The 'tourist bubble' emerged as a common restructuring strategy depicting tourist spaces as destination spots across American cities.[7] Convention centres, theme parks, stadium developments and casino and riverboat gambling reshaped the physical landscape and image of hundreds of dying urban cores. Thus, professional sports and the stadium become part of the new city of leisure that aims to attract locals and visitors, extensively reshaping planning policies and priorities.[8]

The political economy of sports stadium development

Cities across the United States have devoted huge sums of public money to finance the construction of sports arenas. To justify this public expenditure, supporters of these projects have used economic impact studies and multiplier calculations, which purport to measure positive direct and indirect economic outcomes, and have cited various non-economic benefits, notably the community-building and cultural identification functions of sporting events. Yet even with the emerging corporatization of sport and its maturation as a culture industry, there remains considerable uncertainty concerning the utility of these construction projects as tools for economic development and urban regeneration.

From 1970 to 1990 the proportion of publicly owned facilities used by professional sports teams increased from 70% to 80%.[9] Driven by intense inter-municipal competition, huge public investments have aimed to retain or attract professional sports franchises. More recently, from 1993 to 1996, $7 billion dollars was spent on the construction and renovation of major league facilities. The public sector provided 80% of these funds resulting in the introduction of 50 new stadiums across the various US professional leagues.[10] Analogous pressures are felt by smaller cities – the typical homes of minor league sports franchises – which recognize that if they do not pay for the upgrading of local arenas, other cities will accommodate franchises in the hunt for more commodious 'home fields'.[11]

This development craze has persisted in the last few years. For example, from 2000 to 2009, 12 new stadiums have been developed in the National Football League (NFL) at a cost of $5.9 billion (average of $491 million per project). More impressively, the four new stadiums that are either under construction, planned or proposed are at a staggering total cost of $4.2 billion. Two of those under development are for $1.4 billion (New York) and $1 billion (San Diego).

Since 2000, Major League Baseball (MLB) has seen the introduction of 11 new stadiums totalling $4.6 billion. In addition, two new baseball stadiums are under construction for over $1 billion and others are planned or proposed in the league at a cost of $3.3 billion. For example, the new Yankee Stadium in New York City with a capacity of 51,800 opened in 2009 with an astonishing price tag of $1.3 billion.

These massive expenditures are driven by the profit motivation of team owners and the shifting economics of professional sports. By the 1970s, television broadcasts were the primary revenue source for major league teams. Stadium revenues from ticket sales, in effect, became an auxiliary source of profit. As a result, the owners of sports franchises supported the construction of multi-purpose facilities with large seating capacities. The outcome of this trend was a clutch of mammoth sports complexes, both domed stadiums and bowl-like structures, including Three Rivers Stadium (1970) in Pittsburgh, Riverfront Stadium (1970) in Cincinnati and Veterans Stadium (1971) in Philadelphia. By the mid-1980s, the prospect of boosting on-site revenue through the sale of luxury seating and the provision of associated luxury services, led to the physical reconfiguration of many such structures. Luxury seating increasingly became an extremely attractive profit centre.

The economics of upscale sports viewing has also produced a new type of sports arena. The expectation of private viewing environments and the infrastructure requisites for delivering an array of foods, beverages, and other commodities, dictated various design innovations. The current trend in stadiums favours single-purpose facilities that make room for restaurants and taverns, gift shops, and in some cases, overnight accommodations.

When the TD Banknorth Garden, home of the Boston Celtics of the National Basketball Association and of the Boston Bruins of the National Hockey League, opened in 1995 it featured state-of-the-art amenities. Among the facilities' marvels were portable computers providing 'In-Seat Wait Service'. Patrons of the Club Seat section of the arena can use a handheld device to order food and beverages from a full-range menu. The arena's management guarantees that food delivery is performed within a five-minute period from the time of order. These services are now standard and are found across almost all new sporting venues.

Because of these design fads, franchise owners increasingly turned to cities and public coffers to underwrite new facilities. Given the presumed economic and civic benefits derived from the hosting of sports franchises, municipal sponsorship of stadium projects is easily rationalized as a powerful economic development tool. The drive to attract teams is consistent with, indeed integral to, the municipal growth ideology. Cities thus compete with each other to attract existing clubs or to win the honour of hosting an expansion team. The justification for subsidies to often-profitable professional teams grows from the perception that public funding constitutes a form of capital investment and, as such, is akin to other urban redevelopment outlays.

As an inducement to the appropriation of public funds for stadium development, team owners routinely threaten to relocate their franchises, playing one city against another. For example, in the NFL from 1982 to 1997 there were seven team relocations (Oakland Raiders, Baltimore Colts, St Louis Cardinals, Los Angeles Rams, Los Angeles Raiders, Cleveland Browns, and the Houston Oilers), all driven by the prospect of expanded team profitability as a result of stadium replacement or upgrading. Currently, Los Angeles and San Antonio are searching for an NFL team and are prepared to provide considerable financial incentives to succeed.

Another trend has included the construction of new stadiums in downtown areas. From 1998–2009, 15 new stadiums were built in the NFL at a cost nearing $5 billion. Eleven of them were developed in downtown or urban areas and only four in suburban areas. Overall, as Table 1 shows below, more than half of the 32 NFL teams have downtown or urban stadiums. A similar trend can be observed in MLB (Table 2).

The revenues underwriting the construction of sports arenas in the NFL come primarily from taxes and bonds. Property taxes, sales taxes (Cincinnati and Tampa), sports lottery revenues (Maryland for the Baltimore Ravens), motel/hotel taxes (Chicago, Detroit, Nashville, St Louis), rental car surcharges (Chicago, Detroit, Houston), team merchandise and ticket taxes (Nashville), stadium parking surcharges (Seattle), alcohol and cigarette taxes (Cleveland), and restaurant meal taxes (Detroit) are used to fund stadium building.[12] Sales tax revenues are the most common form of sports facility financial stream. The economically regressive impact of sales tax collections means that the poor and underprivileged pay more than their fair share of the stadium development costs.

A new wrinkle in the financing of sports facilities is the location of stadiums within entertainment districts, the latter providing a revenue base to fund construction and upkeep. In California we can observe efforts to underwrite a refurbished Los Angeles Coliseum and in turn, return the NFL to that city. Further south, San Diego is in the process of rebuilding Qualcomm Stadium and financing a new baseball stadium for the Padres (MLB). Both of these efforts are conceptualized around the entertainment district concept.

In 2004, in Washington DC, proposed plans for two stadiums, one for soccer and the other for baseball, not only touted the direct economic impact but also conveyed broader benefits. According to Mark Tuohey, chairman of the D.C. Sports and Entertainment Commission, 'City stadiums are successful where you combine the stadium with economic stimulus in the surrounding area. Having the stadiums in close proximity I think benefits the entire area around them.'[13] In this regard, proponents of this project also outlined an adjacent entertainment district with retail shops, outdoor music in the summer and additional recreational opportunities.

The case of Chicago

By the 1960s and 1970s it became obvious that old port and industrial cities across the United States were in trouble. Chicago fit this profile. Often called 'Beirut by the lake' for its intense and nationally profiled council wars of the 1980s, the phrase could also have been used to describe Chicago's socially and economically depressed neighbourhoods. The city aggressively pursued federal funds until the 1970s, when it increasingly turned its efforts to local economic development. The tourist strategy, which can be traced to the 1950s with the building of McCormick Place (city's convention centre), received a shot in the arm with the election of Mayor Richard M. Daley in 1989.

Table 1. Urban/suburban stadium locations in the National Football League, 2010

Downtown/Urban
- Atlanta Falcons: Georgia Dome (1992) at $210 million
- Baltimore Ravens: M & T Bank Stadium (1998) at $220 million
- Carolina Panthers: Bank of America Stadium (1996) at $248 million
- Chicago Bears: Soldier Field (2003) at $425 million
- Cincinnati Bengals: Paul Brown Stadium (2000) at $453 million
- Cleveland Browns: Cleveland Browns Stadium (1999) at $290 million
- Denver Broncos: Invesco Field (2001) at $364 million
- Detroit Lions: Ford Field (2002) at $500 million
- Green Bay Packers: Lambeau Field (1957) at $1 million
- Indianapolis Colts: Lucas Oil Stadium (2008) at $625 million
- Jacksonville Jaguars: Jacksonville Municipal Stadium (1995) at $134 million
- Minnesota Vikings: Metrodome (1982) at $68 million (currently under negotiations for a new $954 million stadium)
- New Orleans Saints: Superdome (1975) at $134 million (currently under negotiations for a new $450 million stadium)
- Pittsburgh Steelers: Heinz Field (2001) at $281 million
- St. Louis Rams: Edward Jones Dome (1995) at $281 million
- Seattle Seahawks: Quest Field (2002) at $450 million
- Tampa Bay Buccaneers: Raymond James Stadium (1998) at $168.5 million
- Tennessee Titans: LP Field (1999) at $292 million

Suburban
- Arizona Cardinals: University of Phoenix Stadium (2006) at $455 million
- Buffalo Bills: Ralph Wilson Stadium (1973) at $22 million
- Dallas Cowboys: Texas Stadium (1971) at $39 million (Cowboys Stadium opened in 2009 for $1.3 billion)
- Houston Texans: Reliant Stadium (2002) at $352 million
- Kansas City Chiefs: Arrowhead Stadium (1968) at $43 million
- Miami Dolphins: Pro Player Stadium (1987) at $115 million (upcoming renovations are expected to exceed $300 million)
- New England Patriots: Gillette Stadium (2002) at $325 million
- New York Giants/Jets: Giants Stadium (new stadium opened in 2010 for $1.4 billion)
- Oakland Raiders: McAfee Coliseum (1966) at $200 million with recent renovations
- Philadelphia Eagles: Lincoln Financial Field (2003) at $512 million
- San Diego Chargers: Qualcomm Stadium (1967) at $27 million (currently under negotiations for a new $400 million stadium)
- San Francisco 49ers: Monster Park (1971) at $24 million (currently under negotiations for a new stadium)
- Washington Redskins: FedEx Field (1997) at $300 million

Note: construction year in parenthesis; cost in millions.

In response to the anxiety caused by deindustrialization, suburbanization and the general urban decline, the current mayor's father, Mayor Richard J. Daley (1955–1976), aggressively pursued a downtown redevelopment strategy that focused on office construction and the residential expansion of the Loop (Central Business District). But by the 1990s, like many other cities, Chicago was operating within a new set of guidelines, framed by the complex forces of globalization. Achieving economic growth and attracting capital in this recast environment would require the development of a new infrastructure, making Chicago attractive to locals and visitors and economically successful as well.

Richard M. Daley's undertaking of a massive public works programme transformed the city's economy and built environment. Projects have included (among others) the renovation and redesign of Navy Pier (entertainment district) in 1995 ($250 million), the Lakefront Millennium Park project in 2004 ($500 million), the reconfiguration of Lake

Table 2. Urban/suburban stadium locations in Major League Baseball, 2010

Downtown/Urban
- Arizona Diamondbacks: Chase Field (1998) at $355 million
- Atlanta Braves: Turner Field (1996) at $210 million
- Baltimore Orioles: Oriole Park at Camden Yards (1992) at $110 million
- Boston Red Sox Fenway Park (1912) at $14 million
- Chicago Cubs: Wrigley Field (1914) at $250,0000
- Chicago White Sox: U.S. Cellular Field (1991) at 160 million
- Cincinnati Reds: Great American Ball Park (2003) at $290 million
- Cleveland Indians: Progressive Field (1994) at $175 million
- Colorado Rockies: Coors Field (1995) at $300 million
- Detroit Tigers: Comerica Park (2000) at $300 million
- Houston Astros: Minute Maid Park (2000) at $255 million
- Minnesota Twins: Metrodome (1982) at $68 million (in 2010 opened Target Field in downtown Minneapolis for an estimated $545 million).
- New York Yankees: Yankee Stadium (2009) $1.3 billion
- Pittsburgh Pirates: PNC Park (2001) at $230 million
- St. Louis Cardinals: Busch Stadium (2006) at $360 million
- San Diego Padres: PETCO Park (2004) at $450 million
- San Francisco Giants: AT&T Park (2000) at $355 million
- Seattle Mariners: Safeco Field (1999) at $520 million
- Toronto Blue Jays: Rogers Centre (1989) at $570 million
- Washington Nationals: Nationals Park (2008) at $611 million

Suburban
- Florida Marlins: LandShark Stadium (1987) at $115 million (currently under development Miami Ballpark for an estimated $515 million scheduled to open in 2012 in downtown Miami).
- Tampa Bay Rays: Tropicana Field (1988) $130 million
- Kansas City Royals: Kauffman Stadium (1973) $43 million (underwent $250 million upgrades in 2010).
- Los Angeles Angels: Anaheim Angel Stadium of Anaheim (1966) at $24 million (underwent $120 million in renovations in 1999).
- Texas Rangers Rangers: Ballpark in Arlington (1994) at $190 million
- Los Angeles Dodgers: Dodger Stadium (1962) at $21 million
- Milwaukee Brewers: Miller Park (2001) at $385 million
- Oakland Athletics: Oakland-Alameda County Coliseum (1966) at $26 million (underwent a $200 million renovation in 1996)
- New York Mets: Citi Field (2009) at $900 million
- Philadelphia Phillies: Citizens Bank Park (2004) at $460 million

Note: construction year in parenthesis; cost in millions

Shore Drive and the creation of the Museum Campus in 1998 ($110 million), the rebuilding of Soldier Field (stadium) in 2003 ($678 million), and the expansion of McCormick Place Convention Center, first in 1996 ($675 million) and again in 2008 ($850 million). In 2003 the Mayor closed Meigs Field, a small business airport along the lakefront, as a preliminary step to turning the space into a mixed-use natural area. The city's bid for the 2016 Olympics rivals that of any other in the world.

Professional sports in Chicago have a significant value beyond the action on the field. When the Chicago Bears of the NFL threatened to leave the city in the early 1990s, a *Chicago Tribune* commentary responded: 'The Bears have long been a unifying element for a city where North Side, South Side, West Side, and the Loop all distrust one another, where the Sox and the Cubs split the baseball community and where racial divisions run below the surface like so many fault lines.'[14] The same commentary concluded:

The Bears, more than any other Chicago franchise, represent every cherished character trait and every tour-bus cliche that gives the city its identity. Thinking of big shoulders? Think Dick Butkus. The ethnic success story? Think Bears founder George Halas, the son of Bohemian immigrants. Personalities as unforgiving as steel? Think 'Iron Mike' Ditka. Tough but graceful architecture? Think of Walter Payton's bruising and balletic build. The beautiful lakefront? Think Soldier Field. The brutal Chicago weather? Think Bear weather. The Bears are the only reason Chicagoans can take pride in our miserable winter.[15]

It is within this broad framework that Chicago embraced stadium development by replacing and/or upgrading the playing venues of its professional teams. The 'old' Chicago stadiums, Comiskey Park (1910) on the south side and Chicago Stadium (1929) on the west side respectively gave way to the New Comiskey Park (1991), since renamed US Cellular Field, and to the United Center (1994). In 2003 the New Soldier Field replaced the original facility built in 1924. Furthermore, in 1988, Wrigley Field (1914) was updated through the addition of field lighting.

Chicago's stadium stories differ from those of other cities due to their unique real estate location. Three of the above mention stadiums are positioned within residential neighbourhoods. This fact introduces an additional player into the government/corporate ownership arena: the communities themselves. Finally, an analysis of these cases provides us with interesting insights on the complex dynamics of urban stadium development.

Corporate search for profit and the community response

The Chicago cases reveal how corporate interests dominate the genesis of proposed facility development and upgrading projects, leaving local and state governments in positions of reaction, rather than leading the charge for change. Ownership of the White Sox (baseball) called for a new stadium in the 1980s as did the Cubs (baseball) which, during a similar timeframe, expressed their desire for the installation of lights at Wrigley Field and the inclusion of night games. Since the middle part of the 1980s the ownership of the Bears (football) sought a replacement structure and in the late 1980s, the ownership of the Blackhawks (hockey) and of the Bulls (basketball) outlined their need for a new home on the Near West Side. At the core of these plans is the common desire to create new environments capable of producing conditions necessary for expanding profit.

At the same time, the community response to these projects differed. The variation in community mobilization, racial and ethnic make-up, current political capital, history of community organizing and the role of the municipal government produced unique outcomes. Because of these variations, the residents in South Armour Square (New Comiskey Park for the White Sox) and other groups, proved incapable of halting the construction of the new facility. In Lake View (Wrigley Field for the Cubs), a determined, well-organized opposition managed to not only limit the development plans but to also extract the implementation of numerous community protection plans from the city and the team. On the Near West Side (United Center for Blackhawks and Bulls), numerous negotiations between neighbourhood organizations and the team ownership provided limited community-wide benefits while directly addressing the housing needs of those displaced by the project.

The Chicago White Sox: the acquisition of a new, publicly funded stadium

Following the purchase of the Chicago White Sox by a group of investors early in 1981, it quickly became apparent that the new leadership of Jerry Reinsdorf and Eddie Einhorn had a new agenda for their newly acquired franchise and field. Built in 1910, Comiskey Park lacked luxury skyboxes. Furthermore, columns provided structural support to the upper deck but produced 2000 obstructed-view seats. In comparison, newer stadiums like Riverfront (1970) in Cincinnati and Royals Stadium (1973) in Kansas City did not have even one column-obstructed seat.[16]

White Sox ownership successfully declared the structure deteriorated, with serious structural flaws, requiring 'significant expenditures on an annual basis to keep the park in safe and usable condition'.[17] The team then opened up to explore 'the market' and search for a new facility. By the mid-1980s, the White Sox had engaged in talks with suburban Addison, Illinois and St Petersburg, Florida, and made it clear that without public support they would leave Chicago.

Suburban Addison was a legitimate option since it could bring the White Sox near their fan base in wealthy DuPage County and the availability of a 140-acre parcel in the community owned by the White Sox made it an attractive option.[18] The Sox proceeded to outline the extensive economic benefits of $41.4 million for the county and $1.7 million for the city.[19] The effort to relocate collapsed since in a close referendum vote 50.3% voted against the proposal of housing the White Sox in Addison.

Reinsdorf and Einhorn then turned to St Petersburg, Florida, after declaring that the Illinois State legislature and the City of Chicago were not moving fast enough to accommodate the needs of the franchise. South Florida wanted to attract a professional baseball team and the 'troubles' of the White Sox in Chicago made them a likely candidate. City officials expressed their commitment to the team by offering to complete a facility under construction by the start of the 1989 season. The Florida State legislature supported a fast-track release of an additional $30 million to meet that goal.

In Chicago, extensive economic justification arose arguing for retaining the team. In 1986, a Department of Economic Development, City of Chicago, study argued that a new stadium development would have considerable benefits and incentives for the local economies. The study concluded that: 'a team is a substantial source of revenue for the City, County and State'.[20] Furthermore, stories in the local press echoed similar findings, arguing that the White Sox in Chicago would help 'retain an estimated $112 million to $162 million in annual local spending, taxes and economic activity'.[21]

In July of 1988, fearing loss of the team, State of Illinois Governor Thompson signed the White Sox deal. The agreement provided the team with a new, publicly funded stadium costing in excess of $150 million. The legislative act also gave the White Sox exclusive rights to sales within and around the new ballpark and additional ticket purchases would be provided by the state if minimum annual ticket sales were not met. Taxpayer dollars would be used for annual maintenance. The construction of the 'New Comiskey Park' (renamed US Cellular Field in 2003), to be located across from the old Comiskey Park in the community of the South Armour Square, would require the acquisition of land resulting in housing and business removal. The relocation costs were also covered by the act.

South Armour Square was an African-American community located south of the old ballpark. It only covered 15 city blocks and prior to the construction of the new ballpark it had about 1500 residents. This was not an economically thriving community, but it possessed a strong sense of residential identity that dated back to decades earlier. In fact, like other south-side neighbourhoods, South Armour square was the recipient of many African Americans migrating from the agricultural south to the industrial north. But South Armour lacked longstanding community organization structures and the prospect of removing a large section of its housing stock for the new stadium caused anxiety and confusion.

In 1987 and 1988, the residents engaged in organizational efforts under the South Amour Square Neighborhood Coalition group, and held demonstrations in City Hall and other public spaces. Their goal was to attract citywide attention to their plight. They also attempted to utilize the existing political channels by engaging their 11th Ward Alderman Patrick Huels. Connecting with City Hall proved unsuccessful since Huels' political base derived from the predominantly white community of Bridgeport to the north. In the end, 178 privately owned housing units and 12 community businesses were removed to make room for the new stadium.

The Tribune Company: turning the Cubs into a profitable holding

Following the purchase of the Chicago Cubs and Wrigley Field in 1981 by the Tribune Company, the corporation began to explore ways of complementing the teams' activities to its other assets. The Tribune holdings in Chicago included the influential daily *Chicago Tribune*, and the WGN broadcast station (WGN-Radio and WGN-TV). The television arm of WGN at that time was broadcasting programming nationally. From the very beginning, the new ownership considered the Cubs an excellent addition to its media unit.

The Cubs, however, played at historic Wrigley Field in the near north-side community of Lake View. In addition to its unique architectural characteristics, the ballpark was the only facility in the professional baseball league to hold exclusively day games. Without field lights, Wrigley posed a serious drawback to the plans of the Tribune Co., to transform and mass-market its new commodity via programming across the country and increase advertising revenue.

The Cubs pursued a three-prong strategy to meet their goals. First, they outlined the team's contribution to the city's economy. Second, they showcased the importance of the team to the fans; and third, they focused on conveying the value of historic Wrigley Field. If the team did not get approval for lights, its departure to a suburban location would result in the demolition of the ballpark. According to Donald Grenesko, then Cubs vice-president for operations: 'Lights is still our first choice and without them we cannot stay at Wrigley.'[22]

The franchise commissioned a number of studies showing that the Cubs were Chicago's favourite professional team (77.4%) and that the majority of the fans (64.6%) were willing to accept either unrestricted use of lights, or lights at 18–20 games during the season.[23] In another report, the Cubs showed that an overwhelming majority (77.6%) of those living within a half-mile of Wrigley viewed the ballpark as a neighbourhood asset[24] and that the annual contribution of the Cubs to the local economy was $90.7 million.[25] That same year, a City of Chicago Department of Economic Development study concluded that 'the consulting reports prepared come to remarkably similar conclusions about the total impact of a baseball team on the local economy – about $100 million'.[26]

Community organizations in Lake View managed the proposed installation of lights at Wrigley Field much differently than had the Comiskey Park residents. Lake View had been an old established community, with predominantly white residential neighbour-hoods, relatively high family incomes and stable property values. The area experienced population declines following the 1950s. But in the 1980s, housing along the lakefront had become quite pricey, a trend that continued in the 1990s. Historically active community organizations such as the Lake View Community Council (LVCC) rejected the team's proposal. Another group, the Citizens United for Baseball in the Sunshine (CUBS), looked to connect fans and residents in an effort to oppose the corporate ambitions.

The LVCC, the CUBS and the local alderman engaged in an anti-lights campaign arguing that the installation of lights would bring increased traffic, noise, vandalism, rowdiness, drunkenness, decreased property values and related negative community consequences. Community meetings were well attended, often with more than 350 residents on hand, formal press releases, and with the local print and broadcast media present to interview community organizers. The Lake View residents proved a formidable opponent for the Cubs as they employed a multitude of strategies. They engaged in early advocacy on traffic issues through the Wrigley Field Operations Committee, threatened legal action, advanced a non-binding referendum, enlisted local political support, promoted community-wide involvement, and campaigned to eliminate alcohol consumption.

An eventual compromise meant that in exchange for the implementation of lights at Wrigley, the expressed concerns of the residents would be seriously considered and resolved. Those benefits were outlined as part of the neighbourhood protection plan, which required continuous annual review. The Neighborhood Protection and Improvement Plan was central to negotiations and regular discussions among city, community and Cubs' representatives to address and ensure the viability of the neighbourhood. A residential parking permit programme and a police hotline was added. Bus service to the area was expanded. Police presence to assist with area traffic and to address fan-related disorderly conduct was increased, and a new litter control program requiring the participation of the team was instituted. The Cubs also agreed to restrict the sale of beer during the games and to advance the entire plan through their public relations mechanisms.[27]

Sports-driven proposals and eventual compromise in the Near West Side

Located within minutes from the Loop, the Near West Side was viewed in the 1980s as the preferred location for stadium development. The area had originally been mentioned as a potential site for a new White Sox stadium. The Chicago Bears, following their Super Bowl victory in 1986, also sought to construct a playing facility there in the late 1980s. Eventually, the United Center (1994) did make the area its home. The facility was built for the Bulls (NBA) and for the Blackhawks (NHL), replacing the ageing, nearby Chicago Stadium (1929).

In August of 1988, the ownership of the Bulls and Blackhawks proposed an alternative to the Chicago Stadium. Lacking luxury seating, restaurants and new concession areas meant limited profit potential, especially at a time when Michael Jordan and the Bulls were unquestionably the 'hottest' ticket in town and a national and international sports attraction. Chicago Stadium owner Bill Wirtz described the Chicago Stadium as 'economically obsolete' and according to a source close to the owner: 'There comes a point when you realize that you could hurt the health of the franchise by not making a move. The numbers right now don't favor keeping things the way they are.'[28]

The Near West Side was subjected to massive losses of capital in the late 1960s following the destructive riots after the death of Martin Luther King Jr in 1968. Continuous loss of manufacturing jobs and businesses to the suburbs and other states in the 1970s and 1980s exacerbated the problem. These trends created available land, resulting in large-scale institutional construction projects such as the Henry Horner Homes, a high-rise public housing development. Later developments included the University of Illinois at Chicago, Malcolm X College and the expansion of the nearby Medical Center. Predominantly lower income and African American, the Near West Side experienced intense poverty and other social problems. As a result it came to be viewed by developers and the local media as a politically, economically and physically disorganized community.

Led by the Interfaith Organizing Project (IOP), a coalition of clergy and lay-persons, area residents questioned this form of urban redevelopment. The group was formed in 1985 to battle a massive, twin-stadium proposal advanced by the Chicago Bears, the

Chicago White Sox and the nearby Medical Center. That sports complex would have replaced half of the area neighbourhoods. The plan came to be viewed as a land grab by white developers, and as a case where the poor would lose out to the wealthy downtown interests. Residents participated in numerous marches and protests. They attended meetings with city officials and held mock-funerals of their neighbourhood. The lack of community-wide support for this stadium-development plan and the uncertainty of financial revenue provided by the federal government made Illinois State legislators indifferent to the proposal.

After observing the scrimmages between the local community and the Bears on the proposed stadium construction, Jerry Reinsdorf, owner of the Bulls, said regarding his approach to the building of an indoor arena in the area: 'we were determined not to do battle with the community. That is what Mike McCaskey [President of the Bears] did, and he lost. One person can never win these battles – everyone has to get something ... times have changed.'[29] The community also took a different approach to the proposed basketball and hockey facility. According to a community organizer: 'This second time around we wanted to use this opportunity to get something out of it.'[30] Finally, Mayor Daley's position provided more leverage to the local community. According to Daley: 'What this community needs most is jobs and economic development, but not at the expense of homes and neighborhoods.'[31]

Extensive negotiations between the Stadium Joint Venture (corporate body) and the IOP resulted in a deal for a new stadium. The agreement included the removal of 40 homes, in exchange for replacement housing for affected residents. Additional community benefits included funding for the re-opening of a community health centre, a new public library and park, a no-interest loan for the development of 75 'for sale' homes, and parking spaces for affected local churches.

Politics, corporate success and culture-driven urban identity

Soldier Field redevelopment issues have been in the forefront of media coverage in Chicago for over 20 years. Home of the Chicago Bears football team, the facility has been part of the lakefront since its construction in the early 1920s. Following the 1986 Super Bowl victory, the team expressed its desire for a new stadium, embarking on a series of proposals. Some of these included locations in the city (Near West Side, South Loop), suburbs (Elk Grove Village, Hoffman Estates) and nearby Gary, Indiana. However, securing a new facility proved uncharacteristically difficult, especially when many other teams in the league successfully managed to acquire extensive public financial support for revamped or brand new facilities.

There were 60 luxury suites at Soldier Field and 20% of the income went to its owner and operator: the Chicago Park District. Most new stadiums could integrate as many as 240 luxury skyboxes and that meant substantial team profits. The election of Mayor Richard M. Daley brought about consistent opposition from City Hall to any proposals that required the use of public expenditure. Daley portrayed himself as a supporter of the working-class taxpayer and a strong opponent of corporate welfare. This populist stance placed the mayor in sharp opposition to other proposals such as the McDome project, an enclosed sports arena in nearby McCormick Convention Center, promoted by then State of Illinois Governor Edgar. The deteriorating relationship between the team and the mayor induced the Bears to threaten to leave Chicago. Throughout these developments, Daley remained committed to a renovated Soldier Field.

The mayor slowly began to identify Soldier Field as part of a macro-gentrification strategy of massive downtown-focused public-works improvements. Frequently underwritten by tax increment financing, this focus resulted on streetscape and parks beautification; support for arts, entertainment, and university development; as well as targeted neighbourhood investment. The mayoral advancement of a playing field for the Bears on the lakefront complemented this larger redevelopment agenda.

In the summer of 2000, Bears officials and Mayor Daley began to jointly promote an ambitious renovation of Soldier Field and its surroundings. This $600 million proposal would provide a new, state-of-the-art sports facility to be completed in 2003. The team would contribute $200 million while the remaining $400 million would be financed by Chicago's 2% hotel-motel tax. At the same time the Mayor would take another step in his campaign 'to restore the Lakefront', a central piece of his administration's ongoing effort to improve Chicago's downtown and near-downtown public spaces.[32]

The eventual cost of the Soldier Field renovation surpassed the $680 million mark and the Illinois Sports Facilities Authority, an agency created to oversee construction of the New Comiskey Park in the late 1980s, issued bonds to cover the city's share of stadium construction costs. The physical plan specified a new football stadium set within, though also rising substantially above, the classical colonnades crowning Soldier Field's east and west facades. Opposition to this plan was limited and it derived from the Friends of the Park, architectural critics and veterans groups.

Extensive underground parking was added and surface parking areas to the south of the stadium were landscaped, adding more than 15 acres of green space to the lakefront. Overall, 1300 trees of 45 different species were planted, a sledding hill was configured and a children's garden was created.[33] The new facility opened in 2003, and is in concert with the city's larger vision of keeping Soldier Field as part of the lakefront, positioning it as an additional piece to the available entertainment venues along Chicago's front yard.

Conclusion

Professional sports and stadium development in the United States have emerged as part of a culturally based strategy to redefine the city within the post-industrial economy. This approach has resulted in multi-billion-dollar investments in downtowns across the country. The case of Chicago reveals the complicated dynamics of these planning initiatives. Specifically, while considering the intersection between structure and agency we can observe that the interplay between race, class and political representation adds another dimension to understanding the political economy of these developments. Furthermore, the utilization of these construction projects as a means of community revitalization and urban identity results in neighbourhood restructuring and displacement.

This analysis also reveals that local political actors embrace various strategies to achieve support of corporate interests, which are concerned with profit maximization. Numerous factors contribute to these variations. First, the different community responses to the proposed projects presented unique and complex neighbourhood/corporate relation dynamics. Second, the presence of a differentiated political institution and a variety of perceptions of the role of local government in community development further fuelled these complexities. Finally, each case presents a complicated, non-uniformed set of variables given that social and economic background played a significant role in conflict resolution.

Citizens across the country are more aware today than during the 1980s and 1990s of the numerous team-manoeuvring techniques aimed at extracting extensive public support, and of overzealous officials willing to meet their corporate demands. Because of this we can observe more referendums as prerequisites to funding professional sports facilities.

However, given the increasingly short lifespan of stadiums in the United States, we are once again entering into another era of requests for updates and redevelopment which will peak in 2015–2020.

It is expected that private-public partnerships will dominate the next funding cycle even more, but with the private sector playing a greater role. For example, what many have referenced in the media already as the 'eighth wonder of the world', the construction of the new stadium for the Dallas Cowboys was the outcome of considerable private investment. The public portion of the cost was $350 million with the ownership of the team contributing $750 million and the rest of the funds deriving from an array of sources including an admission tax/parking fee, all-access seating, private-auction bonds, personal seat licenses and a relatively small construction loan by the NFL.[34] Proponents and civic officials will continue to connect these projects to municipal strategies for economic development. Hence, as private interests exercise greater control over the revitalization of the built environment, they will also come to determine the complex dynamics of future stadium construction.

Notes

[1] Judd et al., 'Tourism and Entertainment', 73–4.

[2] The post-war response to the economic restructuring in the United States has received extensive coverage in the academic literature, including by Beauregard, *Voices of Decline*; Judd and Swanstrom, *City Politics*; and Judd, *The Infrastructure of Play*.

[3] Beauregard, 'Tourism and Economic Development Policy'.

[4] Law, *Urban Tourism*.

[5] Kotler, Haider and Rein, *Marketing Places*, 311.

[6] Ibid., 227.

[7] Judd and Fainstein. *The Tourist City*, 35–53.

[8] Spirou and Bennett, *It's Hardly Sportin'*, 37–58.

[9] Quirk and Fort, *Pay Dirt*.

[10] Wayne, 'Picking Up the Tab', and Solomon, 'Public Wises Up'.

[11] For the most comprehensive analysis of stadium development in smaller US cities see Johnson, *Minor League*. Mahtesian, 'Major Problems for Minor League Towns', discusses the implications for local government of stadium development investments in smaller cities.

[12] Noll and Zimbalist, *Sports, Jobs, and Taxes*.

[13] Montgomery and Barker, 'D.C. Stadiums', B01.

[14] Papajohn, 'No Bears?', 3.

[15] Ibid.

[16] Bess, *City Baseball Magic*, offers a unique perspective on baseball stadium design issues.

[17] Peter Krallitsch, letter to Jerry Reinsdorf, 21 March 1986 (author's collection).

[18] Hersh, 'Comiskey Park'.

[19] Presecky and Fuentes, 'Sox Dome'.

[20] Department of Economic Development, *The Impact of a Major League Baseball Team*, 8.

[21] Hornung, 'Sox Deal Benefits Team', 10.

[22] McCarron and Burton, 'Are Teams Dealing in Bluffs', 1.

[23] Market Facts, *Chicago Cubs, General Public Survey*.

[24] Market Facts, *Chicago Cubs, Neighborhood Residents Survey*.

[25] Melaniphy and Associates, *Chicago Cubs Economic Impact Analysis*.

[26] Department of Economic Development. *The Impact of a Major League Baseball Team*, 2.

[27] City of Chicago, *Lake View/Uptown*.

[28] Kass, 'Chicago Stadium Replacement Urged', 1.

[29] IOP, *The New 'West Side Story'*, 3.

[30] Schmich, 'Land War', 1.

[31] Reardon, 'Stadium Agreement', 1.

[32] Osnos and Pearson, 'Bears, City Say'.

[33] Ford, 'Soldier Field Landscaping'.

[34] Galloway, 'Jerry Jones Wanted Wow'.

References

Beauregard, Robert. 'Tourism and Economic Development Policy in US Urban Areas'. In *The Economic Geography of the Tourist Industry: A Supply-side Analysis*, edited by Dimitri Ioannides and Keith G. Debbage, 220–34. London and New York: Routledge, 1998.

Beauregard, Robert. *Voices of Decline: The Post-War Fate of US Cities*. Oxford: Blackwell, 1993.

Bess, Philip. *City Baseball Magic: Plain Talk and Uncommon Sense About Cities and Baseball Parks*. Saint Paul, MN: Knothole Press, 1989.

City of Chicago. *Lake View/Uptown Neighborhood Protection and Improvement Plan*. Chicago: City Hall, 1988.

Department of Economic Development. *The Impact of a Major League Baseball Team on the Local Economy*. Chicago: City of Chicago, 1986.

Ford, Liam. 'Soldier Field Landscaping Takes Shape'. *Chicago Tribune*, 26 April 2004 1.

Galloway, Randy. 'Jerry Jones Wanted Wow in Cowboys Stadium, And He Paid For It'. *Star-Telegram*, 20 August 2009 1.

Hersh, Phil. 'Comiskey Park Bears Skid Mark of White Flight'. *Chicago Tribune*, 13 July 1986, 2.

Hornung, Mark. 'Sox Deal Benefits Team, May Shortchange the Public'. *Crain's Chicago Business*, 16 May 1988, 10.

IOP (The Interfaith Organizing Project). *The New 'West Side Story'*. Chicago: IOP, 1992.

Johnson, Arthur. *Minor League Baseball and Local Economic Development*. Champaign, IL: University of Illinois Press, 1993.

Judd, Dennis. *The Infrastructure of Play: Building the Tourist City*. Armonk, New York: M.E. Sharpe, 2003.

Judd, Dennis, and Susan S. Fainstein. *The Tourist City*. New Haven: Yale University Press, 1999.

Judd, Dennis, and Todd Swanstrom. *City Politics*. New York: Harper Collins, 1994.

Judd, Dennis, William Winter, William R. Barnes, and Emily Stern. 'Tourism and Entertainment as a Local Economic Development Strategy: A National Survey'. In *The Infrastructure of Play: Building the Tourist City*, edited by Dennis R. Judd, 50–74. Armonk, New York: M.E. Sharpe, 2003.

Kass, John. 'Chicago Stadium Replacement Urged'. *Chicago Tribune*, 13 September 1988, 1.

Kotler, Philip, Donald H. Haider, and Irving Rein. *Marketing Places: Attracting Investment, Industry, and Tourism to Cities, States and Nations*. New York: The Free Press, 1993.

Law, Christopher M. *Urban Tourism: The Visitor Economy and the Growth of Large Cities*. London and New York: Continuum, 2002.

Mahtesian, Charles. 'Major Problems for Minor League Towns'. *Governing* 7, no. 7 (1994): 48–54.

Market Facts. *Chicago Cubs, General Public Survey*. Chicago: Chicago Cubs, 1985.

Market Facts. *Chicago Cubs, Neighborhood Residents Survey*. Chicago: Chicago Cubs, 1985.

McCarron, John, and Thomas M. Burton. 'Are Teams Dealing in Bluffs to Up City's Ante?'. *Chicago Tribune*, 23 March 1986, 1.

Melaniphy and Associates. *Chicago Cubs Economic Impact Analysis*. Chicago: Melaniphy and Associates, 1986.

Montgomery, Lori, and Karlyn Barker. 'D.C. Stadiums Seen as One-Two Economic Punch'. *Washington Post*, 25 September 2004, B01.

Noll, Roger G., and Andrew Zimbalist. *Sports, Jobs, and Taxes: The Economic Impact of Sports Teams and Stadiums*. Washington, D.C.: Brookings Institution Press, 1977.

Osnos, Evan, and Rick Pearson. 'Bears, City Say This May Be Real Deal for Soldier Field'. *Chicago Tribune*, 15 August 2000, 1.

Papajohn, George. 'No Bears? We'd Be a City on the Fake'. *Chicago Tribune*, 13 August 1995, 3.

Presecky, William, and Gabe Fuentes. 'Sox Dome is No Wild Pitch'. *Chicago Tribune*, 24 November 1985, 1.

Quirk, James, and Rodney Fort. *Pay Dirt: The Business of Professional Team Sports*. Princeton, NJ: Princeton University Press, 1992.

Reardon, Patrick. 'Stadium Agreement Has A Winning Look'. *Chicago Tribune*, 10 May 1991, 1.

Schmich, Mary. 'Land War Turns to Mutual Respect'. *Chicago Tribune*, 24 June 1992, 1.

Solomon, John. 'Public Wises Up, Balks at Paying for New Stadiums'. *USA TODAY*, 1 April 2004, 13A.

Spirou, Costas, and Larry Bennett. *It's Hardly Sportin: Stadiums, Neighborhoods and the New Chicago*. DeKalb: Northern Illinois University Press, 2003.

Wayne, Leslie. 'Picking Up the Tab for Field of Dreams'. *New York Times*, 27 July 1996, 39.

Sport and economic regeneration: a winning combination?

Larissa E. Davies

Sheffield Hallam University, Sheffield, UK

In recent years, there has been a favourable shift in UK urban policy towards the use of sport as a tool for regenerating declining areas. Sporting infrastructure has been constructed in various British cities with a view to addressing the dual aims of sporting need and urban regeneration. However, evidence to support the notion that sport can underpin regeneration goals is highly variable. This paper will explore the growth of sport-related regeneration in the UK and examine the evidence base for this. In particular, it will focus on the economic literature and evaluate the strengths and weaknesses of emerging evidence. It will suggest that with investment in sport likely to increase as a consequence of the London 2012 Olympic Games, there is a need to develop a greater understanding of the role of sport in the regeneration process, to maximize the potential benefits and to justify public expenditure on sport in the future.

Introduction

The use of sport as a tool for regenerating British cities has become increasingly widespread in recent years. Initially used in Sheffield in the early 1990s (World Student Games, 1991), the use of sporting strategies for urban regeneration has grown in popularity throughout the UK, with Manchester (Commonwealth Games, 2002) and London (Olympic Games, 2012) being more recent high-profile examples of cities adopting such strategies. Over this period, it has become increasingly recognized by policymakers that sport can be used to address a wide range of issues relating to urban policy and specifically urban regeneration, including economic development, neighbourhood renewal and social cohesion.

Sport has been a feature of British cites for a significant period of time. Historically, urban areas have provided opportunities for participation in a wide range of sporting activities and served as hosts to sporting events of varying magnitudes. Nevertheless, over the last two decades there has been a shifting emphasis in investment, from investment in 'sport for sports sake', to investment in 'sport for good'.[1] The use of sport to address regeneration objectives has largely stemmed from the belief of government and other sporting and non-sporting organizations that it can confer a wide range of economic and social benefits to individuals and communities beyond those of a purely physical sporting nature, and can contribute positively to the revitalization of declining urban areas.[2] Indeed, much of the increased investment in sport that has been seen from the Lottery and other sources has been advocated on this basis. However, despite the growth of regeneration through sport in British cities, evidence to support the notion that sport can generate benefits in areas and neighbourhoods that have been subject to urban decline is limited, and although anecdotal support for regeneration through sport is growing, there remains a need for further robust evidence to support claims of regeneration made by city authorities and sporting organizations, especially those involved in bidding for public funding for sport-related infrastructure and associated initiatives.

This paper will review the evidence for sport and regeneration, focusing primarily on the UK-based literature. It is beyond the scope of the paper to comprehensively review all dimensions of sport and regeneration; therefore it will primarily consider the economic literature, with a view to establishing the current baseline level of knowledge and understanding in this area. The paper will first explore the growth of sport-related regeneration in the UK by examining the different models of regeneration through sport that are emerging in British cities and by outlining the policy context of this growth. It will then go on to examine the strengths and weaknesses of emerging economic themes of evidence and discuss the relevance of the research to policymakers concerned with sport-related regeneration. Finally, it will conclude by suggesting the need to move towards evidence-based decision-making and propose an agenda of research priorities that need to be addressed. It will argue that, with investment in sport-related initiatives likely to increase significantly in the period leading up to the London 2012 Olympic Games and beyond, there is a need to develop a more comprehensive understanding of the role of sport in the regeneration process to maximize the potential benefits offered by sport-related developments and to justify and sustain public expenditure on sport in the future.

Sport-related regeneration in the UK

Defining 'sport-related' regeneration

'Sports-led regeneration', 'sports regeneration' and 'sport and regeneration' are terms that are becoming more widely used in both academic literature and policy-related documentation. However, these terms are used very broadly to cover a wide range of activities. Prior to exploring the growth of sport-related regeneration in the UK, it is therefore necessary to establish a working definition of this term.

To understand sport-related regeneration, it is first essential to consider the meaning of regeneration, which itself is contested. Percy argues that: 'Traditionally, it has been thought of mainly in economic and environmental terms, but recently more emphasis has been placed on the social and community aspects of regeneration.'[3] A holistic and all encompassing definition is provided by Roberts, who defines urban regeneration as:

> comprehensive and integrated vision and action which leads to the resolution of urban problems and which seeks to bring about a lasting improvement in the economic, physical, social and environmental condition of an area that has been subject to change.[4]

It therefore follows that sport-related regeneration refers to the way that sport can be used to revitalize an area economically, socially, environmentally and physically, with sport being taken from the European Sport Charter[5] as:

> all forms of physical activity which, through casual or organised participation, aim at expressing or improving physical fitness and mental well being, forming social relationships or obtaining results in competition at all levels.[6]

This broad definition, which is also acknowledged by Sport England, thus extends far beyond traditional team games to incorporate individual sports and fitness-related activities including walking, cycling, dance activities and aerobics. Furthermore, it extends from casual and informal participation through to serious, organized club sport and elite level activity.[7]

A comprehensive definition of sport-related regeneration should encompass both the immediate short-term impacts generated from sport-related activities, together with the lasting medium and longer-term legacy impacts on the surrounding environment.

Models of sport-related regeneration

While the use of sport as a catalyst for the regeneration of British cities has grown in recent years, as with culture-related regeneration, this has taken many forms. Sport has developed from being a dimension of cultural and other regeneration programmes, to being a catalyst for regeneration in its own right. Using the work of Evans,[8] it is possible to identify three broad models through which sport has been incorporated into the regeneration process in the UK over the last two decades. The models are summarized in Figure 1.

In the first model, Sports-led regeneration, the sports activity (e.g., an event) or development (e.g., a sports stadium) is seen as the catalyst or key player within the process of urban regeneration. It may take the form of a flagship project or development and is likely to have a high profile. These developments or activities tend to be unique, distinctive and raise awareness or excitement in regeneration schemes as a whole. Wembley Stadium is an example of this type of development. It is a flagship iconic development for London and the stadium is being used as a catalyst for the regeneration of the surrounding area and the borough of Brent. Similarly, the 2012 Olympic Games is an example of a sporting event being used as a flagship project to drive the redevelopment of East London. In both examples, sport is cited as the symbol of regeneration and used to propel real estate and other developments.

In the second model, Sports regeneration, the sports activity or development is integrated more fully into an area-based strategy alongside other activities. In this model, the activity or development is likely to be integrated into mainstream policy and planning at an early stage. An example of this model would be the redevelopment of East Manchester though the 2002 Commonwealth Games. In East Manchester, sport has very much been a key aspect of the area-based initiatives and used to link together various regeneration initiatives in the east of the city.

Finally the third model, Sport and regeneration, is probably the most common type of regeneration through sport in the UK, and is defined by Evans[9] as the 'model by default'. In this sporting model, activities and developments are not fully integrated into the

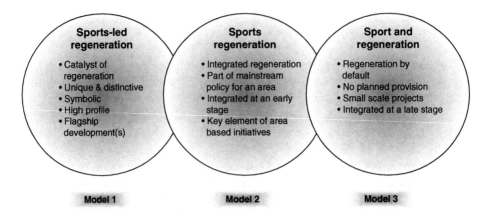

Figure 1.   Models of sport-related regeneration.

strategic development of an area. Rather, interventions are often small and in many cases with no planned provision. Such interventions are often added as a component of a regeneration strategy at a later stage and may not form a particularly large part of the mainstream regeneration strategy. Nevertheless, these activities and developments can often enhance existing or planned services and facilities. Examples of this model are numerous and include smaller-scale community sports facilities and activity programmes, for example as illustrated by the activities of the Beacon Councils or Sport Action Zones.[10]

The models outlined above are quite generalized, and are intended to give a sense of order to the different levels of sporting involvement in regeneration schemes rather than rigid categorization. However, as Evans[11] notes with regard to culture, the models of sport-related regeneration are not necessarily mutually exclusive, especially over time.

The policy context

The transition of sport from primarily being a physical activity, to playing an increasing role in society, has seen its emergence within a number of public policy agendas in the UK. The following discussion will briefly outline how sport has become a growing part of modern urban policy initiatives but also how sport policy has developed to incorporate regeneration issues within its agenda.

The health benefits of sport to society have been acknowledged for many years.[12] However, the notion that sport and leisure may be contributors to the process of urban regeneration more generally only began to emerge in the early 1980s. One of the earliest examples of urban funds being used to support sporting initiatives was the Urban Programme, which was initially launched by the Home Office in 1968 and later transferred together with responsibility for urban policy, to the Department for the Environment. Although in the 1980s, sport in society was still very much regarded as part of the product of affluence, rather than its producer, by 1986/7, the Urban Programme was providing significant funds to sporting projects, contributing £33.7 million to some 1200 separate projects.[13]

Since the 1980s, there has been a growing recognition that sport can contribute to the urban policy agenda and funds have been leveraged from a range of more recent initiatives including the Single Regeneration Budget, which was a major form of support for regeneration in the UK until 2000; the New Deal for Communities, which is currently a key programme in the governments strategy to tackle multiple deprivation in the most deprived neighbourhoods in the country and the Neighbourhood Renewal Fund, made available to the most deprived neighbourhoods in the country to improve services.

In parallel to the growing use of sport in urban policy, there has been a reorientation of sports policy to address the broader issues of urban regeneration. Traditionally concerned with the issues of raising sports performance and increasing participation, sports policy under the New Labour government in the UK since 1997 has become increasingly concerned with the wider economic, social and physical impacts of sport on society.[14] There has been a greater emphasis placed on developing a strategic agenda for sport, with national policy documents relating to the delivery of sport, such as Game Plan[15] and the Framework for Sport in England[16] highlighting the potential benefits of sport to various public policy agendas including health, crime prevention, education, neighbourhood renewal and social inclusion.

As a consequence of growing synergies between urban policy and sports policy, there are emerging examples of government and sporting agencies working together on a growing number of sport-related regeneration initiatives in the UK. For example, Sport

England has set up a Strategic Alliance Team to work with various government departments on a number of urban-related initiatives, with representatives currently working with the Community Cohesion Unit (Home Office), the Neighbourhood Renewal Unit (Department for Communities and Local Government), the Department for Health and the Department for Educations and Schools to promote and deliver the wider benefits of sport.[17]

Monitoring and evaluating sport-related regeneration

With increasing public and private investment in sport, together with a growth in the use of sport across various policy agendas, there is a greater than ever need to measure and evaluate the benefits of sport. Sport England argues that:

> The benefits sport brings to individuals and communities may be obvious to many. In the competition for scarce resources, however, sport must face up to the challenge of justifying in more tangible ways why public money should be invested in it.[18]

At present, the evidence base for sport-related regeneration is highly variable. For example, the Sport England Value of Sport Monitor,[19] suggests that the strongest evidence regarding social issues is in relation to health outcomes, with evidence in other areas of social policy such as crime reduction, drug use and education, less convincing.[20] This variability is commented upon by others in relation to economic objectives.[21] As noted earlier, it is beyond the scope of a single article to comprehensively examine evidence across the broad spectrum of regeneration; therefore the discussion will focus on the economic literature. Within this section, the paper will examine the strengths and weaknesses of the evidence base, together with the main methodological issues and problems of monitoring and evaluating the contribution of sport to economic regeneration. It will also consider the relevance of the evidence base to policymakers.

Evaluating the economic contribution of sport to regeneration

Evidence on the economic contribution of sport to regeneration is wide-ranging and published in a variety of forms, including peer-reviewed journals, government reports and sponsored impact evaluations. It includes examples of both macro and micro economic studies. Nevertheless, despite the growing emphasis on sport to deliver economic returns, the evidence base remains fragmented, with limited cohesion between the various research themes. In recent years there have been attempts by UK Sport and various Sports Councils in the UK to provide some strategic direction to the research through the commissioning of various studies, yet the evidence available to policymakers, particularly at the local level, remains somewhat variable.

Within the UK literature, there are two key themes of research evidence emerging: firstly, macro-economic impact studies of sport and the economy, focusing on the contribution of sport to output and employment; and secondly, economic impact studies of major events. A further theme, which has received less attention in the UK but is evident from the US literature, is around professional teams and sports stadia. Each of these themes will now be examined in detail.

Sport and the economy

Until the early 1980s, very little work was published on the economic impact and importance of the sports industry in the UK or elsewhere, despite its increasing prominence in the international economy as a large growth area for output and employment.[22] However, since this time, a significant body of literature has emerged in the area. In the UK, the research is largely based on using macro-economic analysis to measure the importance of sport and sport-related expenditure at the national and regional level, with the Henley Centre for Forecasting, Cambridge Econometrics and the Sport Industries Research Centre (formerly the Leisure Industries Research Centre) leading the research in the area.

The earliest macro-economic study of sport in the UK was undertaken in the mid-1980s[23] and it formed part of a European report on the impact of sport in various member states.[24] The principal aim of this study was to provide a snapshot of the role of sport in the economy and thereby to raise general awareness of that role. A subsequent number of similar studies have since been commissioned by various organizations as illustrated in Table 1. The majority of these studies have been carried out at the national or regional level and have used the National Income Accounting Framework to estimate consumer expenditure on sport, (gross) value-added by sport and sport-related employment.

The UK studies throughout the 1990s were relatively successful in raising the profile of sport as an industrial sector within the academic environment, although their policy relevance remained limited due to the irregular and snapshot nature of the estimates produced. With an increasing need to justify spending on sport, since 2000, macro-economic impact studies have been commissioned on an increasingly regular basis, reflecting the strategic decision by sporting bodies such as Sport England and other Sports Councils in the UK to build an evidence base around the economic importance of sport. Moreover, as a consequence of various factors, including the movement towards greater regional determination of policy in the 1990s, there has also been an enhanced focus on the (English) regions, with additional studies being commissioned on a regular basis at this spatial level. As a result of these developments, there is now a growing evidence base for the economic contribution of sport to the national and regional level in the UK, allowing policymakers to identify a much fuller and clearer picture of the parts of the sports economy generating wealth and employment over a longer period of time.

While the generation of longitudinal data on the economic contribution of the sports economy is a positive development in the literature, there are ongoing issues relating to the quality of data used within these reports. At the national level, although much data is derived from published sources, there are some measures of sport-related economic activity that are not recorded and assumptions and estimates are inferred from the wider economic context.[25] Moreover, this is a greater issue for data reliability and validity at the regional level, where not only are the models essentially replicated and downsized from the national models without fully considering the changing nature and inter-related functions of the regional economy but also because fewer published statistics exist at this spacial scale, there is a greater need to extract the relative statistics from the UK figures using regional proportions and further assumptions, which are sometimes but not always based on credible evidence.

Since the 1980s, there have undoubtedly been improvements in the quality, consistency and transparency of data used to produce the estimates of the economic value of sport. As studies have developed, there has been greater use of reliable published data sources and estimates have been adjusted where it has become apparent that data was previously incorrectly approximated, for example in relation to the overvaluing of consumer spending on sports gambling.[26] Furthermore, in the latest series of studies, for the first time there are attempts to use sources such as the Annual Business Inquiry to provide a measure of validity, independent of the methodology employed in the reports themselves.[27] However, there are some outstanding issues relating to the reliability and validity of data in the models that remain unresolved. For example Davies[28] notes how the

Table 1.   Measuring the macro-economic impact of sport: UK studies

Scale	Year of study	References
National level		
UK	1985; 1990; 1995; 1998; 2001; 2004	Henley Centre for Forecasting (1986); Henley Centre for Forecasting (1992); LIRC (1997d); LIRC (2000c) ; SIRC (2004b); SIRC (2007m)
England	1995; 1998; 2000; 2001; 2003; 2004–2005	LIRC (1997a); LIRC (2000a); Cambridge Econometrics (2003a); SIRC (2004a); SIRC (2007c); SIRC (2007d)
Wales	1988; 1993; 1995; 1998; 2004	Henley Centre for Forecasting (1990); Centre for Advanced Studies in the Social Sciences (1995); LIRC (1997e); LIRC (2000d); SIRC (2007o)
Scotland	1990; 1995; 1998; 2001; 2004	Pieda (1991); LIRC (1997c); Sportscotland (2001); Sportscotland (2004); Sportscotland (2007);
Northern Ireland	1989; 1995; 1998; 2004	Henley Centre for Forecasting (1992); LIRC (1997b); LIRC (2000b); SIRC (2007f)
Regional level		
Northern Region	1993	Pieda (1994)
East of England	2000; 2003; 2004–5	Cambridge Econometrics (2003d); SIRC (2007b); SIRC (2007g)
East Midlands	2000; 2003; 2004–5	Cambridge Econometrics (2003c); SIRC (2007a); SIRC (2007h)
London	2000; 2003; 2004–5	Cambridge Econometrics (2003b); SIRC (2007q); SIRC (2007e)
North East	2000; 2003; 2004–5	Cambridge Econometrics (2003e); SIRC (2007r); SIRC (2007i)
North West	2000; 2003; 2004–5	Cambridge Econometrics (2003f); SIRC (2007s); SIRC (2007j)
South East	2000; 2003; 2004–5	Cambridge Econometrics (2003g); SIRC (2007t); SIRC (2007k)
South West	2000; 2003; 2004–5	Cambridge Econometrics (2003h); SIRC (2007u); SIRC (2007l)
West Midlands	2000; 2003; 2004–5	Cambridge Econometrics (2003i); SIRC (2007v); SIRC (2007n)
Yorkshire and the Humber	2000; 2003; 2004–5	Cambridge Econometrics (2003j); SIRC (2007w); SIRC (2007p)
Sub-regional/local level		
Bracknell and the Wirral	1987	Henley Centre for Forecasting (1989)
Cornwall Region and the Isles of Scilly	2001	SIRC (2004c)
Sheffield	1996/7	Davies (2002)
South Yorkshire	2000	Gratton *et al* (2001)

voluntary sector is the weakest part of macro-economic impact assessments. Data for the voluntary sector is simply not available in published form, therefore all of the pre-1995 studies, with the exception of the first UK study, carried out primary data collection in the form of bespoke questionnaires. The results of these have been highly variable in terms of sampling, response rates and aggregation. Nevertheless, more recent studies have done little to address the issue of data reliability and validity in the voluntary sector and have not modified or challenged the assumptions made in previous work: 'No data exist to adequately describe the Voluntary sector; for this reason we use relationships that arise from previous studies and surveys to relate the Voluntary sector to the sport economy.'[29]

However, one of the greatest limitations of the literature on sport and the economy is not concerning the research that has been carried out at the national and regional level but relates to the lack of research at the sub-regional and local level. Several studies have been carried out at this scale[30] but they tend to be one-off snapshot studies undertaken to identify the size of the sports industry at a specific point in time and as such provide only limited baseline information. Furthermore, there is a lack of research relating to the economic importance of sport in urban areas, which is where much sport-related expenditure for regeneration purposes is invested. A major obstacle facing studies at this level, and a possible explanation for the limited research undertaken, is the lack published data available. Nevertheless, it is at the local level that policymakers require information to implement urban regeneration policies. Thus a lack of information on sport and the economy at this level is a severe limitation of the evidence base for policymakers and a research priority that needs to be addressed in the near future.

Sports events

Research on the economic importance of sporting events remains the most systematically researched area of the three themes identified. Such has been the development of literature in this area that there is now a strong and growing evidence base for the impact of major events within the UK and elsewhere in the world. Unlike the literature on sport and the economy, the event literature is largely at the local level.

The literature on major events similarly developed from the mid-1980s onwards. Gratton et al.,[31] provide a useful overview of this development, noting that one of the earliest studies undertaken was on the Adelaide Formula 1 Grand Prix.[32] Since this time, a plethora of *ex ante* and *ex post* impact studies have been undertaken on a wide range of major events throughout the world, from those staged as part of annual professional team competition to less regular European and world championships. These studies have been undertaken by a wide range of individuals and organizations, including academics but also consultancy firms and event organizers. Although much of the literature on major events is concerned with analysing the economic impacts, it also covers a wide range of broader issues including sports participation and development, social impact, legacies, tourism and urban regeneration.[33]

Multiplier analysis has been widely used as a method for evaluating the overall economic impact of sporting events. It has also been used for assessing the impact of other leisure industries such as the arts and tourism. Multiplier analysis is used to calculate the direct (initial) impact of additional money spent by visitors in an area, together with the indirect and the induced impacts (subsequent rounds of related spending after leakages) that the additional expenditure generates. There are various types of multiplier in common use including employment, income, output and sales or transactions multipliers.[34] Multiplier analysis is a credible method for analysing economic impact at the regional and local level. However, its application in sport has been widely criticized. UK Sport[35] argue that rarely is the information required available to carry out a comprehensive evaluation and to acquire this information is often costly and complex, with the result that multipliers are regularly borrowed from other sectors of the economy or other studies leading to inaccurate estimates. Crompton[36] summarizes 11 major contributors to the inaccuracies commonly cited, including: using sales instead of income multipliers; misrepresenting employment multipliers; failing to define the impacted area; including local spectators;

omitting opportunity costs and claiming total instead of marginal economic benefits. Nevertheless, despite these inaccuracies, he argues that if implemented knowledgeably and with integrity, multiplier analysis does have value. However, therein lies the problem; economic impact studies are often not impartial or objective. Frequently, the motives of those commissioning studies leads to the generation of economic impact numbers that are supportive of their position,[37] particularly *ex ante* economic impact assessments, which forecast rather than retrospectively analyse the impact of the event.[38]

UK Sport is the organization responsible for coordinating and supporting the UK's efforts to bid for and stage major sporting events. Since 1997, it has played a key role in the development of research relating to the economic impact of major events in the UK, commissioning several reports to understand the impacts generated by sporting events and to provide an appraisal of lottery funding investment.[39] The methodology adopted in the UK Sport research attempts to establish economic impact by calculating only the total amount of additional expenditure generated within a host city or area, which is directly attributable to the staging of a particular event, rather than the more conventional multiplier analysis approach used in many studies and discussed above, which attempts to measure direct, indirect and induced impacts. While conventional multiplier analysis is arguably a more comprehensive measure of economic impact, by only measuring the first round of spending, the UK Sport research avoids the complex and often inaccurate calculation of the multiplier discussed above, together with some of the inaccuracies identified by Crompton.[40] Furthermore, it avoids the exaggeration of any errors in the direct effect that are often compounded when estimating the indirect and induced effects,[41] while at the same time providing a consistent and relatively simple methodology for estimating and comparing the economic impact of a sporting event, albeit a conservative one.

While the economic literature on events has become more comprehensive in recent years, with it now covering a fairly wide range of events, the evidence relates largely to the short-term, immediate impacts. There remains a lack of evidence on the longer-term impacts that events can potentially deliver, despite the fact that hosting an event is often justified on the legacy benefits generated. This is an issue that has been raised previously in the literature,[42] but has so far not been addressed. Even within the broader Olympic research, although there is extensive discussion of regeneration legacy benefits, to date there has never been any longitudinal economic impact study of a Games undertaken. While the International Olympic Committee are attempting to address this by means of the Olympic Games Global Impact study, which was launched in 2000 in an attempt to measure the global impact of the Games, create a comparable benchmark across all future Games, and to help bidding cities and future organizers identify potential legacies[43] there are doubts over whether methodologically this is sound.[44] Moreover, whether it will actually produce evidence of regeneration legacies is debateable as, despite each study spanning a period of 11 years, from the bidding process through to post-games evaluation, it will still end two years after the Games are held, thus failing to capture any longer-term impacts. In summary then, while the literature on the short-term economic impacts of events has become more comprehensive and there is an increased awareness of the limitations of these studies, the evidence for the wider and longer-term economic impacts of events remains less convincing.

Professional sports teams and stadiums

The third and final area of literature linked to the economic regeneration agenda is the body of literature relating to professional sports teams and stadiums. The use of sports stadiums for the purpose of regeneration is a fairly recent phenomenon in the UK, and as such the scope and breadth of literature in this field is relatively limited. In contrast, sports stadiums have been used in tackling urban decline in US cities for many years, therefore much of the evidence for stadiums and economic development is based on this experience.

In terms of the North American literature, a detailed and comprehensive economic analysis of sports stadiums and professional sports teams has been developed.[45] Within the vast literature on professional sports in North America, although there remains considerable debate between proponents and critics, there exists a considerable body of work on the economic benefits of major and minor league sports to communities[46] and the relative merits of public development and subsidization of sports stadiums.[47]

While the North American literature provides an interesting context for discussions of sports stadiums, professional teams and regeneration in the UK, there are fundamental differences underpinning the funding and development of stadiums in the UK and North America, which limits the use of the evidence by UK policymakers. In the UK, there are essentially two types of stadium development. Those primarily seen as serving a 'national need', often built to host major flagship events,[48] and the second more common type are those built for professional sports teams (mainly football). Thornley[49] observes how in the US, cities compete with each other for inward investment and the sports industry. Local states develop stadiums to attract professional sports teams and franchises from other cities, and devote considerable public funds from local taxpayers' money to these projects. However, in the UK this process rarely occurs. Stadiums developed for professional teams tend to be privately owned and operated, and generally do not receive public funding. Moreover, cities do not have the power to determine the use of tax revenues or to propose local tax increases in order to subsidize stadium construction. Additionally, the geographical movement of teams is unlikely thus the need to retain or lure professional teams does not exist.[50] As a result, much of the literature relating to the threat of franchise flight and the loss of perceived economic benefits associated with professional teams, together with the merits of subsidizing stadiums using public funding, is not of relevance to the UK, whose cities will retain their professional club regardless of whether a new stadium is developed. The US literature may have more relevance to the development of 'national stadiums' in the UK, as these stadiums tend to be funded by national public funding or public-private partnerships but, even then, the impacts are likely to be dependent upon the long-term use of the venue, which may or may not include the tenancy of a professional team.

In terms of the UK evidence, little has been written or researched about the link between sports stadiums, professional sports teams and urban regeneration. Unlike the previous research themes discussed, where there has been strategic direction from organizations such as UK Sport and various Sports Councils, there has been no such programme of research commissioned in this area. The evidence base for stadiums and regeneration therefore comprises largely of one-off studies of a relatively small scale. These have also tended to focus on 'national' stadiums rather than those constructed for professional teams. For example, Jones[51] has examined evidence concerning the impacts of stadiums on economic and urban development, primarily using the Millennium Stadium as a case study, and while these papers provide informative accounts of the Cardiff case study and issues arising from the development, they provide little in the way of quantifiable robust evidence that can be used by policymakers in other cities. Similarly, Davies[52] has provided an account of the impacts of stadium development on property, nevertheless concludes that before the findings can be utilized by policymakers, there is a need for further investigation to build an evidence base for the arguments presented, which are largely based on small-scale exploratory research.

A likely explanation for this theme of research having received little attention in the literature is because as noted previously, stadiums built for professional teams in the UK are generally constructed for and operated by the private sector. Although new stadiums comply with the planning process, they are rarely integrated fully into the strategic regeneration and development of an area; therefore any regeneration tends to be *ad hoc*. However, even national stadiums with considerable public subsidy have only been subject to minimal investigation, with limited analysis of how they contribute to the regeneration process. Clearly if stadiums and other major infrastructure developments for sport are to be justified on the basis of the wider regeneration they bring to an area, there is a need to address this omission in the literature.

Utilizing the evidence base for policymaking in sport

There is certainly more information available currently for policymakers about sport and economic regeneration, than there was when Policy Action Team 10 was established in 1998, to look at the contribution sport and the arts could potentially make towards neighbourhood renewal.[53] There is now growing evidence of the regional and national importance of sport to the overall economy and fairly comprehensive information available for policymakers on the short-term economic impacts of sports events and how to measure them. However, it is clear from the preceding discussion that omissions and key weaknesses in the evidence base exist. There are still aspects of sport-related regeneration that have received little attention, and whether current research provides urban policymakers with the relevant evidence they require to justify sport-related initiatives from an economic regeneration perspective is debatable.

While there is increasing evidence of the direct and more observable economic impacts generated by sport-related investment, there is less comprehensive information about the broader economic regeneration issues across the three themes identified. As suggested in Figure 2, the current evidence base tends to focus on the narrower, more discernible economic 'impacts' of sport such as employment, wealth creation and tourism; but it is far less comprehensive in its consideration of broader economic 'regeneration' issues such as how investment in the sports industry impacts on business development and inward investment, job quality, workforce development, innovation and knowledge. Each

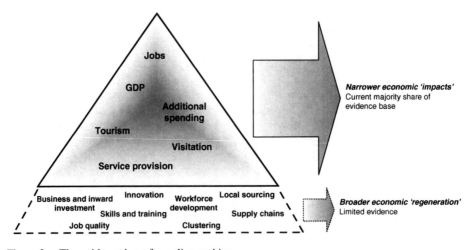

Figure 2.   The evidence base for policy making.

of these wider economic issues are of considerable importance to urban policymakers, yet are seldom evidenced in the sport-related research. In essence, the broad foundation of the pyramid outlined in Figure 2, is missing.

In part, the deficit of evidence relating to the aforementioned economic 'regeneration' issues can be explained by the lack of in-depth research undertaken at the local level. As a consequence of limited published data at this scale, it is difficult methodologically to carry out both macro-economic and detailed micro-economic impact studies without the collection of extensive primary data, which is both time-consuming and expensive, but also difficult to repeat with reliability. Nevertheless, it is at the local level that the detailed economic issues such as those outlined in the base of the pyramid need to be investigated. Therefore this methodological issue must be addressed if the evidence is to become more relevant to policymaking.

There are other empirical reasons why the evidence base does not necessarily produce the information required by policymakers. Measuring the impact of investment in sport-related regeneration is not an easy task. As with culture-led regeneration, measuring the social, economic and environmental impacts attributed to an event or a development is problematic and fraught with methodological difficulty.[54] Isolating the impact of sport-related investments, such as stadiums, from other investment initiatives is a key method-ological issue that needs to be resolved. Furthermore, estimating the opportunity costs of sport-related developments and evaluating whether regeneration would have occurred irrespective of sport-related investment also presents methodological challenges for researchers and policymakers alike. The latter in particular is a key question in relation to London 2012, given that the redevelopment of the Stratford area, where the Olympic Park will be situated, was already underway prior to awarding the 2012 Games to London in 2005. However, the methodological issues identified will again need to be tackled if the evidence base is to become more fully utilized by urban policymakers.

The evidence base for sport-related regeneration is undoubtedly growing; nevertheless there clearly remains gap between the information that currently exists and the information required by policymakers to justify sport-related investments. While some of the pragmatic and methodological reasons for this disparity have been suggested, the final section will now discuss how future research should be developed to address these and other issues raised within the paper.

Towards London 2012 and evidence-based decision making for sport-related regeneration

The London 2012 Olympic Games is the largest sport-related regeneration project the UK has ever undertaken. From the outset, a significant element of the London bid was based around the regeneration legacy that the Games would create for the Lower Lea Valley in East London: 'By staging the Games in this part of the city, the most enduring legacy of the Olympics will be the regeneration of an entire community for the direct benefit of everyone who lives there.'[55] Arguably, no previous Games have ever focused so heavily on regeneration. However, it is clear from the literature reviewed within this paper that the economic regeneration benefits claimed were not based on substantial and rigorous academic evidence. Nevertheless, the decision to host a major event without significant evidence to support the case is not a new phenomenon, as Hall argued nearly 20 years ago: 'Hallmark events are not the result of a rational decision-making process. Decisions affecting the hosting and the nature of hallmark events grow out of a political process.'[56]

While there is no doubt that the London Olympics will generate impacts for the economy of East London, whether these will be long lasting and benefit the local area and well being of local residents remains to be seen. Kasimati argues that: 'Although economic analyses prepared on behalf of Olympic advocates have demonstrated economic advantages from hosting the Games, potential host communities pose the question of whether, in fact, the economic benefits of the Olympics are pragmatic'.[57] He goes on to suggest that although all the *ex ante* economic impact studies between 1984 and 2012 indicate the significant role of the Summer Olympic Games in the promotion of the host economy, he shows that *ex ante* models and forecasts are seldom confirmed by *ex post* analyses.[58] Horne similarly suggests:

> The arguments for hosting sports-mega events are usually articulated in terms of sportive as well as economic and social benefits for the hosting nation ... Yet research has pointed out significant gaps between forecast and actual outcomes, between economic and non-economic rewards, between the experience of mega-events in advanced and in developing societies.[59]

Although the Olympic-related literature does emphasize the long-term consequences for the host city,[60] as noted earlier, no comprehensive longitudinal post-event study has ever been undertaken on the economic regeneration impacts of the Olympic Games. Given these comments, the challenge for London 2012 will be how to deliver high-impact sustainable regeneration to the local area and indeed how to evidence this to justify the £9.325 billion pounds being spent on delivering the Games.[61]

It is probably too late to provide an evidence-based resource for those policymakers involved in planning the regeneration strategy for London 2012. However, it is not too late to put in place an evaluative framework for future sport-related regeneration projects that are likely to be spurred as a result of the 2012 Olympic Games in the UK. Research around sport-related regeneration must now focus on evaluating current projects with a view to not only justifying public expenditure on sport but, more importantly, establishing a baseline of information for policymakers to use. This is fundamental for underpinning future policies and guiding future interventions in sport.

Consequently in terms of a research agenda for sport-related regeneration, a priority must be the robust testing of existing policy interventions, particularly at the local level. Projects utilizing public funding, whether they are stadiums or smaller community facilities or initiatives, must be subject to rigorous evaluation. In particular, there needs to be transparent evidence of what works and what does not work and, perhaps more controversially, an appraisal of what provides value for money. Evaluation at the local level could take the form of macro-economic evaluations, although the issues of data availability are not easily addressed. Moreover, as discussed, macro-economic analysis does not provide information on the broader success of regeneration strategies or the level of detail required by policymakers. Evaluations at the local level therefore need to be designed to incorporate broader measures than just value-added and employment, and attempt to evaluate the tangible and intangible economic regeneration impacts, using both quantitative and qualitative measures. By evaluating local, sport-related regeneration initiatives more comprehensively, knowledge and understanding of sport at the local level will be enhanced, which will address a fundamental weakness in the current evidence base.

As a further priority, there needs to be the generation of evidence relating to the medium and longer term impacts of sport, which at present is lacking. Macro-economic studies at the regional and national level are beginning to generate useful longitudinal data on sport and the economy and should continue, although there needs to be consideration of how broader measures of economic regeneration could be incorporated into these and how data reliability, particularly at the sub-national level, could be improved. At the local level, research into the medium and longer term impact of events, beyond the duration of the event itself, would be useful in helping policymakers identify and maximize the legacy benefits of investment; as would the development of local case study policy evaluations that extend beyond the completion of a sporting development or sporting initiative.

Many parallels can be drawn between the development of culture-related regeneration 10 years ago in the UK and sport-related regeneration today. The challenges facing culture-related regeneration to justify itself and provide more longitudinal research and an improved evidence base are now similarly presenting themselves to sport-related regeneration. Sport should look towards the example of culture to explore how it has tackled the challenge of providing evidence for policymakers and how it has resolved methodological issues around isolating and measuring the impact culture from other activities. Culture by no means has all the answers, but is significantly further developed in the evidence-based decision-making process than sport.

The current evidence base for sport-related regeneration is not without merit. As discussed within the paper, there are elements of it that provide value. However, it remains relatively fragmented, with little synthesis between themes identified. Closer integration of the research themes in the future would strengthen the evidence base; for example, synthesizing the knowledge gained from event studies to enhance studies on sport and the economy. Fundamentally though, as a priority, future research must address the needs of policymakers and facilitate a closer relationship between the evidence base and policymaking. As its stands, the evidence base for sport-related regeneration is in its infancy but if, as suggested, more research is undertaken at the local level and evaluations are undertaken over a longer period of time, it may be possible to begin to build an evidence base around the different models of sport-related regeneration identified in Figure 1. This in turn would facilitate a greater understanding conceptually and empirically of how and why different sporting policy interventions impact on the regeneration process.

This paper has focused primarily on the economic aspects of sport-related regeneration and the recommendations for further research are largely targeted at improving the quality of data and information in this area. While this is clearly important for justifying investment in sport, there needs to be consideration of whether the improvement of data relating solely to economic regeneration will significantly enhance the decision-making process for policymakers involved in sport and urban regeneration or whether there needs to be a more holistic approach to improving the evidence base. Maybe it is not possible or even desirable to separate out the economic impacts from the social and physical impacts, given that regeneration, as defined earlier in the paper, is clearly a much broader phenomenon. Notwithstanding these comments, whether sport-related economic regeneration is re-searched alongside multiple regeneration outcomes or in isolation, if the UK government is serious about utilizing sport as a tool for regeneration, then funding must be forthcoming to evaluate this. Politicians, senior administrators in sport and urban policymakers in the UK are often too quick to support sport-related regeneration initiatives without fully understanding the consequences of investment and this is demonstrated nowhere more clearly than in relation to the decision to host the 2012 Olympic Games in London. However, the 2012 Games has provided London and the UK with a fantastic regeneration opportunity and the lessons learned from this and other sporting initiatives must be evidenced and utilized to maximize the potential benefits of future sport-related regeneration investments in the UK.

Notes

1. Sport England, 'The Value of Sport', http://www.sportengland.org (accessed 25 July 2008).
2. BURA, *BURA Guide*.
3. Percy, *Planning Bulletin*.
4. Roberts, *Evolution, Definition and Purpose*, 17.
5. Council of Europe, 'The European Sports Charter', http://www.coe.int, accessed 26 June 2008. The Charter provides guidance for the Council of Europe's member states to perfect existing legislations or other policies and to develop a comprehensive framework for sport.
6. Ibid.
7. BURA, *BURA Guide*.
8. Evans, 'Measure for Measure'.
9. Ibid.
10. Percy, *Planning Bulletin*.
11. Evans, 'Measure for Measure'.
12. Sport England, *Driving Up Participation*.
13. Department of the Environment, *Developing Sport and Leisure*.
14. For example, DCMS, *National Strategy*.
15. DCMS/Strategy Unit, *Game Plan*.
16. Sport England, *Framework for Sport*.
17. Sport England, 'News and Media: Government and Sport', http://www.sportengland.org/index/news_and_media/news_gs.htm (accessed 25 July 2008).
18. Sport England, 'The Value of Sport', http://www.sportengland.org.
19. Ibid. The Value of Sport is an online monitoring service set up by Sport England detailing research evidence on the contribution of sport to a range of broader social issues.
20. Ibid.
21. Davies, 'Sport in the City'; Davies, 'Sporting a New Role'; Gratton, Shibli and Coleman, 'Sport and Economic Regeneration'.
22. Collins, 'Economics of Sport'.
23. Henley Centre for Forecasting, *The Economic Impact and Importance of Sport in the UK*.
24. Jones, *Economic Impact and Importance*.
25. SIRC, *England, 1985–2005*.
26. SIRC, *England 2003*.
27. SIRC, *England, 1985–2005*; SIRC, *East of England, 2000–2005*; SIRC, *East Midlands, 2000–2005*; SIRC, *London, 2000–2005*; SIRC, *North East 2000–2005*; SIRC, *North West 2000–2005*; *South East 2000–2005*; SIRC, *South West 2000–2005*; SIRC, *West Midlands 2000–2005*; SIRC, *Yorkshire and the Humber 2000–2005*.
28. Davies, 'Valuing the Voluntary Sector'.
29. SIRC, *England, 1985–2005*, 44.
30. E.g., Davies, 'Sport in the City'; Gratton, Coleman and Davies, *Sport Industry*; Henley Centre for Forecasting, *Economic Impact and Importance of Sport in Two Local Areas*; SIRC, *Sport Economy in Rural Cornwall*.
31. Gratton, Shibli and Coleman, 'Sport and Economic Regeneration'.
32. Burns, Hatch and Mules, *Adelaide Grand Prix*.
33. E.g. Brown and Massey, *Literature Review*; Carlsen and Taylor, 'Mega Events'; Smith, 'After the Circus'; Smith and Fox, 'From "Event-led"; Waitt, 'Social Impacts'.
34. Archer, 'Tourism Multipliers'; Jackson, 'Economic Impact Studies'; Kasimati, 'Economic Aspects'.
35. UK Sport, *Measuring Success 3*.
36. Crompton, 'Economic Impact Analysis'.
37. Baade and Dye, 'Impacts of Stadiums'; Baade and Matheson, 'Bidding for the Olympics'; Crompton, 'Economic Impact Analysis'.
38. Kasimati, 'Economic Aspects'.
39. UK Sport, *Measuring Success*; *Measuring Success 2*; *Measuring Success 3*.
40. Crompton, 'Economic Impact Analysis'.
41. Baade and Matheson, 'Bidding for the Olympics'.
42. Brown and Massey, *Literature Review*; Carlsen and Taylor, 'Mega Events'; Gratton, Shibli and Coleman, 'Sport and Economic Regeneration'.

[43] Olympic Review, 'Focus: Olympic Games Global Impact', June 2006, http:www.olympic.org (accessed 23 July 2008).

[44] Leonardsen, 'Planning of Mega Events'.

[45] Baade, 'Stadiums'; Baade, 'Professional Sports'; Coates and Humphreys, 'Growth Effects'; Danielson, *Home Team*; Noll and Zimbalist, *Sports, Jobs and Taxes*; Rosentraub, *Major League Losers*.

[46] Baade and Matheson, 'Home Run or Wild Pitch?'; Colclough, Daellenback and Sherony, 'Estimating the Economic Impact'; Euchner, *Playing the Field*; Johnson, 'Local Government'; Johnson, *Minor League Baseball*; Lertwachara and Cochran, 'An Event Study'; Rosentraub and Swindell, 'Just Say No?'.

[47] Baade, *Evaluating Subsidies*; Baade and Dye, 'An Analysis'; Baade and Dye, 'Sports Stadiums'; Baade and Dye, 'Impact of Stadiums'; Chema, 'When Professional Sports'; Coates, 'Stadiums and Arenas'; Crompton, 'Public Subsidies'; Rosentraub, 'Does the Emperor'; Rosentraub, *Major League Losers*; Shropshire, *Sports Franchise Game*; Swindell and Rosentraub, 'Who Benefits'.

[48] Jones, 'Public Cost'.

[49] Thornley, 'Guest Editorial'.

[50] Jones, 'Public Cost'.

[51] Jones, 'A Level Playing Field'; Jones, 'Public Cost'; Jones, 'Stadium and Economic Development'.

[52] Davies, 'Not in My Back Yard!'; Davies, 'Sporting a New Role?'; Davies, 'Sport and the Local Economy'.

[53] DCMS, *National Strategy*.

[54] Evans, 'Measure for Measure'.

[55] London2012, 'Candidate File, Volume 1', http://www.London2012.com (accessed 25 July 2008).

[56] Hall, 'Politics of Hallmark Events', 219.

[57] Kasimati, 'Economic Aspects', 433.

[58] Ibid.

[59] Horne, 'Four "Knowns"', 85.

[60] Essex and Chalkley, 'Urban Development'; French and Disher, 'Atlanta and the Olympics'; Roche, 'Mega-events and Urban Policy'; Preuss, *Economics of Staging the Olympics*.

[61] DCMS, 'Olympics Minister Tessa Jowell Written Ministerial Statement – Olympic Delivery Authority Budget', http://www.culture.gov.uk/reference_library/media_releases/2260.aspx (accessed 28 July 2008).

References

Archer, B.H. 'Tourism Multipliers: The State of the Art'. *Bangor Occasional Papers in Economics*, no. 2. Cardiff: University of Wales Press, 1977.

Baade, R.A. 'Evaluating Subsidies for Professional Sports in the United States and Europe: A Public Sector Primer'. *Oxford Review of Economic Policy* 19, no. 4 (2003): 585–97.

Baade, R.A. 'Professional Sports as Catalysts for Metropolitan Economic Development'. *Journal of Urban Affairs* 18, no. 1 (1996): 1–17.

Baade, R.A. 'Stadiums, Professional Sports and City Economies: An Analysis of the United States Experience'. In *The Stadium and the City*, edited by J. Bale and O. Moen, 277–94. Keele: Keele University Press, 1995.

Baade, R.A., and R.F Dye. 'An Analysis of the Economic Rationale for Public Subsidization of Sports Stadiums'. *Annals of Regional Science* 23 (1988): 37–42.

Baade, R.A., and R.F Dye. 'The Impact of Stadiums and Professional Sports on Metropolitan Area Development'. *Growth and Change* 21, no. 2 (1990): 1–14.

Baade, R.A, and R.F Dye. 'Sports Stadiums and Area Development: A Critical Review'. *Economic Development Quarterly* 2 (1988): 265–75.

Baade, R.A., and V. Matheson. 'Bidding for the Olympics: Fool's Gold?'. In *Transatlantic Sport: The Comparative Economics of North America and European Sports*, edited by C.P Barros, M. Ibrahimo, and S. Szymanski, 127–51. London: Edward Elgar, 2002.

Baade, R.A., and V. Matheson. 'Home Run or Wild Pitch? Assessing the Economic Impact of Major League Baseball's All-star Game'. *Journal of Sports Economics* 2 (2001): 307–27.

Brown, A., and J. Massey. *Literature Review: The Impact of Major Sporting Events*. London: UK Sport, 2001.

BURA. *BURA Guide to Best Practice in Sport and Regeneration*. London: British Urban Regeneration Association, 2003.

Burns, J.A., J.H. Hatch, and T.J. Mules. *The Adelaide Grand Prix*. Adelaide: The Centre for South Australian Economic Studies, 1986.

Cambridge Econometrics. *The Value of the Sports Economy in England*. Cambridge: Cambridge Econometrics, 2003a.

Cambridge Econometrics. *The Value of the Sports Economy in the Regions: The Case of London*. Cambridge: Cambridge Econometrics, 2003b.

Cambridge Econometrics. *The Value of the Sports Economy in the Regions: The Case of the East Midlands*. Cambridge: Cambridge Econometrics, 2003c.

Cambridge Econometrics. *The Value of the Sports Economy in the Regions: The Case of the East of England*. Cambridge: Cambridge Econometrics, 2003d.

Cambridge Econometrics. *The Value of the Sports Economy in the Regions: The Case of the North East*. Cambridge: Cambridge Econometrics, 2003e.

Cambridge Econometrics. *The Value of the Sports Economy in the Regions: The Case of the North West*. Cambridge: Cambridge Econometrics, 2003f.

Cambridge Econometrics. *The Value of the Sports Economy in the Regions: The Case of the South East*. Cambridge: Cambridge Econometrics, 2003g.

Cambridge Econometrics. *The Value of the Sports Economy in the Regions: The Case of the South West*. Cambridge: Cambridge Econometrics, 2003h.

Cambridge Econometrics. *The Value of the Sports Economy in the Regions: The Case of the West Midlands*. Cambridge: Cambridge Econometrics, 2003i.

Cambridge Econometrics. *The Value of the Sports Economy in the Regions: The Case of Yorkshire & the Humber*. Cambridge: Cambridge Econometrics, 2003j.

Carlsen, J., and A. Taylor. 'Mega Events and Urban Renewal: The Case of the Manchester 2002 Commonwealth Games'. *Event Management* 8 (2003): 15–22.

Centre for Advanced Studies in the Social Sciences. *The Economic Impact of Sport in Wales*. Cardiff: The Sports Council for Wales, 1995.

Chema, T.V. 'When Professional Sports Justify the Subsidy. A Reply to Robert A. Baade'. *Journal of Urban Affairs* 18, no. 1 (1996): 19–22.

Coates, D. 'Stadiums and Arenas: Economic Development or Economic Redistribution'. *Contemporary Economic Policy* 25, no. 4 (2007): 565–77.

Coates, D., and B.R. Humphreys. 'The Growth Effects of Sport Franchises, Stadia and Arenas'. *Journal of Policy Analysis and Management* 18 (1999): 601–24.

Colclough, W., L. Daellenback, and K. Sherony. 'Estimating the Economic Impact of a Minor League Baseball Stadium'. *Managerial and Decision Economics* 15, no. 5 (1994): 497–502.

Collins, M.F. 'The Economics of Sport and Sports in the Economy: Some International Comparisons'. In *Progress in Tourism, Recreation and Hospitality Management*, edited by C.P. Cooper, 184–214. London: Belhaven Press, 1991.

Crompton, J.L. 'Economic Impact Analysis of Sports Facilities and Events: Eleven Sources of Misapplication'. *Journal of Sport Management* 9 (1995): 14–35.

Crompton, J.L. 'Public Subsidies to Professional Team Sport Facilities in the USA'. In *Sport in the City: The Role of Sport in Economic and Social Regeneration*, edited by C. Gratton and I. Henry, 15–34. London: Routledge, 2001.

Danielson, M.N. *Home Team: Professional Sports and the American Metropolis*. Princeton: Princeton University Press, 1997.

Davies, L.E. 'Not in My Back Yard! Stadia Location and the Property Market'. *Area* 37, no. 3 (2005): 268–76.

Davies, L.E. 'Sport and the Local Economy: The Role of Stadia in Regenerating Commercial Property'. *Local Economy* 23, no. 1 (2008): 31–46.

Davies, L.E. 'Sporting a New Role? Stadia and the Real Estate Market'. *Managing Leisure* 11, no. 4 (2006): 231–44.

Davies, L.E. 'Sport in the City: Measuring Economic Significance at the Local Level'. *European Sport Management Quarterly* 2, no. 2 (2002): 83–107.

Davies, L.E. 'Valuing the Voluntary Sector: Rethinking Economic Analysis'. *Leisure Studies* 23, no. 4 (2004): 347–64.

DCMS. *National Strategy for Neighbourhood Renewal. Policy Action Team Audit: Report of the Policy Action Team 10. The Contribution of Sport and the Arts*. London: HMSO, 1999.

DCMS/Strategy Unit. *Game Plan: A Strategy for Delivering Government's Sport and Physical Activity Objectives*. London: Cabinet Office, 2002.

Department of the Environment. *Developing Sport and Leisure: Good Practice in Urban Regeneration*. London: HMSO, 1989.

Essex, S., and B. Chalkley. 'Urban Development Through Hosting International Events: A History of the Olympic Games'. *Planning Perspectives* 14 (1999): 369–94.

Euchner, C.C. *Playing the Field: Why Sports Teams Move and Cites Fight to Keep Them*. Baltimore: John Hopkins University Press, 1993.

Evans, G. 'Measure for Measure: Evaluating the Evidence of Culture's Contribution to Regeneration'. *Urban Studies* 42, nos. 5/6 (2005): 959–83.

French, S.P., and M.E. Disher. 'Atlanta and the Olympics: A One Year Retrospective'. *Journal of the American Planning Association* 63, no. 3 (1997): 37–92.

Gratton, C., R. Coleman, and L.E. Davies. *The Sport Industry in South Yorkshire*. Sheffield Hallam University: Leisure Industries Research Centre, 2001.

Gratton, C., S. Shibli, and R. Coleman. 'Sport and Economic Regeneration in Cities'. *Urban Studies* 42, nos. 5/6 (2005): 985–99.

Hall, C.M. 'The Politics of Hallmark Events'. In *The Planning and Evaluation of Hallmark Events*, edited by G. Syme, B. Shaw, M. Fenton, and W. Mueller, 219–41. Aldershot: Avebury, 1989.

Henley Centre for Forecasting. *The Economic Impact and Importance of Sport in the Northern Ireland Economy*. Belfast: The Sports Council for Northern Ireland, 1992.

Henley Centre for Forecasting. *The Economic Impact and Importance of Sport in the UK*. Study 30. London: The Sports Council, 1986.

Henley Centre for Forecasting. *The Economic Impact and Importance of Sport in the UK Economy in 1990*. London: The Sports Council, 1992.

Henley Centre for Forecasting. *The Economic Impact and Importance of Sport in the Welsh Economy*. Cardiff: The Sports Council of Wales, 1990.

Henley Centre for Forecasting. *The Economic Impact and Importance of Sport in Two Local Areas: Bracknell and the Wirral*. Study 33 London: The Sports Council, 1989.

Horne, J. 'The Four 'Knowns' of Sports Mega-Events'. *Leisure Studies* 26, no. 1 (2007): 81–96.

Jackson, M.J. 'Economic Impact Studies: The Methodology Applied to Tourism'. *Occasional Research Paper in Economics*. Bristol Polytechnic: Department of Economics and Social Sciences, 1986.

Johnson, A.T. 'Local Government, Minor League Baseball and Economic Development Strategies'. *Economic Development Quarterly* 5, no. 4 (1991): 313–24.

Johnson, A.T. *Minor League Baseball and Local Economic Development*. Urbana: University of Illinois Press, 1993.

Jones, C. 'A Level Playing Field? Sports Stadium Infrastructure and Urban Development in the United Kingdom'. *Environment and Planning A* 33 (2001): 845–61.

Jones, C. "Public Cost for Private Gain? – Recent and Proposed "National" Stadium Developments in the UK, and Commonalities with North America'. *Area* 34 (2002): 160–70.

Jones, C. 'The Stadium and Economic Development: Cardiff and the Millennium Stadium'. *European Planning Studies* 10, no. 7 (2002): 819–29.

Jones, H. *The Economic Impact and Importance of Sport: A European Study*. Strasbourg: Council of Europe, 1989.

Kasimati, E. 'Economic Aspects and the Summer Olympics: A Review of Related Research'. *International Journal of Tourism Research* 5 (2003): 433–44.

Leonardsen, D. 'Planning of Mega Events: Experiences and Lessons'. *Planning Theory and Practice* 8, no. 1 (2007): 11–30.

Lertwachara, K., and J.J. Cochran. 'An Event Study of the Economic Impact of Professional Sport Franchises on Local US Economies'. *Journal of Sports Economics* 8 (2007): 244.

LIRC. *The Economic Importance of Sport in England in 1995*. Report to the Sports Council Sheffield: Leisure Industries Research Centre, Sheffield Hallam University, 1997a.

LIRC. *The Economic Importance of Sport in England in 1998*. Report to Sport England Sheffield: Leisure Industries Research Centre, Sheffield Hallam University, 2000a.

LIRC. *The Economic Importance of Sport in Northern Ireland in 1995*. Report to the Northern Ireland Sports Council Sheffield: Leisure Industries Research Centre, Sheffield Hallam University, 1997b.

LIRC. *The Economic Importance of Sport in Northern Ireland in 1998*. Report to the Northern Ireland Sports Council Sheffield: Leisure Industries Research Centre, Sheffield Hallam University, 2000b.

LIRC. *The Economic Importance of Sport in Scotland in 1995*. Report to the Scottish Sports Council Sheffield: Leisure Industries Research Centre, Sheffield Hallam University, 1997c.

LIRC. *The Economic Importance of Sport in the UK in 1995*. Sheffield: Leisure Industries Research Centre, Sheffield Hallam University, 1997d.

LIRC. *The Economic Importance of Sport in the UK in 1998*. Report to the UK Sports Council Sheffield: Leisure Industries Research Centre, Sheffield Hallam University, 2000c.

LIRC. *The Economic Importance of Sport in Wales in 1995*. Report to the Sports Council for Wales. Sheffield: Leisure Industries Research Centre, Sheffield Hallam University, 1997e.

LIRC. *The Economic Importance of Sport in Wales in 1998*. Report to the Sports Council for Wales. Sheffield: Leisure Industries Research Centre, Sheffield Hallam University, 2000d.

Noll, R.G. and Zimbalist, A., eds. *Sports Jobs and Taxes: The Economic Impact of Sports Teams and Stadiums*. Washington, D.C: Brookings Institution Press, 1997.

Percy, R. *Planning Bulletin, Issue Ten: Sport and Regeneration*. London: Sport England, 2001.

Pieda. *Sport and the Economy of Scotland*. Research Report No 18 Edinburgh: The Scottish Sports Council, 1991.

Pieda. *Sport and the Northern Regional Economy*. The Sports Council, Northern Region 1994.

Preuss, H. *The Economics of Staging the Olympics: A Comparison of the Games 1972–2008*. Cheltenham: Edward Elgar Publishing, 2004.

Roberts, P. 'The Evolution, Definition and Purpose of Urban Regeneration'. In *Urban Regeneration: A Handbook*, edited by P. Roberts and H. Sykes, 9–36. London: Sage, 2000.

Roche, M. 'Mega-events and Urban Policy'. *Annals of Tourism Research* 21 (1994): 1–19.

Rosentraub, M.S. 'Does the Emperor Have New Clothes? A Reply to Robert A. Baade'. *Journal of Urban Affairs* 18, no. 1 (1996): 23–31.

Rosentraub, M.S. *Major League Losers: The Real Cost of Sports and Who's Paying For It*. New York: Basicbooks, 1997.

Rosentraub, M.S., and D. Swindell. 'Just Say No? The Economic and Political Realities of a Small City's Investment in Minor League Baseball'. *Economic Development Quarterly* 5, no. 2 (1991): 152–67.

Shropshire, K.L. *The Sports Franchise Game: Cities in Pursuit of Sports Franchises, Events, Stadiums and Arenas*. Philadelphia: University of Pennsylvania Press, 1995.

SIRC. *The Economic Importance of Sport: East Midlands 2003*. London: Sport England, 2007a.

SIRC. *The Economic Importance of Sport: East of England 2003*. London: Sport England, 2007b.

SIRC. *Economic Importance of Sport: England 2003*. London: Sport England, 2007c.

SIRC. *The Economic Importance of Sport in England 2001*. Report for the English Sport Council Sheffield: Sport Industries Research Centre, Sheffield Hallam University, 2004a.

SIRC. *The Economic Importance of Sport in England, 1985–2005*. London: Sport England, 2007d.

SIRC. *The Economic Importance of Sport in London, 2000–2005*. London: Sport England, 2007e.

SIRC. *The Economic Importance of Sport in Northern Ireland*. 2007f. http://www.sportni.net/research/RecentResearchPublications.html (accessed 10 August 2008).

SIRC. *The Economic Importance of Sport in the East of England, 2000–2005*. London: Sport England, 2007g.

SIRC. *The Economic Importance of Sport in the East Midlands, 2000–2005*. London: Sport England, 2007h.

SIRC. *The Economic Importance of Sport in the North East 2000–2005*. London: Sport England, 2007i.

SIRC. *The Economic Importance of Sport in the North West 2000–2005*. London: Sport England, 2007j.

SIRC. *The Economic Importance of Sport in the South East 2000–2005*. London: Sport England, 2007k.

SIRC. *The Economic Importance of Sport in the South West 2000–2005*. London: Sport England, 2007l.

SIRC. *The Economic Importance of Sport in the UK 2001*. Report for the English and Scottish Sports Councils Sheffield: Sport Industries Research Centre, Sheffield Hallam University, 2004b.

SIRC. *The Economic Importance of Sport in the UK 2004*. Sheffield: Sport Industries Research Centre, Sheffield Hallam University, 2007m.

SIRC. *The Economic Importance of Sport in the West Midlands 2000–2005*. London: Sport England, 2007n.

SIRC. *The Economic Importance of Sport in Wales 2004*. Sheffield: Sport Industries Research Centre, Sheffield Hallam University, 2007o.

SIRC. *The Economic Importance of Sport in Yorkshire and the Humber 2000–2005*. London: Sport England, 2007p.

SIRC. *The Economic Importance of Sport: London 2003*. London: Sport England, 2007q.

SIRC. *The Economic Importance of Sport: North East 2003*. London: Sport England, 2007r.

SIRC. *The Economic Importance of Sport: North West 2003*. London: Sport England, 2007s.

SIRC. *The Economic Importance of Sport: South East 2003*. London: Sport England, 2007t.

SIRC. *The Economic Importance of Sport: South West 2003*. London: Sport England, 2007u.

SIRC. *The Economic Importance of Sport: West Midlands 2003*. London: Sport England, 2007v.

SIRC. *The Economic Importance of Sport: Yorkshire 2003*. London: Sport England, 2007w.

SIRC. *The Sport Economy in Rural Cornwall and the Isles of Scilly*. Cornwall Enterprise Limited, 2004. http://www.ruralcornwall.co.uk/docs/SAZ-EIAfinal.pdf, accessed 31 July 2008c.

Smith, A. 'After the Circus Leaves Town: The Relationship Between Sport Events, Tourism and Urban Regeneration'. In *Tourism, Culture and Regeneration*, edited by M.K. Smith, 10–85. Wallingford: CAB International, 2007.

Smith, A., and T. Fox. 'From "Event-led" to "Event-themed" Regeneration: The 2002 Commonwealth Games Legacy Programme'. *Urban Studies* 44, no. 5 (2007): 1125–43.

Sport England. *Driving Up Participation: The Challenge for Sport*. London: Sport England, 2004.

Sport England. *The Framework for Sport in England*. London: Sport England, 2004.

Sportscotland. *The Economic Importance of Sport in Scotland 1998*. Research Digest No. 60. Edinburgh: Sportscotland, 2001.

Sportscotland. *The Economic Importance of Sport in Scotland 2001*. Research Digest No. 95. Edinburgh: Sportscotland, 2004.

Sportscotland. *The Economic Importance of Sport in Scotland 2004*. Research Digest No. 101. Edinburgh: Sportscotland, 2007.

Swindell, D., and M.S. Rosentraub. 'Who Benefits from the Presence of Professional Sports Teams? The Implications for Public Funding of Stadiums and Arenas'. *Public Administration Review* 58, no. 1 (1998): 11–20.

Thornley, A. 'Guest Editorial: Urban Regeneration and Sports Stadia'. *European Planning Studies* 10, no. 7 (2002): 813–8.

UK Sport. *Measuring Success*. London: UK Sport, 1999.

UK Sport. *Measuring Success 2*. London: UK Sport, 2004.

UK Sport. *Measuring Success 3*. London: UK Sport, 2005.

Waitt, G. 'Social Impacts of the Sydney Olympics'. *Annals of Tourism Research* 30, no. 1 (2003): 194–215.

Fitting a square stadium into a round hole: a case of deliberation and procrastination politics

Michael P. Sam[a] and Jay Scherer[b]

[a]School of Physical Education, University of Otago, New Zealand; [b]Faculty of Physical Education and Recreation, University of Alberta, Canada

From the perspective of city officials, proposals to build new stadiums are tenuous because of the dual local government imperatives of having to be both visionary (i.e., entrepreneurial) and conservative (i.e., fiscally responsible and publicly accountable). Based on case data in Dunedin, New Zealand, we investigate two related dilemmas that emanate from that city's stadium deliberation process. The first is with regards to the dichotomy between politicians and bureaucrats, and the degree to which deliberations on a new stadium should be politically or technocratically driven. The second concerns the extent to which local authorities favour independence or accountability in gathering information. Here we suggest that deference and delegation to an 'independent' body became tantamount to procrastinating – that is a case of holding the process up in order to progress it. Our analysis demonstrates that such dilemmas demand immediate responses that, while seemingly benign in the short term, alter the balance between a city's entrepreneurial outlook and its view towards citizen responsiveness.

Introduction

A prominent theme with respect to sport's connection with cities has been the persistent optimism that the subsidy of stadiums can stimulate urban development. To an extent, this optimism stems from a broader confidence in the capacity of governments to manage their economies through a range of instruments such as the marketization of public services (e.g., privatised enterprises, public/private partnerships) or the provision of industry-specific subsidies (e.g., land acquisitions, infrastructure improvements, financing and regulatory relief). Translated into local politics, these doctrines have encouraged an entrepreneurial outlook and furthered the belief that cities can be re-engineered or re-invented to meet the challenges of rapid economic and social changes. Accordingly, cities wanting to shed their post-industrial images have pursued a range of policy strategies such as the alteration of public spaces into branded tourist and urban entertainment destinations and/or the pursuit of mega-event hosting rights.[1]

Sports stadiums are perhaps one of the most costly and contentious instruments of such urban reinvention and development schemes.[2] Indeed while they are often promoted by urban elites as generating 'psychic income' and producing civic identity,[3] their engagement with democratic processes is inherently tenuous and contingent. Moreover, beyond the sheer amount of public financing required to underwrite these developments, local stadium debates are inevitably related to competing claims as to whose 'vision' of a city and urban space is to be accepted. In addition to these ideological divides, more concretely, stadium proposals also raise a number of practical dilemmas with very real and long-term political consequences. Are planning experts more qualified or competent in determining public value(s) than elected officials? How can civic planning 'visions' (in which stadiums are often an essential component) be legitimized and defended in public, yet responsibly scrutinized at the same time? If, as Hendriks and Carson suggest, deliberative ideals have become 'commercial goods' increasingly linked with the consultancy market, what are the consequences of 'commodifying' the processes of investigation and public deliberation that underpin local stadium debates?[4]

The intersections between stadiums and the political processes of deliberation are important for two additional reasons. First, if we accept the unique place of sport within culture, the debates over the dedication of public funds for stadium developments represent both a litmus test for the relative social significance of sport and a measure of democratic politics in local municipalities. In this way, local stadium debates often reveal concerns about the appropriate scope of government in public-private partnerships, and the 'boundaries of the public'.[5] Indeed, insofar as cities are becoming increasingly entrepreneurial in their outlooks and approaches to policy development, stadium developments are routinely emblematic of strategies that 'naturalize the private interest of capital to appear in the public good'.[6] Second, an emphasis on the tensions and dilemmas faced by local authorities in these debates encourages a closer examination of the political mechanisms that guide and shape public deliberation over the subsidy of stadium developments. While there is a visible shift towards the 'neoliberal city' and entrepreneurial urban policymaking contexts, paradoxically there are also renewed pressures on local governments to democratize the decisions that produce urban space.[7] More than ever, cities now regard public engagement and consultation as an imperative and one not easily exploited in light of contemporary demands for governmental transparency and procedural compliance.[8]

In relation to these issues, our aim is to explore the challenges facing local authorities in Dunedin, New Zealand, who are navigating the deliberative process of a contentious public debate over the construction of a new, world-class rugby stadium to replace the existing rugby ground, Carisbrook. More specifically from the City of Dunedin's perspective, we investigate two related dilemmas that emanate from the dual local government imperatives of having to be both 'visionary' (i.e., entrepreneurial) and conservative (i.e., fiscally responsible and publicly accountable). The first tension is with regards to the dichotomy between politicians and bureaucrats, and the degree to which deliberations on the new stadium should be politically or technocratically driven. It can be granted that achieving this balance has been challenging for politicians not least because existing decision forums (such as the annual planning or budgetary processes) cannot easily cope with an issue that is so divisive and arises so rarely in the lifetimes of civic leaders. Indeed, some have even suggested that local stadium debates constitute 'extraordinary' political circumstances.[9] It is not surprising, then, that the deliberation processes around stadium subsidies are largely characterized by haphazard, piecemeal, and temporary institutional arrangements (such as referendums).

The second, related quandary is in relation to the nature of the public-private partnerships surrounding the Carisbrook debate. The tension can be more easily recognized as a 'trade-off' in which local decision-makers have to balance aspects they want but cannot possibly have – in this case wanting *independent* (evidence-based) investigations, while also meeting the expectations for fostering economic development/cooperation through a public-private partnership. In the Carisbrook case, the principal trade-off appears to be the make-up of the investigating groups that ultimately inform City Council, and whether these groups should consist of interested stakeholders including the provincial rugby union, corporate stakeholders and private consultants. As our analysis demonstrates, such dilemmas demand immediate responses that, while seemingly benign in the short term, alter the balance between a city's entrepreneurial outlook (and its propensity to pursue risky ventures), and its view towards public accountability and citizen responsiveness.

Our analysis proceeds on three fronts. First we locate our work within two prominent approaches used to study stadium debates and processes. We then briefly outline the Carisbrook case with a focus on key events and changes in political context. Finally, we discuss the tendency for such quandaries to result in procrastination and delay that generates opposition and local resistance to stadium developments, while creating a substantive inertia for proponents.

Studying the process

A prominent dimension to stadium subsidy issues concerns the rhetorical, ideological and discursive nature of debates. Such a perspective highlights the near-universal discourses underpinning new stadium development proposals and draws attention to how elites create and/or exploit notions of 'progress', civic identity and/or national pride. For our purposes, Schimmel's work is particularly instructive because it highlights the 'gamble' city officials are willing to undertake with public funds in order to retain the status of a premiere, competitive city.[10]

A second near-universal feature of stadium subsidy debates relates to the coalitions that emerge from public and private sector interests, and exert considerable influence in decision-making processes.[11] That such coalitions or 'regimes' so often succeed in securing public funding is relatively unsurprising: they are typically 'first movers' on the issue and initiate much of the investigative work that subsequently frames public debates.[12] Indeed, the growth coalition thesis suggests a degree of rationality or 'path dependence' in which members of the coalition: (1) are self-interested; (2) have clear and similar policy goal preferences; and (3) purposefully design the institutional environment to meet their demands. Certainly, the first is easily defended, though there is some question as to whether this self-interest is based on material interest or other motives such as status and/or the desire to create a 'lasting legacy'. Similarly, the second of these assumptions is reasonably straightforward since there are rarely many alternatives to deliberate in stadium debates; though admittedly over-simplified, one is either a proponent or opponent of a stadium public subsidy.

Of particular interest here is the third of these characteristics – the extent to which pro-stadium coalitions can manage or exploit the deliberation process. There are potentially two primary reasons to question this aspect. The first relates to the infrequency of these debates in the lifetimes of the coalition members themselves, an argument we would suggest is perhaps more relevant in smaller urban centres than larger ones. Second, it is unlikely that the designers of local government legislation had stadiums in mind and thus did not foresee their attendant public contentiousness, visibility and connections with civic, national and global identity. That is, if we accept that the debates around sport stadiums are often presented as 'crises' or what Kingdon would call 'focusing events', we are likely to see the galvanization of interest groups at a rate beyond the normal capacity of mechanisms to address it.[13] Indeed, while these sporting crises may well provide for opportunistic interests to exploit a sense of urgency, how they are able to do so is a function of the system of checks and balances available within local democracies (or a lack thereof). In this regard, we suggest it vital to critically examine the power relations and institutionalized dilemmas in local government that make them more (or less) susceptible to capture by coalitions and regimes.

Case background

While the debates over the existing Carisbrook stadium and a new replacement stadium have been ongoing since 2003, there have been several key milestones to this process.[14]

The first relates to the recent changes to the Special Consultative Procedures (SCPs) mandated by the amended Local Government Act (2002). As a result of these amendments, local authorities are now required to consult on proposals introducing 'significant' changes to the community plan. With respect to the stadium debate in Dunedin, the SCPs became a significant source of uncertainty for city councillors and bureaucrats, particularly given the largesse of the change, the probable involvement of two levels of local government, and the connection with professional rugby and the Otago Rugby Union (ORU) – the owners of the existing Carisbrook stadium. Indeed, when the issue of a substantial stadium subsidy first came to the attention of the Dunedin City Council (DCC) in 2003, the SCPs were relatively new and their requirements had been untested. Thus, the city began to navigate the consultative procedures without the benefit of any existing guidelines or institutionalized practices.

The second milestone was the establishment of the Carisbrook Working Party (CWP) that included the CEOs of the DCC, the Otago Regional Council (ORC), Sport Otago, the Community Trust of Otago, the ORU, and a local businessman. In 2004, the Dunedin City Council's CEO formed the CWP, a steering group charged with investigating and consulting with the public on three options regarding the city's existing stadium. Those options were to: (1) do nothing; (2) progressively upgrade the stadium; or, (3) build a new stadium. While consultations in rural regions were generally uncontested and mostly supportive of a progressive upgrade, the CWP encountered substantial resistance amongst city residents.[15] Against this urban animosity, and despite inconclusive survey data, the CWP announced that the preferred option was to upgrade the existing stadium at a cost of between $25–40 million.[16] However, after submitting its report to City Council, the CWP faced mounting public criticism aimed especially at the supposed 'independence' of its membership which consisted of a number of individuals with a vested interest in the outcome of this debate, most notably the CEOs of the ORU, the DCC, and the ORC. Additionally, against the claims of support for an upgrade of the existing stadium, the Dunedin Ratepayers and Householders Association circulated a petition against a city-funded upgrade which garnered over 3000 signatures. In the months that followed, a consulting company completed two separate refurbishment design options for the city, both of which were ultimately rejected by city councillors who cited the initial survey data that showed a small percentage (10%) of residents indicating a preference for a new stadium.

The third key event in the process is marked by the dissolution of the CWP in late 2005, as a direct result of it failing to win council consensus on the upgrade of Carsibrook stadium. This, along with the announcement that New Zealand had won the rights to host the 2011 Rugby World Cup spurred the subsequent formation of the Carisbrook Stadium Trust (CST), a self-appointed committee chaired by former city councillor and businessman Malcolm Farry. Notably, the CST's membership consisted of heads of construction companies and hotel consortiums as well as two University of Otago council representatives. The CST took over the remaining investigative budget from the CWP and, in August 2006, released its 'vision': a new, covered stadium situated on the harbour front. The 'coup de grace' was the University of Otago's proposed connection with the project. From that point onward, the Trust forever changed its role from that of 'investigator' to that of advocate, promoter and civic booster. For example, within a week of this announcement, the CST took out the following advertisement to hire a CEO, or in their words, a 'Leader of the Pack':

the vision for a new Carisbrook stadium includes a roof, a flexible entertainment layout and a unique partnership between sporting events, sports science and education . . . It represents a once in a lifetime opportunity for a passionate and dynamic Chief Executive to **turn the vision into reality** [emphasis added].[17]

A month later, the City Council instructed the CST that, while it supported the vision 'in principle', it should also 'investigate and present a range of options on the [existing stadium] Carisbrook upgrade'.[18] This left little doubt that the exploration of alternate options was no longer intended to re-open public deliberations, but to achieve minimal compliance in relation to the Local Government Act (LGA) and SCPs. Indeed, such incongruities between the City Council's expectations/requirements of due process and the autonomy of the CST became the hallmark of subsequent events and ensuing public debates. The next section of this paper is thus dedicated to tracing two key dilemmas that gave rise to these seemingly contradictory institutional arrangements.

Dilemma 1: politicians or bureaucrats?

Before changes to the LGA, policy roles for the two sub-levels of local government in New Zealand (Regional Councils and Territorial Local Authorities) were relatively distinct.[19] However, the new amendments included provisions for greater sharing of responsibilities (and costs), such as those associated with regional developments like harbour fronts or sports facilities. In this respect, instances of cooperation between the city and region had been rare. For example, the ORC had no historical role in developing or maintaining sports and recreation facilities. As one of the CWP members observed,

> there's not a lot of love lost between the TLAs [Territorial Local Authorities] and the Regional Council. And there's certainly not a lot of love lost between the DCC as the major authority tongue, and the other TLAs around it, such that in other issues, if the DCC isn't interested in what is an issue for one of the other local authorities, the DCC sort of just disregards it or doesn't give it due attention. . . . And so when the DCC looks to the other local authorities for buy-in to this project, then their instant reaction is one of hackles up, and 'stuff you, mate, where were you when . . . '. (personal communication)

Thus, beyond the 'newness' of the stadium subsidy issue, the CEO of the DCC felt he was limited by the process itself, which required the support of many levels of local government. Indeed, any decision to create an *ad hoc* body to include these interests would have immediately placed the issue into the political realm. The city's CEO said:

> In terms of political involvement, that's problematic because if you are wanting regional support and you put political people on, then you need a mechanism. Well, you would have to put the Regional Council on, you'd have to put the city on and you would need a mechanism to put the districts on. It's not impossible but you would have had three. (personal communication)

However, as he would later point out, there was general agreement that the issue of Carisbrook was a technical matter and one better situated with professionals with administrative expertise. The 'thinking at the time,' he said,

> was getting the information together, working through different stadia design and all of that – that's more of a technical and professional exercise. The actual decision is a political exercise, so I think certainly we would have turned our mind probably a bit more to the political involvement, but the councillors of the day were more than comfortable with that arrangement. (personal communication)

There was thus a strong belief that removing the issue from politicians would have the effect of de-politicizing the process, taken narrowly to mean that the work emanating from a group of 'experts' could avoid the parochial politics between the city and outlying municipalities. In this light, Fischer has argued that the use of experts was intended to replace the 'virtual enemy' of rational social organization, namely politicians and interest groups.[20] More significantly, the delineation between politics and planning would highlight the belief that planning lies firmly in the domain of bureaucrats and much less so with politicians.

Dilemma 2: structuring for autonomy or accountability?

The politics of planning also introduced a second interrelated tension – that between the imperative to work in partnership with the stadium owners (the ORU), and the need to maintain a level of objectivity or independence. For example, from initial discussions, the CEO of the DCC recognised that the ORU had neither the capacity nor the resources to negotiate the consultative requirements within the LGA. Other CWP members echoed the hesitancy of bringing the issue into the political realm too early. As the steering group's private consultant recalled:

> So I think it was....what forum can we use to debate these issues and how do we get a group of people around the table that have got some knowledge to drive this thing forward, how do we take it out of the strict council environment? (personal communication)

Two important points can be gleaned here. One is that the reason councillors agreed to have investigations proceed in this way was that they wanted the CWP to be independent. Having established that the issue as a technical matter, it thus made sense to include the owners of the stadium, the ORU. Also appropriate, then, was to have membership representing the amateur sport community and the business sector. Nevertheless, throughout the process, members of the CWP perceived their role as facilitators to the ORU, and not as independent investigators of a public issue. They were there, as one of the CWP members noted, 'to help facilitate the process of the Rugby Union [ORU] building up its case'.

Clearly, the CEO of the ORU perceived the consultation process in this way, as we frequently observed him speaking out as an advocate and proponent of a new or refurbished stadium.[21] His colleagues were not always comfortable with the approach, warning that, to some members of the public, this kind of 'bravado' might be seen as a loss of control and overly 'provocative'.

Certainly, this kind of posturing points to a tension residing beyond politics/adminis-tration and further into the perceived expediency of private sector management. One of the private sector members of the CWP, in fact, warned that the overly prescriptive requirements of the LGA, and by extension those who 'use it as their Bible', might determine the outcome of the stadium debate. 'But,' he said,

> you've got to manage that process, and accept that that's part of it and you can't just ignore it. So it's about using your management skills to work with people that you know are box tickers and just accept that that's part of it and work with them you know? (personal communication)

However, the 'box tickers' were at odds also, in part because sport facilities were seen to be firmly within the jurisdiction of the city and not the ORC. But more significantly, they were at odds over the particulars of the consultation process, and whether a survey and five public meetings would be sufficient in terms of providing evidenced-based policymaking. As the regional council's CEO expressed:

> Under the direction of the City itself or under the City-MWH liaison ... there got to be this issue that by racing out with the pamphlet and having these meetings around the region, with you know ten [or] sixteen people attending, everybody could agree it's a regional facility and it's regional funds and therefore it's all there, it's all done. We've done the consultation. You know I've been cautioning for a long time before that: 'hey guys, this is not the consultation that's required to get this Council involved'. (personal communication)

Even though there seemed to be agreement on the desired outcome between members of the CWP (i.e., the need for a new or refurbished stadium), the tensions between the public-sector accountability requirements and private-sector interests were continually apparent. For example, disagreements intensified over the very way in which public consultation should occur. While the consultants felt that the role of the CWP was to inform the public, the CEO of the ORU felt that,

> [Y]ou really want to be a bit bolder and go in and say 'right this is what we're going to do [Joe] Public and this is how we're going to fund it' but it [the LGA] doesn't allow you to do that because that then opens you up to review in some cases to the extent of judicial review because you didn't follow the correct consultative process. You can be deemed to have already preconceived outcomes before you've gone though the consultation. Whereas at the end of the day that's actually what people want. Just tell us what this thing is going to be, tell us how much its going to cost and then we'll get it all out in the newspapers and then we'll forget about it and just get on with life. (personal communication)

These words would, in fact, prove prophetic. After the dissolution of the CWP, the CST would ultimately produce a 'stadium vision' under a shroud of secrecy and without public input.

In 2007, and in the build-up to the CST's report that would detail the feasibility of a new stadium relative to upgrading the existing one, city councillors expressed their satisfaction with the Trust arrangements.[22] Many of them indicated that the CST's strength as investigative body was its independence from the political arena. 'The process,' as one councillor observed, 'had been 100 percent the right way to go'.[23] Meanwhile, the Deputy Mayor noted that by taking it out of the public arena, the council would be better informed to make a decision. And indeed, the CST was left to its own devices, with any interim contact with the City Council conducted well out of the public eye. For a few councillors, this independence and autonomy became something of an issue, a point we return to in the next section.

In late February 2007, and one week after the CST's briefing to the city, the council voted to support the stadium's inclusion in the community plan. Only after, did city officials decide to consult with the public and only with regards to the architectural designs, and options for how it should be funded. Thus, despite originating from within the special consultative procedures under the LGA, the formation of both the CWP and the CST became subsumed under what Bedford et al., called the traditional 'prepare-reveal-defend' process of planning delivery.[24]

Discussion: marketing the 'public interest' to ourselves

There is an old adage that policy can never be too far 'ahead' of the people it is intended to serve. In liberal democracies, this is meant to serve as a warning to political leaders who 'think big' or appear to ignore the general wishes of the public. Yet, it also highlights one of the fundamental tensions in local politics – that is, the degree to which city officials should be entrepreneurial (and take risks) while remaining publicly accountable (and fiscally responsible). One of the contemporary ways in which this tension becomes manifest is through the development of ever-more complex institutional arrangements designed to champion both the principles of civic engagement, and the appearance of a 'business-friendly' city.

Our case demonstrates that the attempts to reconcile this dilemma produced a number of consequences for the deliberation process. First and foremost, the use of an 'autonomous' body like the CST allowed city officials to set aside the political question of whether local government *should* provide a substantive subsidy. To be sure, there is arguably good reason to 'put off' making a decision of this magnitude. It is prudent for any government to seek public opinion, conduct feasibility studies and investigations, all of which take considerable time and effort, especially if they are to be conducted by 'disinterested' parties. However, within such investigations, the question of government subsidy was treated as a given by the city, and as a matter of economic and cultural common sense. Moreover, the fundamental political/normative questions of what problems the stadium was intended to solve in the first place (e.g., the city's drift away from its status as a major centre, the loss of hosting privileges for large-scale events), or whether local government should be the primary funder, were continually set aside in favour of seeking solutions to technical questions: in this case, turf growth, roof height, and the nuances of different taxation schemes.

Furthermore, after a year of such investigations, political questions remained off the public agenda because the CST had not formally asked the City Council for money. However, in light of this inevitability and the fact that the City Council had paid the CST over \$6 million to carry out its investigative activities, some councillors became concerned at the widening disconnection between the council and the CST. In response to one city councillor's complaints, the CST Chairman defended the arrangement this way: 'Seeing as we have not asked for any funding, it's not appropriate for us to go reporting like a little schoolboy at her [the councillor's] whim'.[25] During this period, the City Council continued to sanction delays in the CST's reporting while continually excluding the public in council and committee meetings on the grounds that land sale deals for a new stadium were commercially sensitive.

Issues of transparency aside, we suggest that such deference to the CST became tantamount to procrastination in public affairs or what Andreou would call putting off late 'what one should, relative to one's ends and information, have done sooner'.[26] Thus, we suggest the City Council procrastinated not only on publicly debating the need for a new stadium, but also on reviewing the investigative work carried out by its quasi-autonomous agents. We have noted elsewhere that this lack of 'checking' was achieved by insulating consultant forecasts from public scrutiny. Indeed, the CST continually assured the public that its revenue projections, estimates of costs and the like were accurate simply because they had been 'thoroughly challenged and debated' internally.[27]

Beyond that, the city's continuing deference to the CST has had perverse consequences for the system of democratic local politics. We use the word perverse here to suggest that the outcomes were likely unintended and unanticipated at the time these arrangements were developed.[28] So, while insulating the CST from political scrutiny allowed it to conduct its investigations without 'interference', this arrangement also allowed the CST time to 'build its case' and to aggressively market its vision to both the council and the public. In May 2007, for example, the CST commissioned consulting firm Colmar Brunton to gauge residents and businesses support for the new stadium development.[29] Expectedly, the results showed 'clear' support, mainly because the consultants used an online survey in which the CST provided its 'vision' as background but also because the 'representative sample' of 'corporates' (business and company representatives) was provided by the CST. To further sway the Council regarding the viability of private funding, the CST also commissioned an 'independent' report from consultants 'the Marketing Bureau Ltd'. Typifying its findings in December 2007, the writers concluded that the proposed stadium:

> is a key piece in the beginning of the rest of Dunedin's life – a centerpiece, an innovative, world class, civic, academic and community hub, providing a focus, a base and an icon for the future of Dunedin's place in the world.[30]

To win consent from the wider public, the CST paid for a series of full page adverts in the city's newspaper to promote the 'truth about the new multi-purpose stadium' and to 'thank the public for their support and encouragement'.[31] It also took out a series of half-page newspaper advertisements to present 'fact versus fiction' in relation to the 'great stadium debate 2007'.[32] The CST aired similar messages using various internet sites as a means of articulating its unfiltered findings and conclusions.[33] Perhaps most problematic is that, during the time of a city-council-commissioned survey to gauge public opinion on the new stadium, the CST embarked on a regional 'road show' to 'Brief you regarding the new multi-purpose stadium and provide information you may require to complete and return the public consultation questionnaire'.[34]

Taken together, these strategies also point to the currency of promotional politics, where most elements of communication, including those from the public sector, now contain a promotional message.[35] Of course, it is no small irony that the promotional efforts of the CST and its private boosters were dependent on, and appropriated, public funds in order to market their vision of the 'public interest' to the citizens of Dunedin. Indeed, the very fact that this preferred vision for the city was essentially developed in secrecy and out of the public eye speaks to the unease around how such projects can (or should) be brought onto the public agenda. Equally problematic is that the vision's subsequent deliberation became a product to be bought and sold – a case of citizens paying private consultants and advertisers (i.e., the ads noted above) to sell an idea back to the citizens themselves so that the public might hopefully agree to pay for it. In this light, the city's sanctioning of an autonomous body became arguably 'perverse' in that it weakened the credibility/legitimacy of the arrangement *and* countered one of the principal concerns it was intended to address: an independent assessment of the project's public value that was reduced altogether to the imperatives of marketing.

Conclusion

From the perspective of city officials, proposals to build new stadiums are tenuous because they are profoundly tied to both the prospect of growth and the prospect of political risk. They reflect the fundamental tensions in local governance between needing to act (i.e., the imperative to foster economic growth) and needing to listen (i.e., the imperative to be responsive to citizen preferences). Within these tensions we have proposed two inherent dilemmas underpinning the deliberative processes of a stadium subsidy proposal. The first dilemma concerns the degree to which these issues should be addressed by elected officials or bureaucrats. Insofar as a new stadium requires a careful negotiation of territorial boundaries, bureaucrats had the capacity to temporarily set aside parochial politics and thereby allow for the more technical concerns of cost and feasibility. However, 'doing things right' could not necessarily reconcile the political value of 'doing the right things' – in this case deliberating on the fundamental issue of public subsidy and whether such a project should be included on the planning agenda in the first place.

The second challenge is in regards to the extent to which cities favour autonomy and independence in gathering information versus the value of holding such investigations to account. We have suggested here that deference and delegation to an 'independent' body became tantamount to procrastinating – that is, a case of holding the process up in order to progress it. There are thus two equally plausible views that emerge from this perspective. The first is that cities put off their decisions in the hopes that the projects will eventually fall over, without councillors having to appear as against 'progress'. The second is that cities (and their dominant coalitions more particularly) procrastinate to ultimately gain enough time to market and promote their positions over a prolonged period, thereby allowing it to gain inertia and public acquiescence. In the context of the entrepreneurial city, both views are understandable if not also reprehensible.

They may be understandable in the context of the neoliberal imperative to become a competitive city, where the way in which to do so is to take chances, be visionary and lead. But what this also implies is that local governments not only feel that they must market themselves globally (a point frequently raised in academic writings), but they must also take considerable time and effort to market sport and sport edifices to the city itself, as matters of economic and cultural common sense. To an increasingly cynical public these actions can seem reprehensible, for there is an increasing expectation that local governments will be responsive and engage in extensive and meaningful public consultation, and not simply replace the institutionalized planning practice of 'prepare, reveal and defend' with a newer mantra of 'delay, market and sell'.

Notes

[1] See Belanger, 'Sport Venues'; Hannigan, *Fantasy City*.
[2] Eisinger, 'Politics of Bread'.
[3] Crompton, 'Beyond Economic Impact'.
[4] Hendriks and Carson, 'Can the Market Help'.
[5] Ferlie, Lynn and Pollitt, 'Afterword', 723.
[6] Schimmel, 'Political Economy of Place', 346.
[7] Purcell, 'Urban Democracy'.
[8] Bedford, Clark and Harrison, 'Limits to New Public'.
[9] Delaney and Eckstein, 'Urban Power Structures'.
[10] Schimmel, 'Deep Play'.
[11] Hannigan, *Fantasy City*.
[12] There are ongoing nuanced debates about both growth coalition and urban regime theories and thus for our purposes treat both of these interchangeably.
[13] Kingdon, *Agendas, Alternatives*.
[14] For details of this study's methods, see Scherer and Sam, this volume.
[15] Scherer and Sam, 'Public Consultation'.
[16] Sam and Scherer, 'Steering Group'.
[17] Otago Daily Times, 30 September 2006. Available at www.odt.co.nz.
[18] Dunedin City Council, Minutes.
[19] Territorial Local Authorities (TLAs) are elected councils situated in rural towns. Regional councils are made of representatives of the TLAs.
[20] Fischer, *Technocracy*, 24.
[21] Scherer and Sam, 'Public Consultation'.
[22] A. Rudd and D. Loughrey, 'Most Councillors Satisfied with Stadium Process', *Otago Daily Times*, 14 February 2007, 4.
[23] Ibid.
[24] Bedford, Clark and Harrison, 'Limits to New Public', 313.
[25] L. McBey, 'When Councillors Feel the Need to Ask Public to Trust Them', *Otago Daily Times*, 21 February 2007, 19.
[26] Andreou, 'Environmental Preservation', 234.
[27] Sam and Scherer, 'Stand Up'.
[28] Hood and Peters, 'Middle Aging'.
[29] Colmar Brunton Ltd, *Measuring Support*.
[30] Marketing Bureau, 'The New Stadium: Private Sector Funding Strategy and Progress'.
[31] CST. 'The Truth About the New Multi-purpose Stadium', *Otago Daily Times*, 28 September 2007, 16.
[32] Our Statium Group. 'The Great Stadium Debate 2007: Fact vs. Fiction', *Otago Daily Times*, 2.
[33] Scherer and Sam, this volume.
[34] CST. 'Notification of Meetings', *Otago Daily Times*, 18.
[35] Wernick, 'Promotional Culture: Advertising, Ideology and Symbolic Expression'.

References

Andreou, C. 'Environmental Preservation and Second-Order Procrastination'. *Philosophy and Public Affairs* 35, no. 3 (2007): 233–48.

Bedford, T., J. Clark, and C. Harrison. 'Limits to New Public Participation Practices in Local Land Use Planning'. *Town Planning Review* 73, no. 3 (2002): 311–31.

Belanger, A. 'Sport Venues and the Spectacularization of Urban Spaces in North America'. *International Review for the Sociology of Sport* 35, no. 3 (2000): 378–97.

Colmar Brunton Ltd. *Measuring Support for a Southern Entertainment Centre and Its Fundraising Initiatives*. Prepared for the Carisbrook Stadium Trust, Dunedin, 2007.

Crompton, J.L. 'Beyond Economic Impact: An Alternative Rationale for the Public Subsidy of Major League Sports Facilities'. *Journal of Sport Management* 18, no. 1 (2004): 40–58.

Delaney, K.J., and R. Eckstein. 'Urban Power Structures and Publicly Financed Stadiums'. *Sociological Forum* 22, no. 3 (2007): 331–53.

Dunedin City Council. *Minutes of the Meeting of the Dunedin City Council on the 25 September 2006*. Available at www.dunedin.govt.nz.

Eisinger, P. 'The Politics of Bread and Circuses: Building the City for the Visitor Class'. *Urban Affairs Review* 35, no. 3 (2000): 316–33.

Ferlie, E., L.E Lynn, and C. Pollitt. 'Afterword'. In *The Oxford Handbook of Public Management*, edited by E. Ferlie, L.E. Lynn, and C. Pollitt, 720–9. Oxford: Oxford University Press, 2005.

Fischer, Frank. *Technocracy and the Politics of Expertise*. Newbury Park, CA: Sage Publications, 1990.

Hannigan, J. *Fantasy City: Pleasure and Profit in the Postmodern Metropolis*. London: Routledge, 1998.

Hendriks, C.M., and L. Carson. 'Can the Market Help the Forum? Negotiating the Commercialization of Deliberative Democracy'. *Policy Sciences* 41, no. 4 (2008): 293–313.

Hood, Christopher, and B. Guy Peters. 'The Middle Aging of New Public Management: Into the Age of Paradox?'. *Journal of Public Administration Research and Theory* 14, no. 3 (2004): 267–82.

Kingdon, John W. *Agendas, Alternatives, and Public Policies*. 2nd ed. New York: HarperCollins College Publishers, 1995.

Marketing Bureau Ltd. *The New Stadium: Private Sector Funding Strategy and Progress*. Auckland: The Marketing Bureau, 2007.

Purcell, M. 'Urban Democracy and the Local Trap'. *Urban Studies* 43, no. 11 (2006): 1921–41.

Sam, M.P., and J. Scherer. 'Stand up and Be Counted: Numerical Storylines in a Stadium Debate'. *International Review for the Sociology of Sport* 43 (2008): 53–70.

Sam, M.P., and J. Scherer. 'The Steering Group as Policy Advice Instrument: A Case of "Consultocracy" in Stadium Deliberations'. *Policy Sciences* 39, no. 2 (2006): 169–81.

Scherer, J., and M.P. Sam. 'Public Consultation and Stadium Developments: Coercion and the Polarization of Debates'. *Sociology of Sport Journal* 25, no. 4 (2008): 443–61.

Schimmel, K. 'Deep Play: Sports Mega-Events and Urban Social Conditions in the USA'. *The Sociological Review* 54, no. 2 (2006): 160–74.

Schimmel, K. 'The Political Economy of Place: Urban and Sport Studies Perspectives'. In *Theory, Sport and Society*, edited by J. Maguire and K. Young, 335–51. New York and London: Elsevier, 2002.

Wernick, A. *Promotional Culture: Advertising, Ideology and Symbolic Expression*. London: Sage, 1991.

Policing the cyber agenda: new media technologies and recycled claims in a local stadium debate

Jay Scherer[a] and Michael P. Sam[b]

[a]Faculty of Physical Education and Recreation, University of Alberta, Edmonton, Alberta, Canada;
[b]School of Physical Education, University of Otago, Dunedin, New Zealand

In conjunction with the extensive growth of new media technologies, stadium debates and competing claims on civic resources are being increasingly played out in cyberspace. Using case material from Dunedin, New Zealand, we critically examine the deployment of popular video sharing websites like YouTube that allow dominant interest groups to articulate their 'unfiltered' ideological positions. We suggest that stadium proponents (in the private and public sectors) are utilizing new media technologies (e.g., websites, blogs, etc.) as part of highly orchestrated public-relations campaigns that are designed to create the impression of popular support and optimistic momentum for development. In bypassing traditional media and skirting oppositional viewpoints, we argue that these types of promotional strategies have profound implications for local democratic politics.

Introduction

As cities continue to adopt a more entrepreneurial approach to urban policy, civic elites regularly articulate the belief that a cosmopolitan image, as a centre of entertainment and sporting culture, helps to attract people and capital of the 'right sort'.[1] This is especially so for peripheral regions and cities that act as gateways 'for the transmission of economic, political and cultural globalization',[2] and have heavily invested in stadium and entertainment developments to signify their arrival on the world stage as attractive destinations for potential investors and the visitor class.[3] Despite being framed by civic elites as benefiting the community as a whole, critics of neo-liberalism have remarked that, since the 1990s, these types of entrepreneurial policies have generated high levels of social polarization as evidenced by the hardening of two kinds of competing claims on scarce public resources. On the right side of the political spectrum, are urban boosters and the business community who push for major capital investments for world-class stadium developments. On the other side, are local community groups and advocates for less affluent citizens who make different claims for extensively supported public services, and more inclusive types of sporting and leisure facilities. As a result of these divergent claims, Eisinger has bluntly argued that, with respect to the subsidy of sporting developments: 'No other type of major capital expenditure – not for roads, schools, wastewater treatment facilities, public buildings, jails, or sewers – has the potential to generate such intense divisions in local politics'.[4]

In this article, we focus on the antagonistic deliberations over the expenditure of public funds to refurbish or rebuild Carisbrook rugby stadium, located in Dunedin, New Zealand:

population of 120,000.[5] To date, the Carisbrook debate has been one of the most divisive urban policy issues as evidenced by: (1) a petition that was spearheaded by the Dunedin Ratepayers and Householders Association (DRHA) and signed by over 6000 residents in opposition to the use of rates to renovate or rebuild the stadium; (2) countless oppositional letters to the editor in the local newspaper the *Otago Daily Times* (ODT); (3) an acrimonious public meeting held in Dunedin in November 2004; and (4) ongoing protests by the DRHA and the oppositional group Stop the Stadium; the most recent of which saw over a thousand citizens take to the streets in a protest march on 31 January 2009.

At the root of the debate over whether Carisbrook should be refurbished or rebuilt is the New Zealand Rugby Union's (NZRU) power to determine where annual international test matches featuring the All Blacks are to be played in New Zealand. In 2003, the NZRU officially informed the Otago Rugby Union (ORU) that Carisbrook no longer met its national stadium requirements to host international test matches. Without offering any financial resources, the NZRU threatened that, unless Carisbrook was renovated or rebuilt altogether, international test matches would no longer be allocated to Dunedin.[6] After two years of initial political deliberations, including the formation of a Carisbrook Working Party (CWP) and initial public consultation processes, the Carisbrook crisis reached a turning point in 2005 when New Zealand was awarded the 2011 Rugby World Cup. This development, in turn, fuelled the pressure to upgrade or rebuild the stadium in time for Dunedin to host World Cup matches. It is also important to note that, at this time, the Carisbrook brief (which was previously managed by the CWP) was taken over by a public-private entity called the Carisbrook Stadium Trust (CST), headed by local businessman and former city councillor Malcolm Ferry. In August 2006, the CST formally announced plans to build a new stadium in conjunction with the University of Otago worth NZ$188 million (a conservative estimate by all accounts). While the announcement was widely lauded by stadium proponents who claimed that the public-private partnership was in the best interest of the community, it has further fuelled opposition to such exorbitant public financing, the majority of which will come from tax rises.

To date, we have critically examined a range of political-economic and policy issues surrounding the Carisbrook crisis including the inherent tensions associated with the use of steering groups and their consultants in relation to their roles as advisors, advocates and policy marketers.[7] We further scrutinized the institutional basis, biases and power relations of public consultation processes held in 2004 to debate the Carisbrook crisis that ultimately reinforced mandates for neo-liberal growth and had profound consequences for democratic politics in local governance.[8] Finally, we have also looked at some of the print-media coverage of the stadium debate in the ODT, focusing specifically on the changing numerical storylines that have been promoted by the CST. Related to this latter study, it is by now familiar to note that there exists a growing body of knowledge that examines how media (newspapers) shape and frame local stadium debates.[9] Historically, of course, local media, especially sports reporters, have routinely supported urban elites and the construction of world-class sporting amenities with public funds.[10] Indeed, thanks in part to the naturalization of the connection between public entertainments and the promotion of community, there is a lengthy history of popular support for the civic provision of land and other subsidies for sport franchises in a range of contexts.[11] However, there are now, more than ever, critical assessments of publicly-funded stadium developments by some journalists and organized opposition groups that are extending their critiques of the new economy of professional sport to include broader analyses of current patterns of capital accumulation and various state policies that normalize them.[12]

In conjunction with the extensive growth of new media technologies, it is arguably not surprising that these types of stadium debates and competing claims on public resources are increasingly being played out in cyberspace. Thus far, however, a critical examination of the deployment of new media technologies in various stadium debates remains unexamined by scholars in the sociology of sport and media studies communities. In this article, we aim to address this void by engaging the utilization of new media technologies by stadium proponents in the Carisbrook debate. Specifically, we examine the promotional websites that were developed by the CST and their supporters, most notably the Our Stadium lobby group. We also discuss the extensive investment in popular video-sharing websites like YouTube that allowed dominant interest groups to articulate their 'unfiltered' ideological positions in cyberspace, thereby avoiding traditional media and skirting oppositional viewpoints altogether.

We suggest that the increasing deployment of new media technologies by stadium proponents is, in part, emblematic of what Jay Rosen refers to as the decertification of the press.[13] For Rosen, there has been a visible shift in the balance of power in the news business: a movement away from informing the public via traditional news networks and the press to smaller news providers (including new media and blogs) and the networks of various state interests. Rosen's broad concerns stem from his criticism of the Bush administration's tactics to control information while casting doubt on other more critical stories in the press. Decertification, then, places journalists in a diminished and discredited position (often by simply excluding them) which, in turn, works to accredit other interest groups and their information as unbiased, factual, and in the general interest of local citizens. In our case, we suggest that stadium proponents (in the private and public sectors) utilized a range of new media technologies (e.g., websites, blogs, YouTube) as part of their highly orchestrated public relations/'astroturfing' campaigns that have been designed to create the impression of popular support and optimistic momentum for the stadium development.[14] As we will argue in the remainder of this article, these types of strategies have profound implications for democratic politics and contentious debates over matters of public policy.

Methods

Our analysis is drawn from interviews conducted with stadium proponents including the CEOs of the ORU, Dunedin City Council (DCC), and the Otago Regional Council (ORC) in 2004. We secured these interviews after attending various regional public meetings earlier in the year and meeting key players. During the interviews we queried participants on a range of issues, including the contentious use of public funds to refurbish Carisbrook, their engagement with local media (specifically the reporters and editors from the ODT), and the issues they faced in terms of articulating their political platform in relation to intense local opposition. We suggest that these difficulties have, in turn, prompted the development and deployment of new media technologies to allow dominant interest groups to circulate their messages and economic predictions via a controlled promotional network.

We then offer a brief critical analysis of the ideological content of these promotional messages and claims that naturalize the mandates of neo-liberal growth under the guise of discourses of community. Moreover, we challenge the economic forecasts, impact studies, and financial 'facts' that were put forward and normalized by proponents about the purported value of the stadium development. While these cybernetic networks may appear to be insignificant in the overall stadium debate, we argue that they need to be understood as inseparable from the overall promotional efforts of dominant interest groups who are likely to outspend and out-manoeuvre opponents in the battle to shape public opinion. It is therefore important to interrogate the types of common sense arguments being made by stadium proponents on their websites, particularly those around questionable economic impact and job creation estimates, because they have the potential to sway even a small number of citizens in future referendums or public consultation processes over contested matters of public policy.[15]

This brings us to a brief commentary on the politics of conducting this type of critical research and its inevitable connection(s) to issues of academic border crossing, activism and public intellectualism. These are, of course, paramount issues for scholars who are committed to a critical pedagogy and challenging neo-liberal growth ideologies while holding government accountable for its actions.[16] It scarcely needs saying that our political beliefs are inseparable from this research process and wider questions of social justice/social inequality. To be clear, as citizens who are deeply perplexed by the use of over NZ$188 million of public funds to retain one international rugby test match per year in Dunedin, we faced several dilemmas concerning our roles as researchers, specifically when we felt pressure to 'take sides'.[17] For example, when we attended the public meetings in 2004, we purposefully avoided any direct verbal participation and debate to facilitate access to key players for future interviews. Arguably, we were granted these interviews because of the status of our academic positions and the desire of civic elites to offer a particular perspective in an academic study pertaining to the Carisbrook issue, but perhaps also due to the very fact that we did not 'disrupt' the consultation process. Furthermore, we were subsequently able to ask some very critical and direct questions about the public consultation process and the broader Carisbrook crisis during our interviews with participants; interviews that, in some instances, were extremely difficult to secure. These interactions resulted in extensive dialogue and, at times, heated exchanges with individuals and interest groups who had a vested interest in renovating or rebuilding Carisbrook.

Thus, despite the tensions of this type of public intellectualism, it is our hope that the following analysis will provide a critical perspective to the issues that have transpired in Dunedin, while contributing to the broader body of knowledge in the sociology of sport community that interrogates the construction of stadium developments in relation to neo-liberal growth ideologies. Moreover, since conducting this specific study, we have continued to dialogue with other concerned citizens and activists who are campaigning against the use of public funds to rebuild Carisbrook and the undercutting of democratic practices by various civic elites. In addition to nurturing these local networks, the second author of this paper published a critical op-ed piece in the ODT[18] outlining his opposition to the stadium development, and also took part in a panel discussion on the Carisbrook debate at the University of Otago that featured other academics from more reactionary perspectives. In short, despite the ascendancy of market fundamentalism and the blurring of public/private boundaries,[19] there are still pockets of opportunities for academics and organic intellectuals to transcend institutional borders and assume critical roles in 'linking learning to social change, education to democracy, and knowledge to acts of intervention in public life'.[20]

Decertifying the press

We begin our analysis by noting the simple fact that each of the individuals we interviewed recounted, rather bitterly, the difficulties they had encountered in terms of communicating and engaging with the traditional press. The following examples, along with critical letters to the editor, illuminate some of their perceived difficulties of dealing with traditional media in the struggle to shape public opinion on divisive policy issues. Consider the comments from the CEO of the ORU who described feeling betrayed by the ODT which had, in his opinion, fabricated an erroneous headline that insinuated the NZRU had threatened the ORU about the state of Carisbrook:

> we had a meeting here with NZRU and we had an agreement...I got a call from the ODT saying 'How did this meeting go?' and I said well it was a joint press statement coming out tomorrow. And they said 'Well we need to put something in the paper tomorrow' ...So I said 'Look, it was a very positive, constructive meeting, it's clear that this facility needs to be upgraded'....The headline the next morning read 'NZRU puts the boot in over Carisbrook'. If you read the article, the article read fine. It's just the headline. It's the sub-editors that do the headlines. Now I don't know who these people are, everyone talks about 'sub-editors'. They must be clandestine people that sit in a room somewhere, and dream up these sorts of things. But they are doing a lot of damage (personal communication, Russell Grey).

In a similar vein, the CEO of the DCC also spoke about the perceived liberties being taken by the editors of the ODT:

> Well, some people have misrepresented the work we have done...I wrote the article, and the headline wasn't the headline we gave them, the headline I gave them was 'Further work to be done before decision is made', and that was exactly the truth...that caused an immense amount of damage...a lot of grief for the councillors and a lot of grief for me personally but that seems to be how these papers work (personal communication, Jim Harland).

Finally, the CEO of the ORC noted the issues facing stadium proponents with respect to the use of traditional media where editorials fluctuate and newspapers take different and, at times, contradictory positions like opposing increases in taxes, but supporting a stadium development that would irrevocably raise taxes. When asked if he was surprised by the type of coverage that the stadium debate was receiving from the ODT, the CEO sardonically remarked:

> it's the usual sorts of things for the ODT...it's interesting that the ODT should have an [supportive] editorial on sport initially isn't it? And when they're every year, year in year out, criticising councils for raising rates or spending money. But I suppose that's the beauty of an editorial; you don't have to have integrity with it, you just have to get words to flow (personal communication, Graeme Martin).

Admittedly, it was somewhat fascinating to hear each of these elites complain about the quality of the media coverage they had received given the amount of research that shows how newspapers systematically bias stories in favour of stadium developments[21] and generally reproduce dominant, taken for granted values and interests.[22] Against this, however, there are no shortages of examples where stories and headlines have been sensationalized for the purpose of selling newspapers, particularly given the range of 'social personalities' of various newspapers which increasingly play up and emphasize dramatic and scandalous elements in stories to enhance their newsworthiness. These strategies, which often utilize spectacular headlines and popular language ('NZRU puts boot in over Carisbrook'), also subtly signify to citizens that the media do not simply adopt the viewpoints of a political party or various economic interests, particularly during various public policy debates.

Nevertheless, what is written beneath a dramatic headline often reproduces the viewpoints of dominant interest groups. For example, despite the headline 'NZRU puts boot in over Carisbrook', the actual content of the article reproduced the dominant position that Carisbrook needed to be upgraded. Indeed, in their seminal piece, the authors of *Policing the Crisis* have written extensively on the social and institutional contexts of news-making processes and the professional ideologies that encourage journalists and editors to code stories and news items into a particular mode of address or language form: one that directly hails its target audience via a public idiom. In other words, the language that is deployed by editors and sub-editors 'will thus be the newspaper's own version of the rhetoric, imagery and underlying common stock of knowledge which it assumes its audience shares'.[23] However, as noted, the coding of stories and news items via popular language and more forceful headings regularly works to 'translate into a public idiom the statements and viewpoints of the primary definers'.[24]

Leaving aside for the moment such contradictory imperatives, it was clear that each of the individuals we spoke to felt aggrieved about the ODT's dramatization of various headlines that inevitably framed and set limits on stories and various political debates. In light of these perceived inconsistencies and difficulties, the CEO of the ORU remarked that, in hindsight, he and other proponents ought to have taken a more entrepreneurial approach and directly lobbied journalists and the owners of the ODT to solicit more supportive headlines and commentary for the pro-stadium position:

> I think we could have done a lot more work with the ODT earlier on...I think with the owners...I know them a lot better 18 months down the track, I think they're the sort of people that if you almost go down and say, 'We can't do this without you guys' we'd get them behind us. Clearly if [the ODT owners] went out to the shop floor and said 'I want to see positive stuff about this' it would happen (personal communication, Russell Grey).

This lack of a close network of connections between the ODT and the ORU is somewhat unusual given Dunedin's relatively small population where most civic elites are familiar with each other. In a much broader sense, there are usually fairly close links between the personnel/management of sports franchises and their counterparts in the media who often operate in similar business networks and social circles and share comparable political-economic viewpoints. In this case, however, the CEO of the ORU was only hired in 2003 and was not originally from Dunedin. He subsequently lacked these types of institutional and political connections. These comments also indirectly acknowledge the power of editors/owners to influence the content of a newspaper and its stance on various political debates in specific stories or editorial balance. Given the social structures and socialization processes of the newsroom outlined by Hall et al., this type of blatant editorial interference is, however, often unnecessary. Still, we have the likes of Conrad Black, Rupert Murdoch, and the Asper family to remind us that levels of coercion and censorship do exist in newsrooms worldwide.

Germane to this case, however, was the sheer level of frustration that each of the proponents outlined in their efforts to communicate with members of the public via traditional media. Consider the following commentary from the CEO of the DCC who admitted that proponents were losing the battle to shape public opinion and the terms of the Carisbrook stadium debate in the press:

> I think it's the difficulty of getting people to understand what the problem is in simple terms ... and the debate hasn't focused on that, it's focused on the blackmail issue, it's focused on the conflict of interest that the chair of the working party supposedly has, and it hasn't focused on the benefits at all and yet that information has been there yet it hasn't really gotten through] (personal communication, Jim Harland).

Here it is important to note that the desire of the CEO to have the stadium debate expressed in simple terms is clearly at odds with the role of the press and the responsibility of reporters to ask critical questions about complex policy issues with profound and long-term consequences for the public coffers. Indeed, the very issues that the CEO of the DCC indirectly identified speak to the very real complexities and tensions of this debate that needed to be held up for critical reflection: whether the CEO of the DCC ought to have been on the CWP; the fact that the NZRU had essentially blackmailed the ORU and citizens to upgrade Carisbrook by threatening to cease allocating future test matches to Dunedin; etc. In light of these concerns, it is somewhat unsurprising, then, that stadium proponents have increasingly sought to decertify the local press by creating and reasserting their own communication networks to establish their positions as credible, apolitical and undistorted by traditional media.

The online battleground: discursive shenanigans

One of the main consequences of these tensions has been the emergence of pro-stadium websites to communicate 'unfiltered' information about the Carisbrook debate to the public. For example, both the CST[25] and Our Stadium[26] lobby group invested in the development and maintenance of extensive promotional websites. Unlike engaging with traditional media, these types of promotional platforms afforded dominant interest groups complete control over the information that appeared at all hours of the day. Here it is important to note both organizations attempted to position their websites as unbiased, while the Our Stadium website noted that it was 'completely independent' from the CST, DCC and the ORC. Of course, the goal of any astroturfing/public relation strategy is to appear as a spontaneous grassroots reaction that is unrelated to a specific formal organization or political entity. Yet, despite their popular guise of independence, these political marketing strategies are often highly orchestrated and intimately connected to individuals or groups promoting a specific political platform. Indeed, given the close connections between stadium proponents in Dunedin, it is somewhat unsurprising that the 'factual' information and economic data that appeared on the Our Stadium website had, in fact, been supplied by the CST.

If we focus on the Our Stadium website, the currency of these communication platforms for stadium lobbyists is plainly visible. This is especially so in relation to the concerns of stadium proponents that the stadium debate was being dominated by critics and oppositional groups, and filtered by journalists and editors from the ODT. For example, the Our Stadium homepage contained an optimistic message from the chairman of the Our Stadium group, Sir Clifford Skeggs who, like other civic elites leaders, routinely argued that a silent majority supported the stadium development. Outlining the purpose of the website and the lobby group, Skeggs noted that:

> Big projects often get captured by a noisy minority who claim to speak for everybody. They don't. Our job is to unite the positive people in the regions and their voices will make the local authorities decision to say YES a much easier task[27].

These comments clearly reveal the ideological work that was undertaken by stadium proponents to unite the region/city, while simultaneously framing any sort of opposition as negative naysayers, special-interest groups and general opponents of the community.[28] They also illuminate the type of pressure that was being applied to local political leaders to say 'yes' to a complex and divisive policy issue with profound consequences for the city's environment and long-term financial stability. Indeed, as we will expand upon shortly, each of the websites attempted to position the new stadium development as simply a matter of economic and cultural common sense for the city and the region.

Central to the arguments of the city's business and political leaders was the belief that the new stadium development was important to everyone (and by extension was beneficial to all citizens), and that 'doing nothing', or simply upgrading the existing stadium (at a significantly lower cost), was nonsensical. Lurking underneath these claims, however, is the timeless blackmail threat that accompanies most demands for the deployment of public funds to build a new stadium: that a sport franchise will fold or be relocated, unless action is taken and a new world-class facility is constructed. In this case, what was continually emphasized was the potential loss of international test matches, but also the Highlanders Super 15 Rugby franchise. Or, as the Our Stadium website argued:

> To the untrained eye Carisbrook may look fine, but doing nothing is not an option. It is in urgent need of a significant upgrade to maintain its existing list of fixtures. It is well known that northern unions are eyeing the Highlanders Super 14 (15) franchise, which is now seriously at risk unless the stadium issues are addressed. Carisbrook is important to everyone who calls the southern region their home, whether sporting fan or not. It plays a vital part of the economic fabric of the region and for it to slip further down rugby's pecking order and ultimately into oblivion will have a significant financial and social impact for the region.[29]

It can be suggested, following Zygmunt Bauman,[30] that these culturally recycled claims are evidence of the ubiquity of fear within contemporary society, and more specifically within the entrepreneurial policy marking contexts of the regimes of even smaller urban centres like Dunedin that are vying to reposition themselves in the (trans)national cultural and economic heirarchy of cities to attract new businesses and people. As Bauman[31] observes, in such a climate of fear, collectively and individually, we 'live on credit' and are prepared to take on substantial debt (including exhausting municipal and regional spending) in search of immediate solutions (like a new world-class stadium development) to complex political-economic issues, with little concern for the long-term ramifications of these decisions. For example, in this case the 'cost of doing nothing' was habitually promoted by civic elites as a dire warning of the significant economic loss that would ensue if a new stadium development was not constructed. By 2006, for example, the estimated economic 'cost of doing nothing' had grown to NZ$223 million over 50 years in the event that a new stadium was not built (Horwarth HTL, 2007). Beyond this, it was this very climate of fear, prompted by the continual threats that Dunedin would slip into economic and cultural oblivion unless a new stadium was built, that seriously hampered meaningful political debate and dialogue over these issues, and the pursuit of alternative investment and development strategies.

Against these claims of loss, the websites also promoted many other bold economic assurances[32] and heralded a new stadium as a symbol of a vibrant and cosmopolitan community: claims that have been often repeated by civic leaders around the world. As will be discussed in the next section, despite bold assurances that a new stadium will serve as an engine of local economic development, the consensus of independent studies indicates that these benefits are substantially overstated.[33] Nevertheless, both websites extolled the importance of the new stadium for Dunedin's future prosperity:

> The new stadium will form a cornerstone for a Dunedin quadrant that flows out from the Octagon, down to the University, across to the stadium, back along the waterfront to the railway station and the Chinese gardens. This will become a new heart for the region. And like Westpac Stadium in Wellington or the Telstra Dome in Melbourne, the stadium will lead a change of land use and is predicted to kick start significant investment in North Dunedin. International and national events attract extensive media coverage and each year television would beam the Otago brand into the living rooms of millions of homes worldwide. Without this exposure Otago would become a forgotten territory, adding an incentive to the northward drift of its businesses and allowing other centres to capture the imaginations of thousands of students.[34]

Here it is important to reiterate that cities are not simply material or lived spaces, but they are also spaces of representation that, in this case, were deeply aligned with neo-liberal discourses of urban development[35] more commonly associated with the entertainment districts in what Hannigan refers to as postmodern fantasy cities.[36] Although his observations are generally reserved for larger urban centers, the power of these discourses can readily be seen in the context of smaller urban centres that are vigorously attempting to reposition themselves through various developments that will revalourize under utilized land.[37] In the fantasy city, 'changes of land use' are deeply aligned with entrepreneurial approaches to the production of private infrastructure for urban leisure as a way to bring new investment and affluent visitors to particular areas: decaying downtowns or, in this case, to 'kick start' investment in North Dunedin. However, it is likely that any form of substantial new investment will take years to materialize, and will certainly not compensate for such a sizeable expenditure of public funds. Moreover, while property values may rise in and around the new stadium, and while some businesses in North Dunedin may also benefit from these developments, these benefits will occur at the expense of investment and businesses in South Dunedin, a less affluent area of the city where the current stadium is located. In other words, while a new stadium may redistribute existing spending patterns and business activity, rarely will it add to overall net growth. Indeed, it can also be suggested that the location of the new stadium development near the University of Otago in North Dunedin will, arguably, heighten disparities between students who are often from more affluent backgrounds and only live in Dunedin for the duration of their education, and local residents (i.e., the classic 'town' versus 'gown' divide).

Nevertheless, what was also on display on these websites was the desire of some civic elites who have traditionally thought of themselves as provincial, to become more ambitious and outward-looking in their aspirations and consumption experiences.[38] These arguments also illuminate that, in an increasingly networked world and promotional culture, every cultural event and every public communication has some sort of promotional/public relations message attached to it; in this instance promoting a synergy of brands (e.g., Dunedin, Otago, the University of Otago, the Highlanders, etc.). These types of sentiments, for example, were equally visible on the CST website:

> The new Dunedin Stadium will be notable for many reasons. One of the key ones is this: It is *not* a stadium. Rather, it is a world class, civic, academic, cultural, sports and entertainment facility with the potential to transform life in the city and the region. Designed as a truly multi functional facility, it will sit on a site that, itself, is one of the finest stadium locations in the world. It will provide a cornucopia of events and activities that will allow every element of our community to enjoy the benefits of this visionary facility in a way that no other stadium in New Zealand currently does.

Through these statements, residents of Dunedin were invited to 'think big' and imagine their city beyond its provincial identity. In so doing, they were also encouraged to embrace a more global outlook and pursue the types of consumption experiences that have been made familiar by global marketing and are now standard in even smaller urban centres around the world.

Also of interest here, beyond these less quantifiable intangible 'benefits', was the ongoing attempts by civic elites to discursively frame the stadium as a multi-use entertainment facility, as opposed to a rugby stadium. Similar strategies of differentiation were evident in the promotional endeavours of stadium boosters and members of the CST. Consider the types of comments that were made by the chairman of the CST, Malcolm Ferry, who, in a posted interview on YouTube, even tried to draw attention away from the name of his organization:

> Well, I prefer not to call it a new stadium because I think that is confusing. It really is a joint venture with the university. We might be called the Carisbrook Stadium Trust but there is a lot more to us than just rugby. So, if you like, it's a complex ... or a square building that happens to have a big atrium in the centre. The atrium happens to be the grass and, you know, some goal posts on so on.[39]

Building on this train of thought, in another YouTube-posted interview, the CEO of the CST, Darren Burden, attempted to explain the culinary potential of this complex:

> if you take the pitch out and look at the buildings that are associated with that, you end up with...the conferences, the exhibitions, the trade fairs, the day meetings, the seminars, potential teaching areas for the university... effectively, what you're making this thing is for use every single day of the year. In fact, just to go further on with that concept; one of the things we have sort of touched on is that we are going to have one of the biggest commercial kitchens in Dunedin located at the stadium. So, there is a possibility... why don't we build a training kitchen rather than a commercial kitchen so that it can be used by students or whatever? You can run courses there potentially through the Polytechnic or other courses like that. And then it's only on event days that you convert it into a commercial kitchen. Now that's just an idea at the moment and we haven't taken it very far.[40]

Regardless of the merit of these proposals, it can be suggested that these types of promotional strategies are little more than discursive appeals to justify the vast public subsidy of what is first and foremost a rugby stadium, and yet another men's cultural centre.[41] As such, we challenge the dominant view that a stadium or a multi-use facility benefits the city or community as a whole, or will even be used frequently by all citizens. Beyond issues of gender, it goes without saying that lower-income residents, let alone those on social assistance, are less likely to benefit from this type of capital expenditure and world-class facility that they will be heavily subsidizing.

The Our Stadium lobby group, in fact, offered a more 'credible' description of the facility:

> A world class, fully enclosed, *boutique stadium* is the vision we are asking the region to embrace. Of all of the options this has the highest price tag, but it is also the best long-term and fiscally robust option. This recommendation provides the region's leaders with a rare, once in a lifetime opportunity to deliver a stunning public facility for the enormous enjoyment of present and future generations (emphasis added).[42]

Both the CST and Our Stadium group lobbied to have the stadium positioned as a novel, innovative, and transformative 'public' complex with a cornucopia of more 'up-market' consumption experiences and leisure opportunities. What is evident in these types of appeals, moreover, is the increasing articulation of private, market-oriented meanings to community development, and new definitions of the public good and citizenship that are increasingly aligned with discourses of boutique consumerism and lifestyle choices. In Dunedin, civic elites were more interested in bequeathing a world-class stadium, along with its exorbitantly high price tag, to future generations as opposed to focusing on social rights and the creation of public spaces centred on more enduring common interests. It was, however, precisely these developments that stimulated so much politcal opposition and protest against bequeathing this facility, and a substantial burden of debt, to those same future generations.

It can also be suggested that these types of entertainment districts, which increasingly act as the foundation for various place-marketing and image-making initiatives of even small market entreprenerial centres, have profound consequences for the urban imaginary, and often transform local distinctiveness into yet another placeless and homogenized environment. While there was never an 'authentic' Carisbrook experience, the stadium is well known for its unique heritage elements, including the terraces that have long-contributed to its much-celebrated, and admittedly mythological, reputation as 'The House of Pain'.[43] Undoubtedly, civic and business leaders will endeavour to articulate these locally rooted traditions and popular memories to the new stadium; but they will then be effectively resold to rugby fans in a manner that legitimizes the new facility as common sense, most likely via the marketing of nostalgia.

Numerical storylines

While we have touched briefly on some of the numerical storylines that were deployed by the CST (e.g., 'the cost of doing nothing'), we now discuss in detail some of the other economic claims that were promoted by dominant interest groups on their websites. For example, with respect to stadium costs, the Our Stadium website provided a range of definitive financial figures. Yet, well below these financial claims were the following caveats: 'conditional upon certain terms and conditions' or 'it is estimated'. Moreover, rather than revealing the voluminous amount of public funds required to construct the new stadium, the Our Stadium website suggested that it was easily affordable by framing a massive capital expenditure in relation to ordinary, every-day purchasing decisions:

> Over 10 years it's only $1.34 a week for an average Dunedin home worth $261,000. In some years it's as low as 13 cents and in the worst year it's $1.74 a week. It's even cheaper if you live in the regions at under a dollar a week on average. That's a lot less than things you buy every day. $2.50 for a sandwich. $3 to park in the Octagon. $3.50 for a latte. $5 for a Speights [beer]. Dunedin City Council wants only $1.34 a week from its ratepayers so they can build a world class, multi-purpose, fully covered stadium that is without rival in New Zealand. We get rugby tests back and we keep our Highlanders here in Otago.[44]

Of course, what the website neglected to impart to readers was that the loan for the stadium actually extended to 20 years (as opposed to 10), that taxpayers were also subsidizing the stadium through their regional governmental authority, and that the amount of city taxation to be collected was being further subsidized by dividends raised through publicly owned civic companies.

We want to suggest that economic claims that minimize and downplay the financial burden that building a new stadium will place on ratepayers speak directly to the socio-cultural bubble[45] that insulates many civic elites and affluent people from any real awareness of the lives and needs of less affluent people and those families who are dependent on social support to just get by. It is in this sense that neo-liberalism 'represents a "secession of the successful" from society, in which elites have sufficiently detached their own fates from those of communities around them that they no longer know or care much about the state of public services, except insofar as these make claims on their taxes'.[46] In these debates, for example, civic and business leaders routinely enjoined citizens to 'just get on with it', and build the stadium with scant consideration of other political-economic realities.

Equally disconcerting were the claims of economic impact promoted by the CST and Our Stadium lobby group on their websites. For example, the CST website made the following predictions about the stadium development:

> The economic impact that would be generated by events, through the spending of visitors, locals, event organisers and media, has been estimated between 24 to 56 million dollars. The higher estimate includes the impact of Otago/Southland people staying at home to attend events, made possible by the stadium, that they would otherwise have had to travel out of the city to attend. The total economic impact for the region of hosting an international rugby test is estimated at $5.3million. This is based on the results of an economic impact study of the Tri-Nations Test between South Africa and New Zealand in 2003 undertaken by Berl. The benefits to the city and region were: Approximately 10,000 extra visitors to the region with an average spend of $302 with the majority of that spent on accommodation, food and beverage.[47]

Interestingly, we can gather from this that 'staying at home' can now be considered an economic impact – a profoundly nonsensical argument in light of what multipliers are intended to produce: a measure of 'new' money and its effects. Equally, this type of distortion breaks down by the very fact that 'staying at home' to attend the events – instead of traveling to Christchurch or Wellington, for example – will mean that fewer seats will be available for visitors thus limiting the transfer of new money to the city. Beyond these issues, we concur with the consensus of academic research that professional sport and stadium developments typically comprise a small portion of a city's economy, and are less important than many lower-profile enterprises in both the private and public sectors.

Similar types of optimistic numerical storylines appeared on the Our Stadium website to promote the potential development of jobs associated with the new stadium:

> During the two year construction phase the stadium will need carpenters, concrete placers, block layers, plumbers, electricians and labourers. It will generate about 600 new jobs. Money raised in the region stays in the region. And when it opens it will need bar staff, waiters, chefs, security and hospitality hosts. That's at least 1000 for a major event day[48].

These types of estimates have regularly been trotted out by civic elites as justification for the public subsidy of stadium developments; estimates that have been widely challenged on both quantitative and qualitative grounds by disinterested academic research.[49] While we take issue with the estimates of job creation in Dunedin, we also question the quality and stability of the jobs created by stadium developments. Beyond offering employment for those in the construction and trade industry over a relatively short-term period, we want to suggest that the resulting facility will not result in the creation of stable, long-term, value-added jobs that would improve the quality of local employment. Indeed, if job creation is one of the primary justifications for public investment, 'governments can realize greater returns on these investments by offering incentives to other kinds of businesses – where substantial internal growth can be expected, where most workers will be employed in skilled and well-paying jobs, and where other private investment may be attracted to the region'.[50]

Finally, it is worth noting that the CST website intimated that a significant amount of private funding would be available to help with the cost of the stadium, in addition to the likelihood of future revenue streams from the sale of luxury boxes/corporate membership which have, of course, become a ubiquitous feature of stadia built in the past 20 years. In an interview posted on YouTube, for example, CST CEO Darren Burden reassured viewers about the level of private sector funding:

> Well, the private funding aspects of this are the things like naming rights, sponsorships, corporate memberships, the brand membership packages; things like that. We undertook some work during the master plan and feasibility stage; benchmarking other stadiums and the types of products they offer. We also looked at how that could be applied to Dunedin, in terms of the socio-economic groups and so on. We came up with the figure of $45.5 million dollars as a target for the private sector funding. Since then we have done some further peer review works and market research and through developing additional products and things like that we now believe that that figure is pretty conservative and it's extremely achievable. Now obviously the knock-on effect of increasing our private sector funding means that other types of funding from the public sector will obviously reduce.[51]

Thus, without any specific information, viewers were informed that the private funding targets were not only conservative, but extremely achievable thanks to extensive, but unnamed, peer-reviewed 'market research'. We have, in fact, long suspected that the figure of 45.5 million was likely substantially inflated given the size and nature of the local corporate sector which has, to date, appeared disinterested in making any substantial investment towards a new stadium or entertainment complex. Indeed, it was recently confirmed that the CST had fallen well short of its original target for private funding by $35 million; a shortfall so significant that it prompted the Mayor of Dunedin to write a letter to the National-led government, pleading for additional public funding for the stadium development.[52]

Despite the enthusiastic and optimistic claims that generally accompany these types of public-private partnerships, the public sector is routinely liable for a significant portion of the development costs and long-term debt that so often results from these types of stadium developments. While public-private partnerships can, at times, function positively, according to the sociologist John Hannigan there needs to be significant measures in place to ensure that the public sector has a substantial degree of control and benefits from its involvement.[53] With respect to the Carisbrook case, we can see no evidence of these types of controls and little reason to be hopeful of any gains that could possibly accrue for the public sector.

Conclusion

In this article, we have sought to explore some of the issues surrounding the utilization of new media technologies and astroturfing strategies by proponents of a stadium development. In so doing, we have raised a number of questions surrounding the potential of these unaccountable websites to decertify the press, while promoting 'exclusive claims' about the common sense economic and intangible benefits of stadium developments. Of course, it goes without saying that there are no guarantees that citizens will simply digest this information in an uncritical manner. As Grossberg argues, 'neither meaning nor subject-positions, once produced, guarantee how such an articulation will itself be inserted to other practices – in particular, to real conditions of existence'.[54] Nevertheless, these websites and communication platforms have the potential to further skew civic deliberations about stadium developments; debates which are often already heavily tilted in favour of the business community and other stadium proponents.

However, despite concerns about the corporate consolidation of the internet, local activist groups are also taking advantage of new media technologies to counter the types of claims being made by dominant interest groups. With respect to this case, for example, both the Stop the Stadium group and the Dunedin Ratepayers and Householders Organization (DRHA) set up websites to challenge the numerical storylines of the CST and the Our Stadium lobby group. Indeed, as a number of critical sport scholars have observed, internet-communication is of increasing importance for a range of sport-related social movements.[55] The benefits of these oppositional websites are potentially substantial, particularly with respect to communicating, informing and motivating local citizens to take action on and offline. For example, in anticipation of the DCC's 'final' decision on the new stadium, the Stop the Stadium group dedicated a significant portion of their website to encourage citizens to attend an 'End the Stadium' march on 31 January 2009. Beyond this, the website offered a range of links to articles, information, and contacts, which had clearly been designed to counter the claims being made by local proponents.

While new media technologies offer some tantalizing possibilities for social movements, we want to offer a final, more cautionary comment about the democratic potential of the internet. Here we follow Knight and Greenberg (2002) who argue that the internet most commonly functions as a medium to inform and communicate with individuals who are already sympathetic to a specific cause, in their case the anti-sweatshop movement. Beyond this, they note that social movements are, in fact, still heavily reliant on more traditional media with respect to exposure and communication. We want to further suggest that, while the internet exists as an invaluable global communications tool, it may also contribute to broader trends of mobile privatization, where citizens take passing interest in political issues that appear on the computer screens in their private homes (or now on mobile phones), at the expense of direct political action.

This brings us to a final comment on the use of new media technologies with respect to policy issues. More specifically, the sheer speed and relative 'simplicity' of new media technologies may be inherently incompatible with the ideals of public deliberation over contested and complex public policy issues. For example, there may be a danger of relying on competing websites and blogs to help citizens distil and synthesize a voluminous amount of information and all the contradictory claims being made by proponents and opponents of stadium developments. Thus, while new media technologies are often heralded as a democratic means for transparency, the volume of fluctuating material and the often mystifying use of economic multipliers amongst other issues, may predispose citizens to uncritically accept what is easily available and, in turn, further decertify traditional media in the eyes of the public.

Notes

[1] Harvey, *Condition of Postmodernism*; Whitson, 'Bringing the World to Canada', 1215–32.
[2] Short et al., 'From World Cities', 319.
[3] Eisinger, 'Politics of Bread and Circuses'.
[4] Ibid., 328.
[5] Carisbrook is owned by a provincial governing sporting organization, the Otago Rugby Union, and is home to the Otago Highlanders, a professional franchise that competes in the Super 15 rugby competition.
[6] Indeed, this case also reveals aspects of the broader transformations of the national sport of rugby union, which has been increasingly pushed out of the reach of ordinary New Zealanders. Since the arrival of full professionalism in 1995, various national networks and structures have been replaced by promotional obligations to media conglomerate News Corporation, global corporate sponsors, and in this case, the demands of rugby administrators and civic elites for world-class stadiums to reposition New Zealand and its urban centres on the world stage (see Scherer, Falcous and Jackson, 'Media Sports Cultural Complex').
[7] Sam and Scherer, 'Steering Group'.
[8] Scherer and Sam, 'Public Consultation'.
[9] Delaney and Eckstein, *Public Dollars, Private Stadiums*; Scherer, 'Globalization'; Scherer and Jackson, 'From Corporate Welfare'.
[10] Scherer, 'Globalization'; Silver, *Thin Ice*.
[11] Gruneau and Whitson, *Hockey Night in Canada*.
[12] Scherer and Jackson, 'From Corporate Welfare'.
[13] Jay Rosen. 'From Meet the Press to *be* the Press.' *PRESSthink*. http://journalism.nyu.edu/pubzone/weblogs/pressthink/2005/03/21/be_press.html (accessed 9 July 2008).
[14] For more information of astroturfing as a political/advertising strategy see: http://www.prwatch.org.
[15] Noll and Zimabalist recount that 'in June 1997 San Francisco and the state of Washington held referenda on whether to subsidize a new NFL football stadium. Both referenda won by tiny margins. In San Francisco proponents outspent opponents by 25 to 1, while in Washington the spending ratio was an amazing 80 to 1. If as few as 2 percent of voters were misled by the incorrect claims about the economic effects of the stadium proposal in these campaigns, the bogus studies determined the outcome in these elections' ('Economic Impact', 85).
[16] Darder and Miron, 'Critical Pedagogy'; Denzin and Giardina, *Qualitative Inquiry*; Giroux, 'Cultural Studies'; Giroux and Giroux, 'Challenging Neoliberalism'.
[17] Denzin, 'Confronting Ethnography's Crisis'.
[18] Sam, 'Stadium Benefits Misrepresented'.
[19] Sheller and Urry, 'Mobile Transformations'.
[20] Giroux and Giroux, 'Challenging Neoliberalism', 28.

[21] Scherer, 'Globalization'; Silver, *Thin Ice*.
[22] Chomsky, *Necessary Illusions*; Hall et al., *Policing the Crisis*; Herman and Chomsky, *Manufacturing Consent*; Winter, *Democracy's Oxygen*.
[23] Hall et al., *Policing the Crisis*, 61.
[24] Ibid.
[25] http://www.carisbrook.org.nz/
[26] http://www.ourstadium.co.nz/
[27] Ibid.
[28] Gruneau and Whitson, *Hockey Night in Canada*; Scherer, 'Globalization'; Silver, *Thin Ice*.
[29] http://www.ourstadium.co.nz/
[30] Bauman, *Liquid Fear*.
[31] Ibid.
[32] Sam and Scherer, 'Stand Up'.
[33] Baade, 'Professional Sports'; Noll and Zimbalist, 'Economic Impact'; Noll and Zimbalist, 'Build the Stadium'; Palmer, 'Bread and Circuses'.
[34] http://www.ourstadium.co.nz/
[35] Bridge and Watson, 'Retext(ur)ing the City'.
[36] Hannigan, *Fantasy City*.
[37] Short et al., 'From World Cities'.
[38] Whitson and Horne, 'Underestimated Costs'.
[39] http://www.ourstadium.co.nz/csinterviews.html
[40] Ibid.
[41] Kidd, 'Men's Cultural Centre'.
[42] http://www.ourstadium.co.nz/
[43] The nickname comes from the All Blacks impressive record of success at Carisbrook.
[44] http://www.ourstadium.co.nz/
[45] Bauman, *Community*.
[46] Whitson, 'Olympic Hosting in Canada', 42.
[47] http://www.carisbrook.org.nz/
[48] http://www.ourstadium.co.nz
[49] Baade and Sanderson, 'Employment Effect of Teams'; Noll and Zimbalist, *Sports, Jobs & Taxes*.
[50] Whitson, Harvey and Lavoie, 'The Mills Report', 148.
[51] Our Stadium Group, 'CST Interview', retrieved from: http://www.youtube.com/watch?v=-f6S24N_cyw&NR=1, 30 January 2008.
[52] Morris, 'Stadium Letter to Government'.
[53] Hannigan, *Fantasy City*.
[54] Grossberg, *Bringing It All Back Home*, 225.
[55] Lenskyj, *Inside the Olympic Industry*; Sage, 'Justice Do It!'; Wilson, 'New Media'.

References

Baade, Robert A. 'Professional Sports as Catalysts for Metropolitan Economic Development'. *Journal of Urban Affairs* 18, no. 1 (1996): 1–17.
Baade, Robert A., and Allen R. Sanderson. 'The Employment Effect of Teams and Sports Facilities'. In *Sports, Jobs & Taxes: The Economic Impact of Sports Teams and Stadiums*, edited by R.G. Noll and A. Zimbalist, 92–118. Washington: The Brookings Institute, 1997.
Bauman, Zygmunt. *Community: Seeking Safety in an Insecure World*. Cambridge: Polity Press, 2001.
Bauman, Zygmunt. *Liquid Fear*. Cambridge: Polity Press, 2006.
Bridge, Gary, and Sophie Watson. 'Retext(ur)ing the City'. *City* 5, no. 3 (2000): 350–62.
Chomsky, Noam. *Necessary Illusions*. Concord, ON: House of Anansi Press, 1989.
Darder, Antonia, and Luis F. Miron. 'Critical Pedagogy in a Time of Uncertainty: A Call to Action'. *Cultural Studies <=> Critical Methodologies* 6, no. 1 (2006): 5–20.
Delaney, Kevin J., and Rick Eckstein. *Public Dollars, Private Stadiums: The Battle Over Building Sports Stadiums*. New Jersey: Rutgers University Press, 1989.
Denzin, Norman K. 'Confronting Ethnography's Crisis of Representation'. *Journal of Contemporary Ethnography* 31 (2006): 482–9.

Denzin, Norman K., and Michael D. Giardina, eds. *Qualitative Inquiry and the Conservative Challenge.* Walnut Creek, CA: Left Coast Press, 2006.

Eisinger, Peter. 'The Politics of Bread and Circuses: Building the City for the Visitor Class'. *Urban Affairs Review* 35 (2006): 316–33.

Giroux, Henry A. 'Cultural Studies as Performative Politics'. *Cultural Studies <=> Critical Methodologies* 1, no. 1 (2006): 5–23.

Giroux, Henry A., and Susan S. Giroux. 'Challenging Neoliberalism's New World Order: The Promise of Critical Pedagogy'. *Cultural Studies <=> Critical Methodologies* 6, no. 1 (2006): 21–32.

Grossberg, Lawrence. *Bringing It All Back Home.* Durham: Duke University Press, 1997.

Gruneau, Richard, and David Whitson. *Hockey Night in Canada: Sport, Identities and Cultural Politics.* Toronto, ON: Garamond Press, 1993.

Hall, Stuart, Charles Critcher, Tony Jefferson, John Clarke, and Brian Robert. *Policing the Crisis: Mugging, the State, and Law and Order.* Houndsmills, Hampshire: Palgrave Macmillan, 1978.

Hannigan, J. *Fantasy City: Pleasure and Profit in the Postmodern Metropolis.* London: Routledge, 1998.

Harvey, David. *The Condition of Postmodernism.* Cambridge, MA: Blackwell Publishers, 1989.

Herman, Edward S., and Noam Chomsky. *Manufacturing Consent.* New York: Pantheon Books, 1988.

Horwarth HTL. New Carisbrook Stadium Development: Financial Feasibility Study and Economic Impact Assessment. Dunedin: Report prepared for the Carisbrook Stadium Trust, 2007.

Kidd, Bruce. 'The Men's Cultural Centre: Sports and the Dynamic of Women's Oppression/Men's Repression'. In *Sport, Men, and the Gender Order*, edited by M. Messner and D. Sabo, 31–43. Champaign, IL: Human Kinetics Books, 1990.

Knight, Graham, and Josh Greenberg. 'Promotionalism and Subpolitics: Nike and its Labor Critics'. *Management Communication Quarterly* 15, no. 4 (2002): 541–570.

Lenskyj, Helen. *Inside the Olympic Industry: Power, Politics, and Activism.* Albany: SUNY Press, 2000.

Morris, C. 'Stadium Letter to Government Was "Private", Mayor Says'. *Otago Daily Times*, 30 January 2009, 5.

Noll, Roger G., and Andrew Zimbalist. 'Build the Stadium – Create the Jobs!'. In *Sports, Jobs & Taxes: The Economic Impact of Sports Teams*, edited by R.G. Noll and A. Zimbalist, 1–54. Washington: The Brookings Institute, 1997.

Noll, Roger G., and Andrew Zimbalist. 'The Economic Impact of Sports Teams and Facilities'. In *Sports, Jobs & Taxes: The Economic Impact of Sports Teams*, edited by R.G. Noll and A. Zimbalist, 55–91. Washington: The Brookings Institute, 1997.

Noll, Roger G., and Andrew Zimbalist, eds. *Sports, Jobs & Taxes: The Economic Impact of Sports Teams.* Washington: The Brookings Institute, 1997.

Palmer, John P. 'Bread and Circuses: The Local Benefits of Sports and Cultural Businesses'. C.D. Howe Institute Commentary No. 161. Toronto, ON: C.D. Howe Institute, 2002.

Sage, George. 'Justice Do It! The Nike Transnational Advocacy Network: Organization, Collective Actions, and Outcomes'. *Sociology of Sport Journal* 16 (1999): 206–35.

Sam, Michael P. 'Stadium Benefits Misrepresented'. *Otago Daily Times*, 30 May 2007, 15.

Sam, Michael P., and Jay Scherer. 'Stand Up and Be Counted: Numerical Storylines in a Stadium Dispute'. *International Review for the Sociology of Sport Journal* 43, no. 1 (2008): 53–70.

Sam, Michael P., and Jay Scherer. 'The Steering Group as Policy Advice Instrument: A Case of 'Consultocracy' in Stadium Subsidy Deliberations'. *Policy Sciences* 39 (2006): 169–81.

Scherer, Jay. 'Globalization and the Construction of Local Particularities: A Case Study of the Winnipeg Jets'. *Sociology of Sport Journal* 18, no. 2 (2001): 205–30.

Scherer, Jay, Mark Falcous, and Steven Jackson. 'The Media Sports Cultural Complex: Local-global Disjuncture in New Zealand/Aotearoa'. *Journal of Sport and Social Issues* 32, no. 1 (2008): 48–71.

Scherer, Jay, and Steven Jackson. 'From Corporate Welfare to National Interest: Newspaper Analysis of the Public Subsidization of NHL Hockey Debate in Canada'. *Sociology of Sport Journal* 21 (2004): 36–60.

Scherer, Jay, and Michael P. Sam. 'Public Consultation and Stadium Developments: Coercion and the Polarization of Debate'. *Sociology of Sport Journal* 25, no. 4 (2008): 443–61.

Sheller, Mimi, and John Urry. 'Mobile Transformations of "Public" and "Private' Life"'. *Theory, Culture & Society* 20, no. 3 (2003): 107–25.

Short, John, Carrie Breitbach, Steven Buckman, and Jamey Essex. 'From World Cities to Gateway Cities: Extending the Boundaries of Globalization Theory'. *City* 4, no. 3 (2000): 317–340.

Silver, Jim. *Thin Ice: Money, Politics, and the Demise of an NHL Franchise*. Halifax: Fernwood Publishing, 1996.

Whitson, David. 'Bringing the World to Canada: "The Periphery of the Centre"'. *Third World Quarterly* 25, no. 7 (2004): 1215–32.

Whitson, David. 'Olympic Hosting in Canada: Promotional Ambitions, Political Challenges'. *Olympika* XIV (2005): 29–46.

Whitson, David, Jean Harvey, and Marc Lavoie. 'The Mills Report, the Manley Subsidy Proposals, and the Business of Major-League Sport'. *Canadian Public Administration* 43, no. 2 (2000): 127–56.

Whitson, David, and John Horne. 'Underestimated Costs and Overestimated Benefits? Comparing the Outcomes of Sports Mega-Events in Canada and Japan'. *Sociological Review* 54, no. 2 (2006): 73–89.

Wilson, Brian. 'New Media, Social Movements, and Global Sport Studies: A Revolutionary Moment and the Sociology of Sport'. *Sociology of Sport Journal* 24 (2007): 457–77.

Winter, James. *Democracy's Oxygen: How Corporations Control the News*. Montreal: Black Rose Books, 1997.

Durban's future? Rebranding through the production/policing of event-specific spaces at the 2010 World Cup

David Roberts

Department of Geography and Planning, University of Toronto, Toronto, Canada and Centre for Critical Research on Race and Identity, University of KwaZulu-Natal, South Africa

As South African cities prepared to host the continent's first FIFA World Cup, one of the host cities, Durban, constructed plans to revitalize its city image through the media attention that accompanied the tournament. This paper explores the three-pronged strategy for the policing of event-specific public spaces during the tournament – the policing of nuisance behaviours, the restriction of protests by social movements, and the use of volunteer Welcome Ambassadors. These three endeavours significantly impacted the way in which public space in Durban was experienced during the World Cup for tourists and Durbanites alike. I argue that these public spaces give us a glimpse into the vision that city planners have for the city of Durban as an elite sports destination. The World Cup and the media coverage that it brings provides a rich opportunity for Durban to rebrand its image. Yet, the question remains as to how this will ultimately impact the future direction of city revitalization.

This paper focuses on the production and policing of event-specific urban spaces in Durban for the World Cup as an explicit strategy to use the media coverage accompanying the tournament to rebrand the city as an elite, international sporting destination. While, certainly, the FIFA World Cup is a large-scale event in and of itself, the planning for the World Cup in Durban is explicitly oriented around laying the foundation for the realization of a future Durban.[1] Thus, as much as the planning has revolved around the safety and experiences of tourists travelling to Durban during 2010, I argue that the work that went into producing and policing event-specific spaces is much more about attracting future tourists and business investors rather than appealing to World Cup tourists. Moreover, in the event-specific spaces created for 2010 we get a glimpse into the geographical imaginations of the city planners in terms of what they believe that an elite sports tourism destination should look like.

Durban, along with the Province of KwaZulu-Nata and federal government of South Africa, devoted significant resources to the production of these spaces for the games. In this paper, I trace three processes through which event-specific spaces were being produced in Durban for the World Cup. I first look at a set of event-specific municipal by-laws that governed the use of public spaces during the tournament with a particular focus on the regulation of 'nuisance' behaviours. I couple this discussion of the policing of individualized 'nuisance' behaviours with an examination of the restrictions on protests or other forms of social-movement organizing during the event. Combined, these two sets of practices worked to produce event-specific spaces where the range of 'acceptable' activities was severely curtailed during the tournament. The production of these newly created (and temporary) spaces was not restricted to the imposition and enforcement of new regimes of behavioural regulation. In conjunction with these processes of policing, the city also devised a volunteer program to enlist local community members to act as 'ambassadors ... to paint the World Cup in the area he stays positively'(sic).[2] These ambassadors, in displaying their national pride and ensuring that tourists have a good time, play a key role in Durban's rebranding. In short, I argue that Durban is hoping to use the World Cup as an opportunity to rebrand the city, setting the ground work for revitalization. To do that they produced event-specific spaces, through: (1) the regulation of behaviours – i.e., nuisance laws; (2) the restriction of protests; and (3) the employment of a volunteer force to act as 'ambassadors' of national pride. In the final section of the paper, I reflect on the fleeting nature of much of the planning for the World Cup in Durban. While, certainly, the World Cup left behind certain structural legacies, such as the newly constructed stadium, some infrastructure development and highly trained police, much of the planning was based on an intensification of resources for the six weeks of the tournament. The spaces produced for the World Cup may provide an insight into the geographical imagination of city planner in terms of their hopes for a future, revitalized Durban. They do not, however, represent permanent additions to the Durban urban landscape. Revitalization is an on-going and contested process. The World Cup offered a significant opportunity to alter the Durban brand. Rebranding and the increased tourism and business investment that may accompany a re-imagined Durban represents a starting point to urban revitalization. I argue that this opens up several questions and possibilities.

Background and methodology

This article is based on fieldwork conducted in South Africa in 2009 and 2010. I was primarily based in Durban. I interviewed city planners, police officers, representatives of community organizations, academics and other South Africans about their expectations for the World Cup and the impacts that it may have on the lived geographies of host cities. During my research, a common theme that ran through many of my interviews, and was echoed in a significant number of media reports, was that as much as the World Cup an event that happened on the ground in South Africa during June and July 2010, it is much more than that as the matches and everything that surrounds the festivities were broadcast globally. In fact, while the Local Organizing Committee projected that 450,000 tourists visited South Africa to attend and otherwise celebrate the World Cup, they estimateed that more than one billion people tuned in each day during the event.[3] While there is room to dispute both of these estimations as being rather hopeful, the fact remains that the World Cup was largely experienced through the medium of television as only a small number, relative to the viewing audience, actually traveled to South Africa to experience the matches and festivities in person. My interviews covered a wide range of topics, but one thing that stood out was that everyone I spoke to was hyper aware of the media coverage that the tournament would receive. A commonly expressed belief is that, if handled correctly, the intense media coverage that accompanied the World Cup could allow the country and host cities to significantly refresh, or completely alter, their media image or brand. The hope is that a rebranded South Africa, or a rebranded Durban as is the case for this paper, would provide the foundation for a refreshed economy. Ultimately, the hope is that the image displayed globally on television will inspire a future boon in tourism and business investment.

Rebranding South Africa

Confronting the negative media images about South Africa in the international media became common practice in the run up to the World Cup. Whether in casual conversation or press conferences at FIFA headquarters in Geneva, the international media bias was called out for unfair portrayals of South Africa. This is not say that South Africa and Durban do not suffer significant issues with crime as well as other social ills, such as poverty, unemployment, lack of housing and HIV/AIDS – these problems do exist. However, Durban and South Africa more generally saw the World Cup as an opportunity to change these images in much the same way as cities like Manchester used the Commonwealth Games to shed their industrial image and gain status as a modern, world-class city. For many of the individuals I interviewed, the World Cup, and the media attention it received, was a prime opportunity to confront South Africa's image and associated bad press. However, this goal of using the World Cup as the catalyst for fundamentally altering global tropes about South Africa, and Africa more broadly, is a formidable task as it confronts a widely held geographical imagination of Africa as an undifferentiated continent in agony – agony caused by underdevelopment, corruption, disease and backward traditional practices, to name just a few of the widely held stereotypical views held about the continent. Following the lead of Said and his theorization of Orientalism[4], scholars such as Treichler have shown how media images rely upon and perpetuate a limited set of common tropes about life in Africa.[5] These images, combined with other images of Africa in popular culture, underscore a geographical imagination of Africa as an undifferentiated continent of misery. For Treichler, the AIDS epidemic and the way it has been treated in the media has only worked to further exacerbate the issue.

In the case of the media coverage of South Africa, the stereotypical approach to the coverage of the AIDS pandemic is far from the only negative press that organizers of the World Cup were attempting to challenge in their planning for the World Cup. From the moment that South Africa was announced as host of the 2010 World Cup there have been questions about safety and security within the country. These concerns led to widespread speculation that there was a possibility that FIFA had clandestinely pursued an alternative location to be used for the tournament if South Africa proved itself to be unable to meet the safety and security requirements of the organization.[6] Moreover, questions of security and safety continued to dominate a significant portion of the international media coverage in the lead up to the tournament.

From national government officials to city planners to police officers, combating the violent and lawless perceptions of South African cities is of a primary concern. Through various programmes, the government has appealed to both the popularity of soccer as well as national pride at the core of tournaments like the World Cup, which pit national teams against each other. To this end, various levels of government engaged in marketing designed to provide South Africans a consistent message about how to talk about South Africa to tourists and foreign press. In many regards, this rebranding took on an explicitly place-based approach. In Durban, there was a concerted effort to produce and police event-specific urban areas to provide alternative images to the negative portrayals that dominate the press. The goal was that these alternative images would provide the catalyst to a rebranding of the city, which in turn would provide for future revitalization.

Given its unique natural beauty and vibrant culture, it could be argued that, 'if it were not for its apartheid history, South Africa would have been one of the most visited places in the world'.[7] In South Africa, Durban stands out as a popular tourist and sporting destination with its year-round warm weather, world-class surfing beaches, proximity to attractions and other amenities. To this end, city planners set their sites on situating the World Cup in Durban as a unique and powerful opportunity to promote a new Durban image. No one has been more vocal about rebranding the city through sports than Mayor Obed Mlaba, who has been mayor of the eThekwini Municipality since 1996. As Peter Alegi writes,

Mlaba leads a pro-business local administration that views international mega-events as engines of economic growth and branding tools for a city eager to reposition itself as 'South Africa's Playground'. Recognizing sport's potential to bring together an urban coalition of public and private actions seeking to attract investment and enhance the city's image, Durban's corporate leaders quickly got behind the stadium project.[8]

The use of the World Cup as a marketing tool at both the national and city levels is not a surprising nor unique phenomena. To this point, David Harvey has argued that the rise of neo-liberalism has led to the abandonment, by city governments, of the 'managerial city' model committed to the social-democratic provision of services in favour of the 'entrepreneurial city' model, which places projects of economic development and the governmental support of capitalist growth within cities.[9] A significant part of the entrepreneurial city is competing with other cities in a global marketplace of limited resources, such as business investment. Thus, the marketing of the city in the global economy has become a primary driving force behind city governance. The World Cup and the media attention it brings provided an unprecedented chance for South African cities to market themselves to the world as either world-class cities for business investment or exotic locations that can function as the playgrounds for jet-setting tourists, or both.

Thus, given the trend of neoliberal entrepreneurialism adopted by cities in South Africa and across the globe, it should not be surprising that host cities seized upon the World Cup as a moment to present themselves as 'world class'[10] locales and implemented planning priorities accordingly. Moreover, the emergence of the entrepreneurial city did not begin in South Africa with the announcement that it would be the 2010 host of the World Cup. Indeed the host-city governments, especially of the larger host cities of Johannesburg, Cape Town and Durban, were already organized in a manner to support entrepreneurial activity. That said, many of the city officials that I spoke to commented on the unique position that they had been placed in given the enormity of the World Cup coupled with the challenge of bringing such an event into an underdeveloped country, especially given some of the on-going social challenges facing South African cities. These comments usually manifested into interviewees mentioning that although city governments had learned a lot from Germany (where the previous World Cup was held in 2006), the significant infrastructure differences between cities in the two countries had placed them in an unprecedented position, where they were basically 'writing the book' on how to host an event of this magnitude in a developing country.

As mentioned previously, in this paper, I trace three processes in which these landscapes are being produced. The first of these processes that I discuss is the imposition of nuisance laws focused on the use of public space during the tournament.

Controlling the use of public space – event-specific nuisance laws

One of the requirements that FIFA places on cities that would like to host World Cup games is the city's willingness to pass event-specific by-laws to 'to enable the efficient running of the Competition'.[11] The by-laws, which were to be implemented specifically during the duration of the World Cup, cover regulations on advertising, controlled access to event-related sites, public open spaces and city beautification, public roads and traffic guidance, and street trading. Of specific concern for this section of the paper are the by-laws that fall under the regulation of public open spaces and city beautification. In particular, I am interested in the by-laws aimed at policing and regulating 'nuisance' behaviours in public spaces.

In tracing the rise of nuisance or civility laws in the United States over the last two decades, Beckett and Herbert note that, 'civility laws have significantly expanded local governments' capacities to regulate urban residents and spaces'.[12] These types of regulations have become a common practice for urban municipalities looking to revitalize their cities and often go hand-in-hand with 'broken window' approaches to policing, first pioneered in New York City. While their origins may be in the United States, their spread has been truly global.[13] Thus, it should not be surprising that such measures were included in the 2010 by-laws provisions. In fact, it ought to be noted that the implementation of these ordinances was not limited to the city of Durban, but happened within each municipality hosting tournament matches at the behest of FIFA. These new provisions expanded the authority of public order policing to police public spaces and other event-specific spaces to ensure that they were free from activities or behaviours that could sully the produced urban imagery that the municipality was trying to create.

Just a short sample of the language of the by-laws gives you an indication of how this process worked while exposing the relatively vague language used:

> 4.2. **General Prohibition**: No Person shall at a Special Event or in a Public Open Space, in particular, or in any other area within the Municipality, in general, without the Approval of the Municipality –
> 4.2.1. cause a Nuisance to other users of a Public Open Space;
> 4.2.2. use abusive or otherwise objectionable language or behave in an abusive, objectionable or disorderly manner towards any other user of a Public Open Space;
> 4.2.3. hamper, disturb, obstruct or harass any other person using and/ or entering a Public Open Space;
> 4.2.10. lie, sit, stand, congregate or walk so as to cause a wilful obstruction, or otherwise cause any obstruction, of any nature whatsoever in a Public Open Space; [14]

What is clear here is that this type of regulation of 'nuisance' behaviour goes hand-in-hand with the production of the types of images of the city and city life that Durban was attempting to put on display during the tournament. Moreover, while these by-laws were enacted as part of the host-city agreement signed between Durban and FIFA, the specific provisions above did not sunset at the end of the tournament. Rather, they 'shall commence upon the adoption, hereof, by the Council and remain in effect for an indefinite period until the Municipality decides otherwise'.[15] Clearly, then, these by-laws cannot be thought of as simply necessary restrictions to ensure an efficient hosting of the World Cup.

The implementation of such restrictions on certain nuisance behaviours works to enforce a furtive creation of a geography of exclusion that is based on the welcoming of a particular deserving public and an exclusion of groups perceived to be a threat to the particular image of public space that Durban is attempting to promote as part of its rebranding strategy. As Ruppert explains,

> regulatory regimes focus on techniques that guide and shape conduct rather than simply exclude particular groups. This is achieved by reconfiguring (rather than removing) liberty through the implementation of myriad constraints that act upon the freedom of choice of the agent and thus the possibilities of taking and making space.[16]

In circumscribing the permissible behaviours within open public space, the new municipal by-laws that address nuisance behaviours, necessarily limit how public space can be utilized and by whom. Through the vaguely worded ban on nuisance behaviours, policing can selectively target both individuals and groups seen as incongruous with the idealized image of Durban's public spaces that were at the centre of rebranding the city during the World Cup.

Combined with this regulation of permissible individual behaviours was restriction on the actions of social movements. There was an expressed fear among some planners for the World Cup that social movements would capitalize on the media attention that accompanies the games to garner attention for their struggles. Of course, this is the same media attention that cities like Durban were hoping to enlist in their rebranding project.

Circumscribing dissent

One of the other common themes from my interviews was the belief/fear that social movements would seize upon the unprecedented media coverage accompanying the tournament to launch protests and other forms of civil unrest in hopes of stealing some of the spotlight of the games. Media stories about these protests and the grievances that social movements have with the South African state were precisely the types of stories that South Africa wanted to keep out of the international coverage.

In an interview I conducted with South African Police Services (SAPS) Captain Govender, he made it quite clear that there would be a management of both the timing and locations of social movement protests through a permit process. Protests were condoned in certain places at certain times with the hope that they would, consequently, not compete for media attention with the event-specific urban spaces created as the cornerstone of the rebranding effort. Attempted protests without permits, that threaten to undermine the idealized images of the World Cup, were met with considerable response from public order policing. As Captain Govender remarked,

> The Gatherings Act stipulates that you as an organizer of a protest march must inform the local authority and seek his permission. So what we are saying, 'yes you can if we have the resources'. It will be pooled to a central point and everyone will be asked, 'can this march take place or should it be stopped?' Then we will go back to the protest organizer and say, 'sorry, we have a bigger event taking place we cannot police your event because we don't have the resources for both. You are not allowed to march.' So if you are not allowed to march, you should not be gathering there in the first place. So if you are gathering you are doing so illegally and we are going to take action against you. So there are steps in place to counteract this. And if you think you are going to hold the country for ransom during the World Cup – say you are Greenpeace – you come here afterwards for permission to march we will put so much restrictions on you – and it can be done legally. So there has to be a win-win situation and I truly believe in negotiating for a win-win. You can't use your authority to say, 'no and I don't have to explain'. You say, 'no, because of A, B, and C and if you go ahead this is what can happen in the future'. But we have contingency plans, extra resources, manpower dedicated to that sort of thing.[17]

Rather than follow the direction of Seattle, during the WTO, and create a no-protest-zone buffer around designated protest sites, the SAPS devised a strategy of limiting protests through the restriction of approvals of permits to protests, using the excuse of limited security resources as the rationale for denying a permit. This is perhaps not an unsurprising strategy. While the World Cup took place over a month's time, there were seven matches played in Durban. It is during these matches that Durban was the centre of the media attention and scrutiny. Thus, it is precisely during these days that city planners was most interested in policing and otherwise producing the urban public spaces that are at the core of the rebranding effort. Social movements were also aware of the heightened media attention during these dates, which set the stage for conflicting agendas on game days – precisely the days with limited resources to police protests.

In the minds of many government officials, the stakes were too high and the possibilities and consequences of failure to live up to the world's expectations for security were too significant not to take action to attempt to keep protests and other negative story lines out of the reporting on the World Cup, as much as possible. Thus, despite a robust array of social movements and grassroots political engagement, the South African state exercised the maximum authority allowed within the law to keep social movements from sharing in the media spotlight. This resulted in an uneven temporal geography of social movement activities, where some spaces in which protests were restricted on game days became available as the media attention shifted to other host cities along with the tournament matches. This created an interesting temporality and allowed the municipality to avoid some of the complications with passing a blanket ban on protesting, while giving authorities a ready-made excuse to deny protests during times when there was significantly greater media coverage.

In practice, this allowed the Durban municipality to essentially police and produce event-specific urban spaces – urban spaces that lacked both 'nuisance' behaviours and disruption/dissension by social movement – selectively. Yet, the production of these spaces went beyond simply the policing of individual and social movement behaviours and activities. The municipality also implemented a volunteer programme to enlist the work of 'ambassadors' from the community.

Enlisting Durbanites to produce the rebranded spaces of Durban

To complete the production of the urban space at the centre of Durban's World Cup rebranding effort, the local division of the SAPS, with the support of local government, established a volunteer programme to tap into community enthusiasm for soccer and national/community pride. As Captain Govender describes,

> But like I said, when the event unfolds, we are looking for people to be patriotic. That is going to help a lot. Because you have a lot of proud people in this country and they want to see it being successful. I am not talking about the politicians – I am talking about the man on the street – they want to see it being successful. And the only way they can do it is if a man has got nothing in his pocket – he has not got a penny in his pocket – he will ensure that as a tourist you have a good time, enjoy your stay, and then go away. If everyone can do that we have won it. We have won it. And we are busy trying to tap into that with our volunteers that are coming in from the various communities. We are training them – letting them be ambassadors. So if we have one volunteer say from an area in which I stay, he is going to paint the World Cup in the area he stays positively and fifty other people are going to know what is happening. That will eventually flow throughout the entire province.[18]

These projects represent, in some ways, the soft side of the approach to managing the messages at the core of using the World Cup as a branding opportunity. Ideally, the widespread sense of ownership and national pride that was so pervasive during the World Cup would showcase South African hospitality over other storylines. On one hand, as I have documented already, the municipality worked to eliminate 'nuisance' behaviours on both an individual level as well as at the level of disruptions by social movements. On the other hand, these 'nuisances' were replaced by a team of volunteers committed to provide a different depiction of Durban's urban culture.

On its surface, the recruitment of a volunteer force to provide a friendly welcome to tourists visiting Durban during the World Cup seems a rather benign and admirable approach to building a sense of community pride in and through the event. The use of volunteers during mega-events is not uncommon and has become an essential part of both ensuring that the events function as planned, as well as contributing to the celebratory spirit of the games. Thus, on its face, I find it difficult to criticize the implementation of the Welcome Ambassadors program within Durban.[19] Steve Herbert, in discussing the appeal of the concept of community-based projects as part of planning the neo-liberal city, explains that 'part of the ideological advantage of governing through community is the benighted status the term possess'.[20] In this, he is pointing out that the general acceptance community participation projects enjoy is due, 'in part because of the widespread and warm associations with the term'.[21]

76

Yet, while on its surface encouraging citizens to be welcoming to visitors and providing support in the form of a volunteer programme is not seemingly problematic, given the wider context of the Welcome Ambassadors programme, there is space to be critical of it. Ambassadors are a common way for business improvement districts and downtown associations to employ a secondary police force to identify precisely the nuisance behaviours that are the subject of the by-laws that Durban implemented for the games.[22] Moreover, when coupled with the intense regulation of public space, as well as the pricing out of many locals from being able to see the games, the Welcome Ambassadors become one of the very few ways that marginalized Durbanites could take part in the games – of course, only those who passed a screening and were willing to adhere to the guidelines of the volunteer programme were allowed this opportunity. In a recent interview on CBC radio, Rich Mkhondo, chief spokesperson for the Local Organizing Committee for South Africa made it clear 'that an event is never intended to benefit people who cannot afford it'.[23] However, while the World Cup may not have been intended to benefit marginalized Durbanites, they still had an active role to play in the production of urban spaces central to capitalizing on the World Cup's potential to rebrand the city. While Mkhondo was clear that the World Cup could not solve the country's social ills, he believes it to be an excellent opportunity to refresh the brand of both South Africa and the continent of Africa. Yet, it is precisely these individuals that cannot afford to attend the World Cup that were called upon to act as an Welcome Ambassadors, providing the human face for what otherwise might seem as an overly policed city.

The rebranding of Durban and the hope that it will lead to a future boom in tourism and business investment was contingent on the production of a revamped urban image during the World Cup through the policing of space and an army of Welcome Ambassadors. Yet, the question remains, will such an intense investment in the control of space over the short term translate into a long-term trajectory of urban revitalization? In the final section of this paper, I provide some preliminary thoughts on post-World Cup Durban.

An icon for the future – some thoughts on post-World Cup Durban

In their article, 'The Global Circus: International Sport, Tourism, and the Marketing of Cities', Whitson and Macintosh ask, 'Who is the city for?'[24] They challenge readers to consider whether the contemporary city is simply a commodity in the global tourism market, 'Or is it a community where people – including those without much disposable income – can, live, work, play and belong?'[25] While Whitson and Macintosh's work focused primarily on the Canadian experience with international mega-events, this question seems all the more relevant in the context of Durban and South Africa, given the many challenges the city and country face. The planning for the World Cup gives an insight on how city planners are approaching this issue.

By their very nature, urban revitalization projects are future oriented and, consequently, imbued with visions of what a city could become given the right set of circumstances. In this regard, the planning for the World Cup that happened in Durban is no different than countless city revitalization projects happening around the globe. The produced urban spaces in Durban during the World Cup represented a glimpse into what city planners hope the future of the city can become through increased international tourism and the infusion of cash that accompanies such visitors. As Tomlinson put it in his chapter, 'Anticipating 2011', 'Durban's economic strategy has long included sports tourism . . . This is not to say that 2010 is not a "big deal" for Durban. Instead, the impression created is that it is at the same time "part of the deal" – an aspect of how Durban has long viewed itself'.[26] One example of this can be seen in the construction of the new World Cup stadium in Durban after the municipality decided that the current stadiums were inadequate for the World Cup. The decision to construct a new stadium was not based on the requirements of the tournament nor requests from FIFA, as Absa Rugby Stadium was already deemed adequate (with a few upgrades) to host World Cup games, including a semi-final. Rather, the city seized upon the World Cup to construct an 'iconic' stadium. As described in the instructions for bid submissions, 'The completed stadium needs to be flexible, cost effective and "ICONIC" such that it is regarded by sports athletes, officials, media, and spectators as having a unique quality and a desirable "sense of place" which will be a hallmark of its reputation in the sports world'.[27] For Durban city officials, the World Cup and the possibility of a new stadium provided an opportunity to further their vision of Durban as a sporting city while setting the stage for a future Olympic bid.

While the question of the desirability of this vision of urban redevelopment falls outside of the work in this paper, the question ought not be ignored; however, given the lack of public consultation on the construction of the stadium in Durban it is somewhat difficult to assess community feelings about the way in which the city has chosen to position its brand. Thus, the decision to build an iconic stadium in a city that continues to suffer from significant social ills such as widespread poverty, unemployment, lack of housing and HIV/AIDS has had little formal opposition. Moreover, the scholarship on the benefits of hosting mega-events indicates that there is a no clear way to rebrand a city. As Gratton explains, 'despite a strong theoretical case in favour of urban regeneration benefits from investment in sporting infrastructure in order to host major sports events, there is also strong arguments that the negative impacts of such investment may even outweigh these benefits'.[28] One must consider that there are often clear trade-offs between a government investing in the construction of 'iconic' stadiums (and other infrastructure for hosting a World Cup) and other things, such as service delivery, that might serve a different set of needs for the city. In considering Cape Town's investment in the beautification of the highway linking the airport and city centre in the run-up to the 2010 World Cup, Newton writes,

> City governments have become increasingly engaged in remodeling their places for the 'visitor class', [and] the needs of the residents have gone out of sight . . . The allocation of public resources to these events and the related needs, such as public transport or neighbourhood renewal, means that cuts have to be made in sectors which are indeed less prestigious, but which might answer the need of local residents.[29]

The vision of Durban that comes into focus in its planning of the World Cup highlights this approach to catering for a 'visitor class' and the revitalization of the city. Thus, in approaching the question of the desirability of this future Durban, the inevitable trade-offs ought to be considered. Thus, I would further question the mechanisms through which Durban's vision is achieved.

While it certainly can be argued that the new stadium has the potential of becoming iconic in the way that it has become an essential part of the Durban skyline, the production of a sense of place in Durban during the World Cup goes well beyond the addition of an iconic piece of architecture as it was being constructed in and through the intense policing of nuisance behaviours, the control of protests and the use of Welcome Ambassadors. The iconic stadium is the centrepiece of an elite sports city; its existence as a permanent element of the Durban skyline does not, however, ensure that the other elements of the city that television viewers saw during the World Cup will endure. In several interviews, individuals associated with planning for the World Cup stressed that the planning effort relied on an intensification of resource deployment, such as policing, for approximately six weeks during June and July,

2010. While my interviewees pointed to legacies that will outlive the tournament, it is clear that many of the measures planned to produce the spaces of the World Cup were phased out shortly after the tournament's final whistle. For example, the security for the World Cup was supported by the largest deployment of the South African military in the history of the republic[30] and supported with upwards of 41,000 additional, event-specific, police officers for the games.[31] While this level of security was designed, in part, to ensure the safety of tourists and athletes, it was called upon to support the production of the spaces of World Cup, as described in the previous section, both in terms of policing the actions of social movements as well as 'nuisance' behaviours. It would be inconceivable and, I would argue, undesirable for South Africa and Durban to maintain that level of securitization post-World Cup.

The fleeting nature of the intense energy used to produce event-specific spaces for 2010 leaves open the possibility for envisioning a different set of futures for Durban. The vision for Durban, as with most urban planning, is politically motivated and thus could change substantially with a change of political leadership. Speaking of the practice of planning in general, Myers and Kitsuse remark, 'current practices in planning address the future in ways that are superficial, shortsighted, or hollow. These approaches may be dictated by the caution required of planners in government agencies or who must seek approval of elected bodies'.[32] Having a grand, politically oriented, vision for the future and seeing this vision through to fruition planning are two very different things. I argue that Durban's approach to the World Cup gives us a glimpse into one possible future of the city, where its ultimate vision of becoming an elite sporting destination is far from a future set in stone. Given the myriad social issues that South Africa faces, the possibility of alternative futures from the ones produced during the World Cup is not a negative prospect. Nor is it negative for Durban to finally receive some good press coverage.

Acknowledgements

I would like to acknowledge FIFA and International Centre for Sport Studies CIES for their financial support for this research through the João Havelange Research Scholarship. I would also like to thank the organizers of the Visualizing the Game conference held in Basel, Switzerland in January 2010. This paper benefited greatly from the insights of conference participants. I am very grateful for the comments of Minelle Mahtani, John Ewing Hughson and Mike Sam on a draft of this paper. This research was conducted while I was a visiting research associate at the Centre for Critical Research on Race and Identity at the University of KwaZulu-Natal. The centre's support has proven to be invaluable to my research.

Notes

[1] Moody, 'Durban's Ambition'.
[2] P. Govender. Personal interview with author, 7 August 2009.
[3] Estimates presented as part of the Local Organizing Committee's progress report to the South African Parliamentary Committee on Sport on 17 June 2008.
[4] Said, *Orientalism*.
[5] Treichler, 'AIDS, Africa and Cultural Thoery'.
[6] Burger, 'A Golden Goal', 5.
[7] Maharaj, Sucheran and Pillay, 'Durban', 278.
[8] Alegi, 'A Nation to be Reckoned With', 409.
[9] Harvey, 'From Managerialism to Entrepreneurialism'.
[10] Harding, 'South Africa Starts 100-day'.
[11] eThekwini Municipality, *2010 FIFA World Cup South Africa By-Laws*, 3.
[12] Beckett and Herbert, 'Dealing with Disorder', 9.
[13] Mountz and Curran, 'Policing in Drag'.
[14] eThekwini Municipality, *2010 FIFA World Cup South Africa By-Laws*, 27–8.

[15] Ibid., 49.
[16] Ruppert, 'Rights to Public Space', 287.
[17] P. Govender, personal interview with author, 7 August 2009.
[18] Ibid.
[19] A short description of the Welcome Ambassadors Program can be found at http://fifaworldcup.durban.gov.za/Pages/Volunteer_programme.aspx (accessed 15 January 2010).
[20] Herbert, 'Trapdoor of Community', 853.
[21] Ibid., 850.
[22] For example, see Amster, 'Patterns of Exclusion'.
[23] R. Mkhondo, interview with A.M. Temonti, *The Current*. CBC Radio, 5 January 2010.
[24] Whitson and Macintosh, 'The Global Circus', 289.
[25] Ibid.
[26] Tomlinson, 'Anticipating 2011', 105.
[27] Emphasis in the original. eThikwini Municipality Strategic Projects Unit, *Expression of Interest*, 6.
[28] Gratton, Shibli and Coleman, 'Sport and Economic Regeneration', 988.
[29] Newton, 'Reverse Side of Medal', 98.
[30] Szabo, '2010 World Cup'.
[31] Donaldson and Ferreira, '(Re-)creating Urban Destination Image', 9.
[32] Myers and Kitsuse, *Constructing the Future in Planning: A Survey of Theories and Tools*, 230.

References

Alegi, P. '"A Nation to be Reckoned With": The Politics of World Cup Stadium Construction in Cape Town and Durban, South Africa'. *African Studies* 67, no. 3 (2010): 397–422.

Amster, R. 'Patterns of Exclusion: Sanitizing Space, Criminalizing Homelessness'. *Social Justice* 30, no. 11 (2003): 195–222.

Beckett, K., and S. Herbert. 'Dealing with Disorder: Social Control in the Post-Industrial City'. *Theoretical Criminology* 12, no. 1 (2008): 5–30.

Burger, J. 'A Golden Goal for South Africa: Security Arrangements for the 2010 FIFA Soccer World Cup'. *South African Crime Quarterly* 19 (2007): 1–6.

Donaldson, R., and S. Ferreira. '(Re-)creating Urban Destination Image: Opinions of Foreign Visitors to South Africa on Safety and Security?'. *Urban Forum* 20 (2009): 1–18.

eThekwini Municipality Strategic Projects Unit. *Expression of Interest: New Iconic Stadium, Kingspark, Durban*, 17 February 2006.

Gratton, C., S. Shibli, and R. Coleman. 'Sport and Economic Regeneration in Cities'. *Urban Studies* 42, no. 5–6 (2005): 985–99.

Harding, A. 'South Africa Starts 100-day World Cup Count Down'. *BBC News*, 1 March 2010. Available at: http://news.bbc.co.uk/go/pr/fr/-/2/hi/business/8543468.stm

Harvey, D. 'From Managerialism to Entrepreneurialism: The Transformation in Urban Governance in Late Capitalism'. *Geografiska Annaler. Series B, Human Geography* 71, no. 1 (1989): 3–17.

Herbert, S. 'The Trapdoor of Community'. *Annals of the Association of American Geographers* 95, no. 4 (2005): 850–65.

Maharaj, B., R. Sucheran, and V. Pillay. 'Durban – A Tourism Mecca? Challenges of the Post-Apartheid Era'. *Urban Forum* 17, no. 3 (2006): 262–81.

Moody, B. 'Durban's Ambition Exceeds World Cup'. *Reuters*, 20 August 2009. Available at http://www.reuters.com/article/idUSLI16655420090820

Mountz, A., and W. Curran. 'Policing in Drag: Guiliani Goes Global with the Illusion of Control'. *Geoforum* 40, no. 6 (2008): 1033–40.

Myers, D., and A. Kituse. 'Constructing the Future in Planning: A Survey of Theories and Tools'. *Journal of Planning Education and Research* 19, no. 3 (2000): 221–231.

Newton, C. 'The Reverse Side of Medal: About the 2010 FIFA World Cup and the Beautification of the N2 in Cape Town'. *Urban Forum* 20 (2009): 93–108.

Ruppert, E. 'Rights to Public Space: Regulatory Reconfigurations of Liberty'. *Urban Geography* 27, no. 3 (2006): 271–92.

Said, E. *Orientalism*. New York: Vintage, 1979.

Szabo, S. '2010 World Cup "Biggest Ever" South African Military Deployment'. *Digital Journal Reports*, 14 October 2009. Available at: http://www.digitaljournal.com/article/280504 (accessed 12 January 2010).

Tomlinson, R. 'Anticipating 2011'. In *Development and Dreams: The Urban Legacy of the 2010 Football World Cup*, edited by U. Pillay, R. Tomlinson, and O. Bass, 96–113. Cape Town: HSRC Press, 2009.

Treichler, P. 'AIDS, Africa, and Cultural Theory'. *Transitions* 51 (1991): 86–103.

Whitson, D., and D. Macintosh 'The Global Circus: International Sport, Tourism, and the Marketing of Cities'. *Journal of Sport and Social Issues* 20, no. 3 (1996): 278–95.

Civic representations of sport history: the New Zealand Sports Hall of Fame

G.Z. Kohe

Institute of Sport and Exercise Science, University of Worcester, Worcester, UK

Sports halls of fame and sports museums have an important role in presenting sport history to a public audience. Utilizing the New Zealand Sports Hall of Fame in Dunedin, I argue that these places construct and represent sport history in particular ways that tend to enhance positive aspects of the sports ethic and a respectful reverence toward sporting figures. I discuss the affective values of historical artefacts, the distinction between sports halls of fame and sport museums, the religious quality of these aesthetic sites, and the importance of nostalgia in creating memorable visitor experiences. I consider how our understanding and critique of these civic spaces can be informed by debates over form and content in historical presentation. A brief review of the Sports Hall of Fame is followed by an alternative proposal that reconceives the role of academic sports historians within the domain of public sports history.

Introduction

While sports museums and halls of fame are popularly regarded as important cultural repositories, sports historians and even curators have long criticized these institutions. They argue there is disjuncture and ambiguity between properly contextualized sports history and the constructions of sporting history for public consumption.[1] Some scholars disagree, and argue that any incongruity between reality, legend and myth in national sports repositories serves an inherent function in engendering the nostalgic recollections and feelings of individual and collective belonging that are important aspects of the hall of fame or museum experience.[2] I, for example, personally enjoy museums for the above reasons. But as an academic historian with an interest in sport, I am still bothered by issues of content, form and representation. This variety of interests plagued my visit to and subsequent analysis of New Zealand's national sports hall of fame and museum. Here it is apparent that the nation's devout interest in sport has not been equally matched with investments into preserving and exhibiting our sporting heritage in ways that necessarily befit its profound and enduring cultural and social significance. The establishment of the New Zealand Sports Hall of Fame in 1990 followed on from the development of the New Zealand Rugby Museum in 1969 and the International Rugby Hall of Fame in 1995.[3] The Hall provides visitors and scholars with an indication of the greater agendas in New Zealand sport. Typically these have been to serve and reflect the country's love of rugby, and immortalize our most memorable sporting achievements and athletic successes.

Drawing upon the debates over public history and academic history, and focusing on the New Zealand Sports Hall of Fame in Dunedin, I look at how the latter has historically constructed and represented New Zealand's sporting and olympic past.[4] I also consider how this construction and representation might contribute to the myths, romanticism and public understanding of our national sporting legacy. Accordingly, in assessing this particular civic repository of sport, I discuss whether sports historians and sports curators share the same agendas and whether they should work together more closely. Their relationship has implications for addressing issues within the discipline of history, in particular concerns over form and content,[5] and future possibilities for the types of historical interpretations halls of fame and museums may provide. I argue that ideally academic research and the public consumption of national sports history should not remain mutually exclusive pursuits. However, I also propose a controversial alternative. I suggest that if the idea of a cultural history of sport is bought into as a sensuous experience[6] then understanding the ability of sporting artefacts to elicit particular affects with audiences becomes particularly important.[7] Following on from recognizing the subjective nature of affective sporting artefacts we might then reconsider the role of sport historians within halls of fames and museums. Perhaps academic historian roles within public history should be seen more comparable to that of the subsidiary role played by art historians or art critics in public art galleries.

Sports halls and museums and the making of affective experiences

Sports museums and sports halls of fame are repositories that reflect the cultural and social significance of national sporting and leisure pursuits. Yet, these sites dedicated to sporting history do not simply involve a passive 'looking back' to an authentic *past*; they are also concerned with the careful construction of select aspects of sporting heritage, tradition, romanticism, memorialization, myth and remembrance. The reconstruction of sporting history in halls of fame and museums is closely aligned to their pragmatic purpose to facilitate and nurture an affective and memorable experience for public consumers, be it educational, nostalgic and/or enjoyable. Accordingly, sports museums and halls of fame utilize highly symbolic constructions and representations of sport and sporting identities to help engender positive feelings among visitors. The type of experience visitors have depends, to an extent, on the symbolic power of the artefacts and exhibits to elicit specific meanings. As an important part of the overall experience, sports museums and halls of fame largely depend on the interpretation of the symbolic to rouse feelings of personal or collective association. These affective associations are a significant aspect of the cultural value imbued in sports museums and halls of fame, particularly in allowing visitors opportunities to acknowledge, appreciate and reflect upon sport's role within national history and their own personal lives. Remarking on the ability of history to engender personal affects, Hughson remarks that 'the cultural history of sport thus takes interest in how sports have been *sensuously known* by people; in how sport has embraced and reflected cultural values and with the symbolic and aesthetic relevance that sport has had to peoples' lives'.[8]

In sports hall of fames and museums sporting artefacts capture the sensuous aspect of cultural history referred to by Hughson.[9] The ability of sporting artefacts to engender emotive responses with audiences has also been discussed in terms of an affective relationship.[10] Booth uses the term 'affective artefact'[11] to denote the way historical material or texts, e.g., magazines, connect with particular audiences by engendering particular emotive responses through their unique form and content.[12] The term is particularly useful for understanding how artefacts within halls of fames and museums may be appreciated not merely because of their historical significance, but because they are valuable texts that have the capacity to stimulate and evoke deeply symbolic personal and collective affects. Drawing on Gibbs and Greggs' arguments that texts stimulate biological responses, Booth suggests that reading historical material may be considered a highly personalized cognitive process.[13] In regards to sports halls of fame and museums visual media, in this case affective sporting artefacts, have the capacity to generate particular affects and evoke certain reactions among specific audiences. The affects of sporting artefacts are varied but may include the ability to inspire, motivate, encourage or temporarily remove ourselves from our present self and consider the alternative possibilities of being. These considerations are employed throughout my following analysis.

What now needs to be foregrounded is how affective artefacts are part of the broader issues of form and content within sports history. Importantly, I want to highlight the idea that civic spaces, like halls and museums, tend to prioritize form over content, and in so doing create an affective experience for public audiences. This experience then needs to be understood on different terms than we might understand more conventional, academic approaches to the same historical material, subject or phenomenon.

With a focus on Australian swimming history, Phillips[14] discusses the concepts of form and content in his work on the different presentation priorities of commissioned histories and historical documentaries. As an academic historian, Phillips concerns himself with the disjuncture between approaches to academic history and other methods of historical presentation. He questions how forms of public history work with the past by essentially asking 'what can be gained by subjecting public history to similar types of analysis and critique that have been applied to written history?'.[15] Although commissioned histories and documentaries require both form and content, the emphasis varies considerably. According to Phillips, 'content centers on the contribution of material reality depicted through traces of the past, exterior real-world events, processes and actions to constructions of the history whether it be written or on film', whereas form 'considers the importance of the ways in which language, the formal structure of narrative and the role of the historian contribute to the structural design and meaning of the written history text'.[16] He suggests that academics of history have tended to believe that content dictates form. However, within the domain of public history, form takes on a particular, significant function.

People's experiences of public history, particularly in places such as sports halls of fame and museums, are predominantly shaped by the form of historical material. The affective value of historical artefacts, specifically the ability of the artefact to engender particular meanings, emotions and nostalgic associations for individuals, largely rests on the specific form of the exhibit. Style, layout and design all contribute to an artefact's particular form. Despite the lack of attention scholars have given to historical form, the artistic aspects of the concept have been employed in realms of public history, in particular films and museums.[17] The innovative and creative ways those in public history approach issues of form deserves recognition. The ultimate affect of the historical artefact is due to their foresight in privileging form over content. Although the particular content of exhibits may be engaging, it is through the overall form of the historical material that the artefacts are able to elicit their principal affects. The visual form of an exhibit is the key way individuals may initially come to *know* and experience the historical material. This idea, though not an initial consideration during my visit, was particularly useful for retrospectively re-evaluating my role as an academic historian interested in public history, and also, reconceiving ways others might approach analysing similar spaces.

Necessary distinctions

Thus far I have used the terms 'sports museum' and 'sports hall of fame' conjointly and interchangeably, however it is important to clarify the distinctions and overlaps between these two specific forms of public sports history. Sport has seemingly struggled to negotiate legitimate space within the landscape of mainstream museums. 'Curiously most non-sports museums appear to have very few sporting artefacts on their accessions register,' says Vamplew, adding that 'even those are rarely documented in detail'.[18] Even at Te Papa Tongarewa, New Zealand's iconic national museum, sport occupies only a marginal place. This is interesting considering the prominent role that sports, especially rugby, have played within the important curatorial themes of colonialism, nationalism and international relations.[19] The reluctance to consider the cultural and social value of sport in mainstream museums has been a partial impetus for establishing specialist sports museums. Like most museums, which 'are containers of things',[20] sports museums are repositories for artefacts, ephemera and memorabilia, dedicated to preserving and recollecting the history of diverse, but often most popular, sporting, recreation and leisure pursuits, with collections ranging from the mundane, trivial, eclectic and profane, to the exceptional, significant, iconic and the sacred. Referring to the National Football Museum in England, Johnes and Mason argue that 'museums provide a multisensory context through the combination of material culture, sound, film, photography, oral testimonies, and stories told through spatial arrangements'.[21]

Sports museums attempt to capture the exciting atmosphere of the sport spectacle and the dynamism of the live physical culture of the sports field through a combination of static, audiovisual, textual and memorabilia-based displays. Moreover sports museums, such as the grandiose International Olympic Museum in Lausanne, are places which educate, entertain and inform people about the history of sport, physical activity, and the sports ethos. Sports museums are typically places where selective sporting traditions, histories and legacies are carefully preserved, exhibited, then consumed by avid public audiences. Ultimately, museums dedicated to sport are civic spaces in which the cloistered domain of academic sports history intersects with the public's insatiable appetite for their shared sporting traditions. However, sports museums do vary in the sports they focus on, the audiences they attract, the range of material they draw upon, their presentation modes, and the versions of history they create. As such the role of history within the sports museum is a matter of some debate.[22] Yet, the popular appeal of sports museums supports the belief that, although they may never accrue the fan bases of live sports, 'sports museums are the best places to replicate the performance, drama, romance, and emotion of sport'.[23]

The emergence of sports museums has simultaneously occurred with the establishment of sports halls of fame. Where sports museum attempt to preserve and honour the value of the sports cult through ephemera, artefacts and memorabilia, sports halls of fame carefully select feats and personalities of iconic sports heroes and heroines to encapsulate the positive aspects of the sport ethic. However, arguably to their benefit, museums do utilize the lives of sports figures to personalize their presentation of history, and halls of fame are inclined to draw on classic curatorial and museological practices in the immortalizations of sports champions. 'The appeal of halls of fames', West argues, 'lies in the fact that they present history through the personalities who helped to form it. Man's [sic] development in sport is told through the means of the talented heroes who have been enshrined', and because of its ability 'to inspire people to appreciate the positive values to be found in sport'.[24]

Sports halls of fame have established indelible places within many sporting cultures and also national cultures as temples of the sport cult, to the point where some have even become heavily imbued with pseudo-religious aura. Speaking of the renowned American National Baseball Hall of Fame in Cooperstown, New York, and its status within the greater American ideology of the 'church of baseball', Grella proclaims,

> The Hall of Fame . . . assumes an even more special place within that church, becoming itself a kind of holy structure to center the history and meaning of the game, to maintain some link with a fundamental theology and worship. Cooperstown then becomes, not only a special place in the great cultural fantasy of America, but also a holy city, a destination for pilgrims, perhaps even exerting for the faithful some healing power.[25]

Moreover, as the name suggests, halls of fame are commonly galleries of sport deities, idolized, immortalized and romanticized figures whose positive public notoriety and athletic supremacy has been deemed sufficient enough to warrant them a place in society's upper echelon. However, not all halls of fame proselytize to this extreme, and certainly the New Zealand Sports Hall of Fame has a more humble agenda: a site 'where champions live on, a place to admire, and a place to live on'.[26]

Sports halls of fame are unashamedly places 'primarily concerned with honouring individual achievement'.[27] Accordingly, despite their goal to enliven the sporting deeds of yesteryear,[28] few halls of fame allocate space to infamy, scandal, unsavoury behaviour or even defeat. Addressing this explicit bias, Vamplew reminds us, 'sports museums in general and halls of fame in particular join the part of the sporting world that is obsessed with winners and winning. Jingoism at national and club triumphs' abounds, and insufficient recognition is given to the more typical competitive sports experience: losing'.[29] Speaking of British club football museums, Johnes and Mason note that there, too, 'the approach is . . . celebratory and selective – overlooking by and large, the controversial, the distasteful and the political'.[30] Where the sports museum may present a more modest overview of sporting culture, tradition and heritage, halls of fame depend specifically on the public profiles and established images of sports stars to portray a particular, positive and appealing version of national sporting history. Be they dedicated to baseball, rugby, football or general sporting culture, halls of fame are hagiographic arcades of sporting achievement that continually perpetuate the legend of the individual and the romanticism of a nation's sporting tradition.

Contested spaces of sporting history

The continued launch of new sports museums and sports halls of fame as sport history for public, or civic, consumption has not occurred without criticism. Debate has emerged over the role these institutions play in the interpretation, construction and representation of sport history as well as their relationship with academic sports history. At the outset of this debate West remarked that,

> The sports historian may want to question their [halls of fame] objectivity. The halls of fame view sport positively and the individuals they honour, they believe are to be admired. Many exist solely to promote a particular sport or the professional organization that sponsors them. Still they fill an important vital gap in the sports history field. With limited resources and personnel they are doing a creditable job in presenting the history of sport to the general public. They are not equipped as yet to undertake extensive objective histories of sport. That is not really their function. They are however quickly accumulating resources in which sports historians would be interested and which they may wish to investigate.[31]

West's comment encapsulates many key points of the debate that has since followed, particularly that the existence and development of sports museums and halls of fame has not been met eagerly by academic research.

Scholars such as Johnes and Mason, Pope, Rosenzweig and Leon, Vamplew, and West suggest several reasons as to why the disjuncture between avenues of public history, particularly sports museums and halls, and academic history has been so difficult to overcome.[32] The first is the lack of objectivity often inherent in sports museums and halls, which belies the more critical requirements of the sports academic.[33] Vamplew argues that despite the best efforts of the curator, 'errors of fact and interpretation persist and myths are perpetuated despite historical research to the contrary'.[34] Moreover, that the 'presentation of information is too simplistic and fails to demonstrate the subtleties of historical argument'.[35] Johnes and Mason too suggest, in regards to British football history, that 'some heritage sites are guilty of sanitising the less savoury aspects of the history they present'.[36] Interestingly, however, this is not a universal complaint with Johnes and Mason noting that the NFM (National Football Museum) has tackled 'football's administrative failings, racism... sexism [and] hooliganism'.[37]

Bruce Kidd acknowledges that 'halls of fame play a strategic role in the public remembering and interpretation of sports'.[38] While they may serve as a useful form of civic education by allowing the past to be relived, understood and experienced, as a form of historical 'text' they are rarely subjected to the same sort of analysis or critique demanded of academic sports history. The expertise of academic sport historians has still not readily found favour among the sponsors and producers of halls of fame. On the other hand, some open-minded academic sport historians are beginning to see halls of fame and sports museums as sites through which they may make their work more accessible to general audiences. Bouchier and Cruickshank lament 'many academic historians sense that they are losing touch with their public audience, that their work rarely transcends traditional academic forms of communications such as the book, the scholarly article, or editorials written for popular magazines or newspapers'.[39] Some sports historians are thus reconceptualizing halls of fames and sports museums as fresh spaces in which to challenge and reconstruct historical interpretations and presentations in an attempt to repave the avenues of public history.[40] Yet despite continued efforts, halls of fame and sports museums are still essentially places that remain clearly devoted to civic edutainment and the nostalgic experience.[41] As Crieghton reminds us, edutainment refers to 'the fusion of education and entertainment offerings, particularly popular or mass culture entertainments that take on educating functions or invoke a pretense of having such functions'. [42]

Nostalgia and sports history

Pope argues sports halls of fame and sports museums 'reside at the intersection of history and nostalgia'.[43] Snyder adds the nostalgia evoked in halls and museums can provide useful ways to understand the significance of sport to people's lives and to their feelings of collective belonging.[44] In his definition, drawn from work on human emotions,[45] Snyder suggests nostalgia is 'a remembrance or recollection of the past, a past that is imbued with special qualities', and that although this reflection is usually positive, it 'may also be tinged with melancholy and sadness because the positive feelings are mixed with negative feelings or because the pleasures are perceived as in a past that cannot be relived in the present'.[46] Fairley adds, the term suggests 'a preference (general liking, positive attitude or favourable affect) towards objects (people, places, experiences or things) from when one was younger or from times about which one has learned vicariously perhaps through socialization or the media'.[47] Fairley and Gammon concur by suggesting 'nostalgia can be defined as a yearning to return to or relive a past period'.[48] Clearly inherent within these conceptions of nostalgia are notions of identity formation and social experience. This link between history and individual and social identity has been explored by Rosenzweig and Thelen in their critical survey of American people's perspectives of history. They uncover that, although people may hold little detailed or accurate knowledge of the past, what historical knowledge they do possess is important and regularly used to give significant meaning and value to their identities and understandings of the contemporary world in which they live.[49]

Recognizing the pertinent place of sport within people's individual lives and collective experiences, sports halls of fames and museums have capitalized on the nostalgic sentiments in their displays to create essential emotive bonds with visitors which serve to traverse the distance between past and present. The use of nostalgia has become an important part of effective sports tourism, particularly in association with the aspects of history, heritage and tradition. Snyder suggests,

> Halls and museums attract people because of their fascination with sport, including the idolized figures and memorabilia from the past...[although]...this is only part of the explanation: the attraction may also be based on the contrasts and incongruity between past and present. This juxtaposition of the past with the present creates the context for feelings of the nostalgia.[50]

Nostalgia is not about remembering the past in actuality, but remembering it as how one believes it was, be it factual or otherwise. With nostalgia the line between myth and reality is considerably blurred to the extent that the past can be selectively recalled, reconstructed and memorialized. Where there exists tension or disenchantment, nostalgia allows the possibility for individuals to negotiate uncomfortable historical terrain by utilizing 'memories which contain a more positive aspect or (experience with) that identity'.[51]

Nostalgia allows opportunity to understand people's visits to sports halls of fame and museums as a subjective process of meaning-making in which sports, sporting champions, sporting events and sporting moments are constantly re-interpreted and reframed around individual and collective sporting experiences. In effect, whilst halls of fame and museums can make concerted efforts to produce displays that are respectful, accurate and authentic, the consumption of history by the general public will always be a matter of personal taste, affectation and interpretation. However, from the accounts available about the New Zealand Sports Hall of Fame, visitor experiences of this form of public history are still typically positive.[52]

The broad range of memorabilia, photographs, archival documents and other ephemera typically on display in sports halls of fame and museums does seem to allow visitors ample opportunities to experience a range of nostalgic feelings.[53] Moreover, these nostalgic feelings may be related to individual's personal sports experiences, such as the display of a particular piece of antiquated sports equipment; or at the social level, the exhibition of the newspaper headlines and photographs from the euphoria of a national sporting success. In any case, the nostalgia ingrained within sports halls of fame and museums requires an emotional investment by visitors, a simple 'buy-in' to the idea that sport is a significant part of our shared common culture, and that sport can have meaning to our own individual lives. If sports halls of fame and museums are about 'the glorification of a sporting heritage',[54] through a heritage which champions an elite minority, then nostalgia may play an important role in allowing visitors to find a symbolic connection with materials on display which otherwise might hold little personal relevance. This understanding of nostalgia and its function within public sports history is useful to the following discussion on the significance of the New Zealand Sports Hall of Fame and the emotional civic representations of the nation's sporting and olympic history.

The New Zealand Sports Hall of Fame

In 1988 members of the Hillary Commission, an essentially charitable sporting organization established by the government to promote sport and physical activity, the

New Zealand Sports Foundation and New Zealand Olympic Committee raised the idea of a site to preserve the legacies of New Zealand sport, specifically the nation's proudest moments of athletic endeavour and success. Accordingly in 1990, and to coincide with the 150th celebrations of the country's Britannic colonization, 'The Sports Hall of Fame' society was created as a partnership venture between with the three organizations. In that year 75 athletes were inducted, representing one for every two years since the formalization of British governance. For the first seven years the Hall of Fame operated largely out of a Wellington office space. Although during this time athletes and sports administrators continued to be inducted, and memorabilia stockpiled, no space yet existed to publically display the champions of New Zealand's sporting history.[55]

By 1997 the governing board agreed that it needed a physical space to showcase the efforts of the growing number of inductees. Subsequent calls went out to local councils. The most practical reply came from the Dunedin City Council, which at that time was underwriting a refurbishment of the city's historic and iconic Victorian gothic-style railway station. The railway station and its impressive façade are a distinct part of the Dunedin city tourist experience. Unfortunately, the Hall of Fame was placed in several rooms on the first floor of the building, and away from the main pedestrian area, thereby losing out on a public profile and potential economic benefits. As chief-executive and curator Ron Palenski colloquially put it, the Hall 'runs off the smell of an oily rag'.[56] Confirming this reality, the most recent annual statement indicates that less than 10% of the Hall's annual income comes from admissions, which tally around 15,000 per annum. Most visitors are New Zealanders but the majority of income comes from grants, donations and sponsorships.[57] Moreover, unlike New Zealand's national museum, Te Papa, the Hall currently receives no regional or central government funding. Yet, despite political and economic issues, the curator has taken efforts to ensure visitors have a memorable and positive experience. The Hall contains many quality exhibits covering more than 115 years of New Zealand's sporting culture, the quality is only compromised occasionally by the lack of information available on some inductees. However, it is here where aspects of form essentially triumph over content in that visitors are still able to affectively engage visually and cognitively with the historical artefact. In 2002 the International Association of Sports Museums and Halls of Fame afforded the Hall a small measure of recognition with an honourable mention for its educational material and books/exhibit catalogues in its annual awards.[58]

The New Zealand Sports Hall of Fame, in name and practice, is a place dedicated to the sporting feats of specific individuals, pairs and teams whose contributions and success in broad sporting culture have been recognized by the governing board and, subsequently, deemed significant enough to warrant induction into the Hall's historical echelon. Accordingly, some visitors to the Hall have been known to remark as to why certain sportspersons are absent, such as cricketer Chris Cairns or equestrian Blyth Tait; or why certain events are not covered, for example the popular rugby international sevens tournaments, or the 1982 World Cup Soccer team.[59] Herein lies another limiting distinction between the site's dual role as a Hall of Fame and a sports museum. Inclusions are specifically related to the biennial inductions of specific athletes or sports administrators. Typically nominees have to be retired for at least five years before their induction is considered. The associated sporting ephemera and memorabilia are then displayed appropriately within the Hall's particular sporting sections. The range of information and material on each inductee is by no means equal, though this is because the Hall does rely on donations, bequests and loans of memorabilia to fill display cases. Much to the dismay of some sports enthusiasts, spatial constraints and a certain amount of curatorial license have necessarily dictated that if material does not relate specifically to an inductee and their sporting feats then it is, for the time being, omitted. Although currently the advertising placard reads, 'Hall of Fame *and* Sports Museum', with the aim of being 'a repository of sporting history', it is unashamedly a place about the history of New Zealand's sporting individuals, more so than about the history of individual sports.

These reservations aside, I personally found my visit to the Hall of Fame a satisfying, informative and enjoyable experience, however critical my agendas might be in the first instance. The renovation of the building's interior has inevitably helped give the Hall a fresh, clean and inviting atmosphere that allows visitors to leisurely absorb a diverse pick 'n' mix history of national sporting achievement and the Hall's overall theme of an enduring celebration of the nation's beloved sports people. The Hall is set out across several adjoining rooms, loosely thematically arranged around specific sports. The first room encountered pays homage to the national rugby fixation. Included here are displays on the 1905 'Originals', the 1924 'Invincibles', the All Blacks 1987 Inaugural World Cup winning team and the New Zealand Expeditionary Forces teams. Players George Nepia, Colin Meads and Maurice Brownlie also receive distinct effigies. As with the majority of exhibits around the hall, the wooden display cases are packed full with assorted memorabilia, notably players' jerseys, caps and boots; newspaper clippings; photographs; cartoons; journal entries; trophies; and other sporting paraphernalia, including the stadium score placard from the infamously disputed three-nil Welsh victory over the All Blacks in 1905. Even for those unenthusiastic about rugby, such as me, or the uninformed, the room effectively creates a jingoistic atmosphere to help engender nostalgic and corporeal feelings of national pride and accomplishment that are crucial to the Hall of Fame experience. Phillips' analysis of historical material offers a way to appreciate that although the content of this room may not be rich in analytical or contextual detail, or necessarily appeal to everyone, the room is still capable of affecting audiences.[60] By placing the emphasis and importance on historical form rather than content, the exhibit is able to maximize the effect the particular sporting artefacts have in eliciting deeply symbolic responses with individuals. Upon moving into the next room visitors are undoubtedly left with a clear impression of the sense of New Zealand's sporting tradition and the iconography of the silver fern on black which has become such an enamoured aspect of our national sporting heritage.

Although the next room contains the typical display cases seen throughout the entire hall, the most obvious feature here is the action display of New Zealand's first female olympic gold medallist, long jumper and multi-sports woman, Yvette Williams, complete with life-size cut-out, mock sandpit and distance markers. In a room that includes displays relating to several other notable olympic champions, such as Peter Snell, Murray Halberg, John Walker and Stan Lay, the façade dedicated to Williams' feats, most notably her 6.24 metre jump at the 1952 Helsinki Games and her 6.28 metre world record,[61] is memorable, impressive and inspiring. Arguably, because the Hall for the most part follows the classical 'glass-case' museum format, based on a 'look and don't touch' approach, there does remain a certain feeling of separation between visitors and historical exhibits that appears difficult to overcome. However, the homage to Williams does go some way to engaging visitors in the dynamism of the lived sports experience, and not merely the stillness of historical record. The curatorial decision to alternate and integrate life-like and static displays with accompanying audio, visual and/or textual information has also effectively worked to engender a nostalgic atmosphere that propels visitors through an identity-shaping and historically engaging journey through New Zealand's sporting past.

Reiterating these sentiments with respect to America's national Baseball Hall of Fame, Grella claims such sites inevitably take on a religious quality whereby sports figures become more like deities, enshrined with reverence, and their associated memorabilia treated as holy relics of the sports cult.[62] Grella notes that 'the hall provides something like an immense reliquary, a receptacle to contain items made precious or even holy by their attachment to some figure'.[63] The Baseball Hall of Fame has even capitalized on the sense of the pseudo-religious by creating a Sacred Ground exhibit that reflects specifically the deeper sensuous experience of the sport, the passionate association with the sports grounds and the enduring admiration fans attribute to their sporting heroes.[64]

This sense of religion and sacredness about sports and sports figures holds true for the New Zealand Sports Hall of Fame, particularly when the language and carefully selected contents of the displays are considered. The case dedicated to world-record holder and triple olympic gold medal miler Peter Snell is a good example. The exhibit includes Snell's running shoes from the 1960 olympic games, where he won gold in the 800 metres, and one of his 1964 olympic gold medals, representative of his wins in both the 800 and 1500 metre track events. If these artefacts do not give visitors a sense of Snell's superior athletic accomplishments, then reading some of the textual commentaries and newspaper clippings may do. As one prominent commentary notes, 'they even call him God-like, the Snell whose power and timing took him into the super league of track athletes'.[65] Undoubtedly Snell's efforts are outstanding, and no other New Zealand track athlete has replicated his three olympic gold medals. So significant, respected and admired are the God-like feats of the olympic milers that they receive further tribute elsewhere in the Hall in a wall display that blurs the past[66] by comparing the feats of gold-winning track stars Jack Lovelock, Peter Snell and John Walker alongside each other with no clear distinction made over the different contexts in which they competed or their varied experiences and perspective. The intent of the Hall of Fame may not be overtly religious in the sense that it verbosely proselytizes about the mythic qualities of New Zealand's sports men and women, but the deep sense of respect, reverence and honour given to the athletes through shrine-like display-cases, is undeniable and arguably in keeping with the site's goal of being 'a place where the champions of yesterday live on'.

Snell's exhibit, with its considered mix of celebratory text, athletic memorabilia, outfits, photos and lively commentaries, is typical of the generally high standard of displays throughout the Hall. Most displays hold a wealth of visual material that will incite personal memories for many people; certainly the plethora of magazine and newspaper front pages lends itself for visitors to relive iconic moments of New Zealand's shared culture. Written text has been kept to a minimum in many displays, possibly a curatorial decision to privilege form over content in order to maximize general public interest. Visitors are, however, able to acquire synopsis sheets on the inductees or the more nostalgic enthusiast may wish to linger. Yet, even the time-conscious visitor can still gain a sensuous experience. This is, indeed, a definite strength of the Hall's design as there are easily recognizable elements of familiarity and visual intrigue. Of particular note in this regard was the cricketing exhibit constructed to represent the quintessential Victorian cricket pavilion complete with picket fence and life-size cut-out. Here legendary cricketers, such as Bert Sutcliffe, Martin Donelly and Daniel Reese, stand alongside the bronze bust of Richard Hadlee. They are presented in a way that reflects positively upon the nation's alleged love of the gentlemen's game. As the supporting induction caption states, 'cricket is the best of our summers. From the sepia tones of long ago to the colour of the present, cricket has been source of passion and a sense of pride'.[67] Continuing on, and in keeping with the all encompassing nature of the Hall, there is also a sheep shearers stock, a golfing putting green and a netball shooters circle; all fitting tributes to the multi-dimensional iconography of the New Zealand sports champion.

There are over 161 inductees to the New Zealand Sports Hall of Fame. Of these inductees there are several inclusions that arguably have remained on the margins of the public's and academic's interest. One of which is Harry Kerr, New Zealand's first olympic medallist, who won bronze in the 3500 metre walk at the 1908 London games as part of the Australasian team. In an era when walking, or pedestrianism, was more widely participated in and followed by spectators, Kerr was a recognized and respected sports figure and national title-holder. The display on Kerr includes the aforementioned small bronze olympic medal, as well as several other commemorative medals, and the unique Australasian team's green and gold cap and shirt, complete with specially designed Australasian Emblem. Although the displays do not elaborate on these items in any great detail, they do raise some interesting historical issues that the more critical visitor or academic may wish to ponder further. The specific 'Australasian' artefacts in this exhibit have in fact been used as historical material in Palenski's discussion on the ambiguous nature of New Zealand's early trans-Tasman sporting relationship. Palenski argues such objects 'reflect(s) the intriguing, contradictory and confusing early olympic history of New Zealand and Australia, the latter one of the few countries which can justly claim it has been represented at each olympic games of the modern era'.[68] However, within the purposeful, celebratory nature of the Hall there is not really the space or necessity to appropriately display Palenski's reflections, and any other alternative sports interpretations, to the broader civic audience. That is simply 'not the point' of the Hall of Fame.[69] We arrive at the point that the Sports Hall of Fame has, in the interest of appealing to a popular market, prioritized form over content. As an avenue of public history, the Hall has been effectively created as a space that has the ability to captivate audiences not by bombarding them with detail but presenting the artefacts simply to generate an affective response.

While for the purist historians of sport the Hall of Fame may be found wanting in its critical assessment of the broader cultural position of sport in New Zealand society, it does offer valuable vignettes about the discourse of meanings on the changing character of our national sports champions. The layout of the Hall, not chronologically dictated, enables visitors to range across time and sport and to juxtapose varying commentaries and reflections on very diverse sports figures. Visitors can admire the classically handsome figure of multiple-winning Wimbledon Tennis champion Anthony Wilding, remarked by one commentator to be 'without doubt one of the finest specimens of manhood physicality ... blest [sic] as well with an ability and steadfastness of character which helped him to reach the highest pinnacle in the lawn tennis world, and his bright, cheery nature made him beloved by all followers of the game'.[70] A few steps further and visitors arrive at the display of one of New Zealand's most memorable female sports champions, squash player Dame Susan Devoy. Her sporting triumphs during the 1980s represented a victory for recognition by minority sports and an attempt to counter the bias toward rugby and the overall masculine sports culture. Yet, aside from her sporting achievements, Devoy was a noted humanitarian. The Hall's website remarks: 'Part of her makeup was not just her excellence on the court, but also her action and demeanour off it, including a trek through New Zealand in 1989 in aid of muscular dystrophy sufferers, a commitment that may have cost her the 1989 world title'.[71] Devoy and Wilding are just two examples where the Hall makes the point that a 'New Zealand sports champion' is not a fixed and predetermined idea, but rather a meaning which has and does change across sports, times, and according to individual's own sporting experiences and constructed and presented public perceptions. If the Hall of Fame can at least retain this message then their approach to sport history should be acknowledged as a success.

The Sports Hall of Fame is about the continued preservation and celebration of New Zealand sport. It need also be said that there is no apparent tackiness or disingenuous feel to the displays, and overall the aesthetic appeal is warm and welcoming. Within the vast contents of the Hall most visitors, even the unenthusiastic about sport, should be able to find something of interest. Despite many suitable inclusions, the exclusions and omissions that have been mentioned are in fact an equally important part of the ongoing practice of complementing our living sports culture by developing representations of, and tributes to, the country's multiple sports histories. Though there are currently spatial constraints to the Hall's content, there is hopefully still room to expand on the displays in ways that enrich visitor's experience and the Hall's academic utility, yet that still remain respectful in honouring and recognizing the legacies and contributions of the inductees. Although the Hall could serve a critical academic function, its primary intent is to focus on educating the public on the specific facts and feats of individuals' and teams' sporting achievement. The agenda could not be simpler. Though critics may lament the lack of context given in the exhibits, the cursory nature of the information displayed, the idealistically laden comments made about sports and sport heroes, or the whimsical ways nostalgia acts as a historical panacea; the Hall's curator and historian asserts that detailing the how and why of sport is not the point, to do so is far too subjective and largely unnecessary.[72]

The sport historian's role: an alternative perspective

Thus far I have argued that the preservation and exhibition of our sporting heritage via sports halls of fames and museums has been at odds with the academic approaches to histories of sport. Furthermore, that this disjuncture necessitates a closer alliance between public sports history and scholarly agendas. It is not necessary to repeat the reasons these two groups are at odds. Instead, I wish to consider an alternative perspective that may partially absolve halls and museums from academic concerns, and academics from subjecting themselves and their work to a potentially unappreciative public. The essence of my argument is that the *presentation,* or form, of the historical material in public spaces, such as the Hall of Fame, is as important, if not more so, than the actual artefact itself. The ability of a particular artefact to engender a specific affect, such as nostalgia, and contribute to individual's overall experience is of primary importance, the content of the artefact is secondary. If it is accepted that sports halls of fame and sport museums are cultural repositories, public sites imbued with an accepted aesthetic and affective value, it stands that they may be interpreted and understood in similar ways as other civic cultural institutions, such as public art galleries. Understanding this perspective requires conceiving the multimedia memorabilia displays within sports halls and museums as valid forms of popular art.

As opposed to the disingenuous commercial production of mass culture, popular art entails some sort of genuine link to tradition or traditional cultural practices and, in doing so, it engenders powerful emotive connections that serve to enhance the audience's experience and appreciation.[73] The aesthetic ingrained within popular art forms allows audiences opportunities to engage emotively and cognitively with artists and art works on deeply personal levels irrespective of their own artistic ability or artistic understanding. Visitors to the local public art gallery can be respectfully awed by Walter Sickert's sinister Victorian paintings, Graham Sydney's Central Otago landscapes or Rita Angus's self portraits,[74] without any great knowledge of art or artistic culture. As such, these visitors should also be able to appreciate the artistic talents clearly evident in exhibits at the local sports hall of fame or museum. In both sites artists have used certain media (paint, print, text, photography or memorabilia) to convey particular messages and ideals. Ideally the intent of the art form, be it landscape painting or sports exhibit, is to invoke an affective cultural experience in which the viewing audience might realize the work's cultural and aesthetic value. As with traditional art forms, within sports halls of fame and museums this cultural realization is, undoubtedly, a highly subjective practice; with the public's experiences potentially ranging from glowing appreciation, general acceptance, feelings of repugnance, ambivalence or indifference. As with conventional forms of popular art, the personal interpretation of exhibits by visitors to sports halls and museums does constitute a valid form of cultural commentary.

If sports halls of fame and museums are considered on a cultural par with public art galleries and, consequently, that visitors' experiences may be as aesthetically enriching, and I reiterate my view that they are, it follows the role of academic sports historians in sports halls of fame may be compared against that of the art critic or art historian's role in public art galleries. Public art galleries are primarily sites dedicated to the visual sense with text typically kept to a minimum to allow visitors opportunity to passively engage with the art forms. Accordingly, typical civic patrons might be described as maintaining an incongniscent air of disinterest, simply satisfying themselves with a cultural pick 'n' mix, perusing various works at leisure. With these predispositions in mind, the role of the knowledgeable art critique or art historian in such places must be deemed not entirely superfluous but rather secondary to the aesthetic of the art, and the public's own, equally valid, interpretations, understandings and personal associations. Aside from gratuitously adding to the descriptive text, and in doing so arguably skewing interpretation, the offerings of art historians and critics could be seen as largely irrelevant and unnecessary in augmenting people's understandings of art and its general cultural value or their own aesthetic appreciations.

When this logic is applied to sports halls of fame and sports museums, retaining a practical and theoretical distinction between public sports history and academic sports historians' agendas can perhaps be better appreciated. While historians may see it necessary to move beyond the scope of their traditional academic forms,[75] the critical and subjective nature of their occupation does lie at odds with the general aim of halls and museum sites to not only entertain and inform, but to invoke meaningful, personal and sensuous visitor experiences. With specific regard to the New Zealand Sports Hall of Fame and Museum, and in keeping with Hughson's previously discussed thoughts on cultural history,[76] such an experience should allow visitors to come to know sport and its place within the nation's collective culture, and its significance and symbolism within people's own individual lives. Though sports historians and critics may offer subjective insights into sport, sports champions and the context of sporting cultures, their involvement does lie outside the purpose of halls of fames to celebrate, educate, but most importantly respect the legacy and athletic endeavour of sporting champions. To invite speculation, moral judgement and unnecessary critique is, in the opinion of some, an irreverent and unnecessary practice.

Conclusion

Ultimately, sports halls of fame and sport museums are key cultural sites where the preservation, interpretation and presentation of sporting histories serves to create important opportunities for visitors to sensuously connect with sport's aesthetic values. Primarily, through the form of presentation at sports halls and museums visitors might come to affectively *know* sport, its cultural value and its relevance to their own lives, and collective feelings of belonging. As an important aspect within popular culture, the role of sports halls of fame and sports museums in championing the cultural and social significance of sport and sporting figures does deserve continued recognition. In response, Moore suggests 'academics have made the study of popular culture acceptable, even respectable, in the university in a way that it is still not in the museum. Yet the study of artefacts has been relatively neglected, a reflection in part of a lack of awareness of the methodologies which can be employed to interpret them'.[77] Despite the tenuous connection between sports halls/museums and academic sport historians, their various respective approaches to sport history should be respected, and their relationship perhaps reconceived in the future as a bond of a respectful reciprocity. Ideally, 'museums should ... similarly seek to develop partnerships to mutual advantage with academics'.[78] However, Moore adds that 'the relationship is a delicate one, because academics inevitably perceive the subject and its representation in a very different way, producing literature, not exhibitions, for a limited specialist audience, rather than the public in general'.[79]

In this paper I explored the role of sports halls of fame and sports museums in the representation of sporting history within civic spaces. By focusing on the local New Zealand Sports Hall of Fame in Dunedin, I argued these public sites do construct sport history in particular ways, specifically enhancing positive aspects of the sports ethic and the respectful idolization of sporting figures. However, to the potential umbrage of some academics, the ways in which halls and museums present sporting history does not appear to detract from satisfying visitor experiences.[80] Through the respectful and carefully considered displays, which aid in engendering collective and personal feelings of nostalgia, visitors can come to sensuously know sports' place within popular culture. As Moore states, such spaces

> Offer an environment to explore the meanings of popular culture in ways that academic texts cannot, primarily because the material culture can be directly experienced ... [Moreover, they are] public space[s], open potentially to the widest possible audience, presenting a dissection of the meaning of popular culture in an accessible manner ... [They] offer a unique forum to succeed where the academics have failed.[81]

Moore's comment also points to the implicit function sports halls and museums serve as spaces of aesthetic value. I extended this thesis by considering that sports halls and sports museums were contentiously comparable to the contents of public art galleries. The comparison also had implications for re-approaching the role of sport historians within domains of public history.

In the ongoing diversification of cityscapes sports halls of fame and sports museums will continue to provide appropriate places to publically and academically debate the relevance of sport, sporting cultures and sports figures. The popular place of sport and the interest in sporting history within cultural life will undoubtedly persist. Consequently halls and museums will maintain a key role in this practice of making meaning through sport and sporting figures. Future efforts should be directed toward investigating changes sports halls and sports museums may need to undertake to retain their academic and civic interest.

Acknowledgements

I am grateful first to Ron Palenski, director of the New Zealand Sports Hall of Fame and Museum, for the warm hospitality he offered during my visit, for the time and resources so freely given, and for the expertise offered during the collation of this paper. Thank you also to Professor John Hughson who made 'Sport in the City' a reality, and my mentor Professor Doug Booth who provided important form and content advice during the draft stages. Lastly, thank you to the editors for accepting this manuscript for publication.

Notes

[1] Crawford, 'New Zealand Rugby Museum'; Bouchier and Cruikshank, 'Reflections'; Johnes and Mason, 'Soccer'; Phillips, 'Public History'; Vamplew, 'Facts and Artefacts'; West, 'Halls of Fame'.

[2] Fairley and Gammon, 'Something Lived, Something Learned'; Snyder, 'Sociology of Nostalgia'.

[3] Crawford, 'New Zealand Rugby Museum'.

[4] In defence of using a lower case 'o' for the olympics I align with Doug Booth's argument that 'the olympics do not warrant the veneration of a capital letter. The ancient games were held at Olympia, hence the use of the upper case as a recognised geographical name. Any resemblance that the modern sport pageant may have to the ancient version or to the place called Olympia is remote and allusional-hence the lower case "o"', (*The Field*, 222).

[5] Phillips, 'Public History'.

[6] Hughson, 'What is Cultural History?'.

[7] Booth, '(Re)reading the Surfers' Bible'.

[8] Hughson, 'What is Cultural History', 20.

[9] Ibid.

[10] Booth, '(Re)reading the Surfers' Bible'; Gibbs, 'Contagious Feelings'; Gregg, *Cultural Studies' Affective Voices*.

[11] Booth, '(Re)reading the Surfers' Bible', 21.

[12] Booth's concern is to move standard textual analysis by exploring how the form and content of surfing magazine *Tracks* can be analysed as an affective artefact; in this case, as a medium that has aligned its images and language to convey to a particular surfing audience the aesthetic and corporeal aspects of the surfing experience.

[13] Gibbs, 'Contagious Feelings'; Gregg, *Cultural Studies' Affective Voices*; Booth, '(Re)reading the Surfers' Bible', 21.

[14] Phillips. 'Public History'.

[15] Ibid., 1.

[16] Ibid., 4.

[17] Ibid.

[18] Vamplew, 'Facts and Artefacts', 269.

[19] Crawford, 'A Secular Religion'; Phillips, *A Man's Country*; Ryan, *Tackling Rugby Myths*; Ryan, 'Sport in 19th Century Aotearoa/New Zealand'.

[20] Vamplew, 'Facts and Artefacts', 268.

[21] Johnes and Mason, 'Soccer', 120.

[22] Crawford, 'New Zealand Rugby Museum'; Johnes and Mason, 'Soccer'; Vamplew, 'Facts and Artefacts'; West, 'Halls of Fame'.

[23] Vamplew, 'Facts and Artefacts', 279.

[24] West, 'Halls of Fame', 55.

[25] Grella, 'The Hall of Fame', 157.

[26] www.nzhalloffame.co.nz (accessed 20 September 2007).

[27] West, 'Halls of Fame', 55.

[28] www.nzhalloffame.co.nz (accessed 20 September 2000).

[29] Vamplew, 'Facts and Artefacts', 272–3.

[30] Johnes and Mason, 'Soccer', 120.

[31] West, 'Halls of Fame', 56. West's views are grounded in a particularly modernist and reconstructive perspective of history in that he approaches historiography as a purely objective phenomenon, rather than as highly subjective practice of interpretation and judgement. With caution, West's comments are useful in highlighting the emerging concern over public presentations of history and the noticeable division with directions in the academic discipline.

[32] Johnes and Mason, 'Soccer'; Pope, 'Sports Films'; Leon and Rosenzweig, *History Museums*; Vamplew, 'Facts and Artefacts'; West, 'Halls of Fame'.

[33] West, 'Halls of Fame'; Vamplew, 'Facts and Artefacts'.

[34] Vamplew, 'Facts and Artefacts', 270.

[35] Ibid., 271.

[36] Johnes and Mason, 'Soccer', 120.

[37] Ibid., 126.

[38] Kidd, 'Making of a Hockey Artefact', 328.

[39] Bouchier and Cruickshank, 'Reflections', 309.

[40] Pope, 'Sports Films'; Bouchier and Cruikshank, 'Reflections'.

[41] Creighton, '"Edutaining" Children'; Hannigan, *Fantasy City*; Soren, 'Museum as Curriculum Site'.

[42] Creighton, '"Edutaining" Children', 35.

43 Pope, 'Sports Films', 310.
44 Snyder, 'Sociology of Nostalgia'.
45 Davis, *Yearning for Yesteryear*; Denzin, *On Understanding Emotions*; Hochschild, *Managed Heart*.
46 Snyder, 'Sociology of Nostalgia', 229.
47 Fairley, 'In Search of Relived Social Experience', 288.
48 Fairley and Gammon, 'Something Lived, Something Learned', 183.
49 Rosenzweig and Thelen, *Presence of the Past*.
50 Snyder, 'Sociology of Nostalgia', 229.
51 Fairley and Gammon, 'Something Lived, Something Learned', 184.
52 Comments from visitor books of the New Zealand Sports Hall of Fame, kindly lent to the author by Ron Palenski, September 2007.
53 Personal communication with Ron Palenski and comments from visitor books of the New Zealand Sports Hall of Fame.
54 Snyder, 'Sociology of Nostalgia', 229.
55 The information on the New Zealand Sports Hall of Fame presented in the paper has been taken from the author's research visits to the Hall, the Hall of Fame's recent annual report, inductee literature, visitors books, and most significantly, discussions with the Hall's curator, administrator and primary sports historian, Ron Palenski (chief-executive of The Hall of Fame society and Hall of Fame Board member).
56 Personal communication with Ron Palenski, 21 September 2007.
57 Palenski, *New Zealand Sports Hall of Fame*.
58 The International Association of Sports Museums and Halls of Fame is a non-profit United States based organization 'dedicated to helping member institutions better preserve history and educate future generations on the importance of sport as history' (www.sportheritage.org, accessed 24 September 2007).
59 Personal communication with Ron Palenski, 21 September 2007
60 Phillips, 'Public History'.
61 Romanos, *New Zealand's Top 100*.
62 Grella, 'Hall of Fame'.
63 Ibid., 159.
64 http://www.baseballhalloffame.org/history/2005/050619.htm. This site contains Dan Holmes review of the Sacred Ground exhibit of American ballparks and the fan experience, dated 20 May 2005.
65 Peter Snell Exhibit, New Zealand Sports Hall of Fame, Dunedin, 2007.
66 The concepts 'the past' and 'history' are not synonymous. The past refers what actually happened at a specific time, place and context. History refers to the process by which we come to *know* the past. Importantly, history is a highly subjective process that relies specifically on interpretations and judgements (Booth, *The Field*).
67 Sir Richard Hadlee Exhibit, New Zealand Sports Hall of Fame, Dunedin, 2007.
68 Palenski, 'When New Zealand and Australia', 1.
69 Personal communication with Ron Palenski, 21 September 2007.
70 Anthony Wilding Exhibit, New Zealand Sports Hall of Fame, Dunedin, 2007.
71 http://www.nzhalloffame.co.nz/page.pasp?searchtext=Susan+Devoy. Accessed 26 September 2007.
72 Personal communication with Ron Palenski, 21 September 2007.
73 The position on sport as popular art is developed by Hughson et al., via Hall and Whannel. Hughson, Inglis and Free, *The Uses of Sport*; Hall and Whannel, *Popular Arts*.
74 All of these popular works, personally seen by the author, have been exhibited over the past few years at Dunedin city's public art gallery, located in The Octagon, Central Dunedin.
75 Bouchier and Cruikshank, 'Reflections'.
76 Hughson, 'Sport a Cultural History'.
77 Moore, *Museums and Popular Culture*, 100.
78 Ibid., 99.
79 Ibid., 99–100.
80 Comments from visitor books of the New Zealand Sports Hall of Fame.
81 Moore, Museums and Popular Culture, 105.

References

Booth, D. *The Field: Truth and Fiction in Sport History*. New York: Routledge, 2005.

Booth, D. '(Re)reading The Surfers' Bible: The Affects of Tracks'. *Continuum: Journal of Media & Cultural Studies* 22, no. 1 (2008): 17–35.

Bouchier, N.B., and K. Cruikshank. 'Reflections of Creating Critical Sport History for a Popular Audience: The People and the Bay'. *Journal of Sport History* 25, no. 2 (1998): 309–16.

Crawford, S. 'A Secular Religion: The Historical Iconography of New Zealand Rugby'. *Physical Education Review* 8, no. 2 (1986): 146–58.

Crawford, S. 'The New Zealand Rugby Museum'. *Journal of Sport History* 23, no. 3 (1996): 338–40.

Crieghton, M.R. '"Edutaining" Children: Consumer and Gender Socialization in Japanese Marketing'. *Ethnology* 33, no. 1 (1994): 35–52.

Davis, F. *Yearning for Yesteryear: A Sociology of Nostalgia*. New York: Free Press, 1979.

Denzin, N. *On Understanding Emotions*. San Francisco: Jossey-Bass, 1984.

Fairley, S. 'In Search of Relived Social Experience: Group Based Nostalgia Sport Tourism'. *Journal of Sport Management* 17, no. 3 (2003): 284–304.

Fairley, S., and S. Gammon. 'Something Lived, Something Learned: Nostalgia's Expanding Role in Sport Tourism'. *Sport in Society* 8, no. 2 (2005): 182–97.

Gibbs, A. 'Contagious Feelings: Pauline Hanson and the Epidemiology of Affect'. *Australian Humanities Review*, December 2001. Available at: http://www.lib.latrobe.edu.au/AHR/archive/Issue-December-2001/gibbs.html.

Gregg, M. *Cultural Studies' Affective Voices*. Houndmills: Palgrave Macmillan, 2006.

Grella, G. 'The Hall of Fame and the American Mythology'. In *Baseball and American Culture: Across the Diamond*, edited by E.J. Rielly. New York: The Haworth Press, 2003.

Hall, S., and P. Whannel. *The Popular Arts*. London: Hutchinson, 1964.

Hannigan, J. *Fantasy City: Pleasure and Profit in the Postmodern Metropolis*. New York: Routledge, 1998.

Hochschild, A. *The Managed Heart*. Berkeley: University of California Press, 1983.

Hughson, J.E. *The Making of Sporting Cultures*. London: Routledge.

Hughson, J.E. 'What is Cultural History?'. In *Sport: A Cultural History*. forthcoming.

Hughson, J.E., D. Inglis, and M. Free. *The Uses of Sport: A Critical Study*. London: Routledge, 2005.

Johnes, M., and R. Mason. 'Soccer, Public History and the National Football Musuem'. *Sport in Public History* 23, no. 1 (2003): 115–31.

Kidd, B. 'The Making of a Hockey Artefact: A Review of the Hockey Hall of Fame'. *Journal of Sports History* 23, no. 3 (1996): 328–34.

Leon, W. and Rosenzweig, R., eds. *History Museums in the United States: A Critical Assessment*. Urbana: University of Illinois Press, 1989.

Moore, K. *Museums and Popular Culture*. London: Cassell, 1997.

Palenski, R., ed. *New Zealand Sports Hall of Fame Annual Report 2006*. Dunedin: New Zealand Sports Hall of Fame Inc, 2007.

Palenski, R. 'When New Zealand and Australia were one (except at rugby)'. Dunedin: New Zealand Sports Hall of Fame and Museum Resource Collection.

Phillips, J. *A Man's Country: The Image of the Pakeha Male*. Auckland: Penguin Books, 1987.

Phillips, M.G. 'Public History and Sport History: Evaluating Commissioned Histories and Historical Documentaries'. *Journal of Sport History* (forthcoming).

Pope, S.W. 'Sports Films and Hall of Fame Museums: An Editorial Introduction'. *Journal of Sports History* 23, no. 3 (1996): 309–12.

Romanos, J. *New Zealands Top 100 Sports History Makers*. Wellington: Trio Books, 2006.

Rosenzweig, R., and D.P. Thelen. *The Presence of the Past: Popular Uses of History in American Life*. Columbia: Columbia University Press, 1998.

Ryan, G. *Tackling Rugby Myths: Rugby and New Zealand Society 1854–2004*. Dunedin: University of Otago Press, 2005.

Ryan, G. 'Sport in 19th Century Aotearoa/New Zealand: Opportunities and Contraints'. In *Sport in Aotearoa/New Zealand*, edited by C. Collins and S. Jackson, 2nd ed., 96–111. Auckland: Thomson Press, 2007.

Snyder, E.E. 'Sociology of Nostalgia: Sport Halls of Fame and Museums in America'. *Sociology of Sport Journal* 8 (1991): 228–38.

Soren, B. 'The Museum as Curricular Site'. *Journal of Aesthetic Education* 26, no. 3 (1992): 91–101.

Vamplew, W. 'Facts and Artefacts: Sports Historians and Sports Museums'. *Journal of Sport History* 25, no. 2 (1998): 268–82.

West, J.T. 'Halls of Fame in North America: Are They Relevant to the Sport Historian?'. *North American Society for Sports History, Proceedings and Newsletter*, 55–6. 1978.

The Southern Man city as cultural place and Speight's Space: locating the masculinity-sport-beer 'holy trinity' in New Zealand

Sarah Gee and Steve J. Jackson

School of Physical Education, University of Otago, Dunedin, New Zealand

This paper explores a particular place where the production, representation, consumption and regulation of a commodity stimulates and reproduces a particular space and vision of masculinity in New Zealand. Here, we focus on a 'local' brewery and beer brand in New Zealand – Speight's – where we tease out the ways in which masculinities are constructed in and through a specific space in addition to how certain places become gendered as masculine. Our cultural conception of the city of Dunedin, New Zealand, as a socially constructed *Speight's Space* (a 'holy trinity' space) becomes evident through our critical, contextual examination of particular places, events and media that not only help define a city but also influence the production and consumption of masculinity, beer and sporting spectacle.

Introduction

> Spaces, then, may be constructed in different ways by different people, through power struggles and conflicts of interest. This idea, that spaces are socially constructed and that many spaces may co-exist within the same physical space, is an important one. It suggests the need to analyse how discourses and strategies of inclusion and exclusion are connected with particular spaces.[1]

Within the context of globalization, transnational corporations continue to seek out new markets in order to reach new consumers. However, what is too often forgotten is that all global corporations started as local enterprises. That is, they were conceived, organized, authorized and located in a particular 'place'. This is true whether we are speaking about McDonald's, Coca-Cola, Exxon, Nike or beer companies. We highlight this point to reinforce the growing body of literature that addresses the complexities and contradictions associated with globalization and, in particular, its impact on local culture and identity.[2] Furthermore, we emphasize this line of reasoning as a reminder that, inasmuch as we live our lives in a highly mediated, technology-driven and often virtual postmodern context, we remain located and dependent upon 'place' whether it is defined as home, city, region or nation. In short, global processes and local places are intimately interrelated and it is essential that any analysis of globalization recognizes the 'material conditions, production sites and "place-bounded-ness"' of the local.[3] This raises some important questions about how we can and should understand the concept of 'place'. According to Longhurst and Wilson, 'places are more than objective physical locations because "real" places can exist only through historical, cultural and social practices'.[4]

The aim of this essay is to explore a particular place where the production, representation, consumption and regulation of a commodity stimulates and reproduces a particular space and vision of masculinity in New Zealand. We centre on a brand of alcohol because the historical and cultural links between masculinity, sport and beer are strong and resilient, and form a theorized 'holy trinity'.[5] As McCracken notes:

> Beer is no mere incident of masculinity ... beer is crucial to the way in which young men present themselves to other males. Beer is not just one of the things that happens to be invested with maleness in our culture; it is at the very heart of the way maleness is constructed and experienced.[6]

While masculinity is undoubtedly constructed through a variety of social practices and signifiers, one paramount activity is the consumption of beer. We agree with McCracken, but we would also suggest that there is a spatial dimension to beer consumption such that both the place of consumption and the meanings associated with beer brands play a key role in identity formation, and in particular the construction of masculinity.

In this paper we specifically focus on Speight's – a 'local' brewery and brand of beer from the city of Dunedin, New Zealand[7] – and its wider cultural connections, including its articulations with sport – to examine the places and spaces through which a particular localized representation of hegemonic masculinity is produced, represented and consumed. Although referring more specifically to nations and national identity, we suggest that Bell's comment – 'By showing the product or service in a (romanticized, idealized) New Zealand context ... not only is the consumer item appropriate to the place, but the consumption of it is somehow in the national collective interest'[8] – is equally valid when applied to the provincial or regional location of Speight's places and events. Speight's, as embodied by its unique Southern Man identity and popular promotional campaign, is a strategic brand for analysis in the following ways: (1) in 1992, it became the first beer brand to advertise on New Zealand television, marking a significant moment in the regulation of alcohol advertising in New Zealand; (2) the television campaign has an enduring quality – it is the longest-running campaign of its genre on New Zealand television; and (3) in a newly created promotional culture of beer in New Zealand, Speight's formed a 'holy trinity' with men and sport via Otago rugby. Therefore, as a brewery and beer brand, Speight's effectively emerged as the glue that binds together the 'holy trinity', particularly within the southern region of New Zealand.

We concur with others who, while acknowledging the primacy of 'place' within the context of globalization, suggest that the media play an increasingly important role in not only representations *of* place but also our relationships *with* place. As Burgess and Gold note, the media 'are an essential element in ... shaping the relationship between people and place.'[9] In essence, our sense of place, community, and identity are constitutive of and constituted by a range of traditions, practices, interactions and images all of which are progressively being experienced and interpreted through the media. This point is of particular relevance to our focus on the process by which a geographically bounded, yet placeless, Southern Man identity was invented, represented and circulated. We identify Speight's Southern Man image and identity as a national cultural symbol that speaks to the collective imagination of New Zealanders, paralleling Kenway, Kraak and Hickey-Moody's analysis of similar phenomena in their book *Masculinity Beyond the Metropolis*. They support the notion that:

> Such representations often, in one way or another, tap into the national psyche ... producing new and reproducing old myths and stereotypes and sociospatial divisions. They help generate such things as longing and belonging, fear and desire, separation and distinction. They speak to cultural anxieties as well as aspirations. They may steer actual or imagined movements of people in and out of place, and illustrate and influence local and other perceptions of the historical and current links between place, change, masculinity and gender dynamics.[10]

Our analysis speaks to the links between the idea of places and spaces, in terms of how they impact on masculinity and contemporary gender relations. In particular, we tease out the ways in which masculinities are constructed in and through a specific space, in addition to how certain places become gendered as masculine. Moreover, we examine these links as they are harboured in tangible masculine places (i.e., buildings and structures), embodied through (somewhat traditional) masculine practices and events – such as sport – and represented by masculine images in promotional culture. We acknowledge the important role that space plays in an ever-changing and increasingly globalized society, and agree with Wenner and Jackson's observation that: 'in today's world, cultural space often trumps place in terms of stability'.[11] Here, our cultural conception for a particular *Speight's Space* is framed by: the representation of brick-and-mortar places, the practices of people in events within this socially constructed space, and the references to Southern Man masculinity in Speight's advertising and marketing campaigns. In this vein, we discuss particular buildings in Dunedin affiliated with Speight's and sport, certain traditional events associated with the student culture from the University of Otago in Dunedin, and the Speight's promotional campaign that provides a visual representation of the 'place-bounded-ness' landscape of the Otago region and its related bucolic, romanticized, white Southern Man masculinity. Taken collectively, these places and events, as well as the corresponding publicity, serve to figuratively locate Dunedin as a mnemonically defined *Speight's Space* – where the production and consumption of both beer and sporting spectacle help define a city. As such, it imparts an enormous sense of nostalgia to stimulate memories, perform histories and symbolize identities for past, present and future inhabitants of this 'holy trinity' space. We begin by identifying specific notable places (e.g., the Speight's Brewery, Carisbrook Stadium and Otago Rugby) and notorious student-centred events (e.g., Flat Rescue, Cook-a-thon and Undie 500) that bolster our conception of a *Speight's Space* and the image of the Southern Man's city. Following this, our analysis extends to the Speight's 'Southern Man' advertising and promotional campaign to illustrate how, through its promotional culture, it strategically articulates a particular mythical form of white, rural masculinity that 'is at once everywhere and yet nowhere, known and yet unknowable, had and yet un-*have*-able'.[12]

The Speight's brewery, brand and heritage centre

> For Southerners, Speight's is a badge of belonging. It expresses what makes them feel good about being from the South. For Northerners, Speight's represents the South, which is a nostalgic ideal, the last bastion of treasured New Zealand values of a bygone era.[13]

This overview of the history and development of the Speight's Brewery and brand is necessarily brief given that other authors discuss it in greater detail.[14] Notably, the focus of this section is on how Speight's, as a beer brand and brewery, began to carve a place for itself within New Zealand's beer marketplace and also its tourism industry.

The Speight's Brewery was founded in 1876 by James Speight, Charles Greenslade and William Dawson, and currently remains in full working production occupying the original Rattray Street site in Dunedin.[15] Given its historical and cultural significance to Dunedin and the Otago region, the 'Speight's Brewery has become one of Dunedin and Otago's biggest icons'.[16] Throughout the first 30 years of the Brewery's existence numerous changes occurred including: the acquisition of rival breweries, the growth of production capacity and shipments to the North Island. As one example of the impact state regulation had on the organization of New Zealand's beer industry, in 1923 – under the threat of prohibition – Speight's amalgamated with nine other companies to form New Zealand

Breweries Limited (NZB). In the 1960s, NZB faced increasing competition and looked to streamline production, resulting in the introduction and mass production of 'Lucky' beer. Distributed nationwide, Lucky simultaneously displaced many local beers from the market, including Speight's. Yet within months the public outcry forced the company to resurrect the Speight's brand.

Following the abolishment of the six o'clock swill on 9 October 1967,[17] transformations in the New Zealand beer industry were assimilated with the restructuring of the economy in general. In the merger-mania of the 1980s, LD Nathan bought out NZB to create Lion Nathan and expanded the company internationally into Australia.[18] Indeed, New Zealand's locally established brewing companies were slowly becoming engulfed by larger transnational corporations as part of a growing, globalized world economy. At the same time state regulations became more lenient on where and when public drinking could occur. In tandem, these changes led to the increasing availability of international beer brands in New Zealand and the subsequent delocalization of New Zealand beer identity, through the 'loosened consumers' familiar local ties with traditional drinking locations like the local pub with its Brewery links. Beer could now be consumed in cafés, restaurants and bars alongside wine or coffee'.[19] Without a doubt New Zealand beer brands, including Speight's, had lost their monopoly on the local market. However as we discuss in the next section, sports sponsorship and various promotional campaigns would eventually enable Speight's to regain its status as 'not just the "Pride of the South" [but] one of New Zealand's most loved beers'.[20]

Today, the Speight's Heritage Centre is one of the must-see places for tourists to Dunedin in order to get a taste of the city's living heritage, according to City of Dunedin tourism. The Heritage Centre offers 'first class guided tours through the working brewery and museum',[21] which 'shows over 100 years of brewing history'.[22] At the end of the Heritage Centre tour, visitors are encouraged to taste the selection of brews that Speight's produces. Indeed, the Speight's Brewery itself signifies an iconic place of production in Dunedin, inasmuch as it is a cluster of conjoined buildings that have produced a consumable commodity for over a century, but it also is a place that is historically and culturally invested with producing a brand that has become synonymous with Otago rugby and symbolic of a particular hegemonic form of masculine identity.

Speight's and Otago sports culture

The endless scope of sport sponsorship by beer companies undoubtedly serves to reinforce the 'holy trinity'.[23] Sport in New Zealand has long been associated with the consumption of alcohol, predominantly beer, and Speight's is certainly no exception.[24] This holds true not only in terms of its liquid consumption at sporting events, but also the company's historical involvement with sport sponsorship, particularly that of rugby.

In 1977, Speight's formal links with sport were established when the company sponsored the Dunedin senior rugby union competition under the name of 'The Speight's Championship'. This prompted a locally driven controversy regarding the moral issues of a brewery sponsoring sport. Indeed, Speights' decision to initiate sport sponsorship was a trailblazing effort linking beer and sport. The result would only prove to be the beginning for future sport sponsorship deals in New Zealand in addition to the commercialization and commodification of sport as we now know it. In particular, rugby in New Zealand has experienced a significant transformation 'from a weekly practice that enjoyed the widespread participation of New Zealand men as players and spectators to a symbolic commercial commodity consumed by an audience who may never have played or attended a live rugby match'.[25] Furthermore, in the same year controversy over Speight's newspaper advertising surfaced. Using the slogan 'Speight's Great', the weekly promotion featured an athlete worthy of the title. The tagline of the ad stated: 'Look after No. 1. Take home the great beer'.[26] A letter of complaint was published in *The Southland Times* and appealed for a re-evaluation of alcohol-sponsored advertising.

Despite these controversies, Speight's sponsorship of sport continued. In 1989, Speight's became the major sponsor for the local Otago franchise in New Zealand's premier domestic rugby competition (National Provincial Championship, NPC) basking in the glory of the team's historic win in 1991. The success of the Otago team 'was based on an adventurous style of rugby, which for many observers epitomised "Otago values" of innovation and integrity.... Loyalty to the [Otago] team among fans was easily transferred into loyalty to [Speight's] beer'.[27] Indeed, sports sponsorship was a vehicle through which Speight's could tactically advertise the Speight's brand, especially considering the alcohol advertising restrictions for radio and television at the time.[28] In 1995–1996 rugby union in New Zealand went through a radical transformation from an amateur game to professional sport, offering new forms of sponsorship opportunities for Speight's. The then newly created Super 12 (currently Super 14, and in 2011 to become the Super 15) competition consisted of 12 teams: three from Australia, four from South Africa and five from New Zealand, including one from the Otago region. Speight's sponsorship of the Otago Highlanders was a strategic move in promoting the brand on an international scale given that the team travelled to both Australia and South Africa for regular season league games. Additionally, all matches were broadcast globally on Rupert Murdoch's SKY Sport.[29] Ten years later, the synergies between the media, rugby and the Speight's Brewery were further strengthened when Speight's became the Super 14's broadcasting rights sponsor on SKY TV, branding New Zealand's coverage of the competition with the tagline 'Live with Pride'.

When Speight's' sponsorship of the Otago NPC team (and later the Highlanders franchise) was initiated, not only did a 'Speight's Rugby' emblem appear on the players' jerseys advertising the Speight's brand, but the company also held naming rights to a particular section of seating in Dunedin's legendary Carisbrook Stadium after they donated $250,000 towards the redevelopment of the stadium.[30] This donation presented Speight's with an incredible advertising opportunity at the time. That is, part of the donation went towards the reconstruction of what is now a significant characteristic in the stadium: the Speight's Stand, a specific zone that features blue and white coloured seats organized to spell 'SPEIGHTS'.

Carisbrook is Dunedin's premier sports stadium, home to the Otago Highlander's professional rugby franchise and the Otago NPC rugby team. Carisbrook also typically hosts an annual international rugby test match that features New Zealand's national team, the All Blacks. Also known as the 'House of Pain', Carisbrook 'is famous the world over for its epic rugby battles',[31] and is a celebrated place of pride in Dunedin. According to the Otago Rugby Union's website, Carisbrook 'is the place where hopes are realised and where the dreams of opponents go to die, it is a stage on which has been enacted all the elements of drama, and a stage for the big matches that envelop all of the city and province'.[32] Such a description confirms Bale's assertion that, 'sport places provide a potent source of affection. Different senses – mainly sight but also smell, sound and nostalgia – contribute to a positive sense of place'.[33] Indeed, there is a palpable sense of pride attached to the historic success of rugby at Carisbrook and the historicity of the stadium itself as a cultural landmark in the cityscape of Dunedin.[34] In this regard, we consider Carisbrook a concrete place that not only sutures and neatly packages the masculinity-sport-beer constituents of the 'holy trinity', but does so by fostering the congregation of men with their mates to collectively experience a live rugby match while drinking beer.

Yet, we must caution against the romanticized reproduction of this particular historic masculinized place given that, like almost all sporting venues, it has a darker side.[35] Consider, for example, some of the fan behaviour that occurs on the Carisbrook terraces, a standing-only area in the stadium typically populated by students because of its cheap ticket price. Admittedly the terrace-dwellers are known for their energy, spirit and costumes, and are the central crowd at the stadium to whom any pre-game, half-time or post-game entertainment is targeted. It is not uncommon to stand in the terraces at a Highlander's game or an All Blacks test match and experience every stadium's infamous display of fandom, the Mexican wave. Yet here, when the Mexican wave advances to the terraces, beer vessels (both aluminium cans, plastic and glass bottles, regardless of whether they are full, half-drunk, or empty) are tossed into the air at random. While the thought of these actions are disgusting they are also harmful to any innocent bystanders who also happen to be standing in the terraces. Equally concerning are the yellow streams of urine that trickle from the top to the bottom of the terraces when crowd size makes a trip to the toilet either prohibitive or not worth the bother – a familiar concept to some football fans in the UK.

More recently, the traditional boisterous behaviour of fans on the Carisbrook terraces escalated to the point of outright loutishness. In June 2009, the All Blacks played France at Carisbrook. For many All Blacks fans, the match was a must-win for the New Zealand side to avenge their loss to France in the quarter-final of the 2007 Rugby World Cup. Unfortunately for the All Blacks, they lost again but it was an historic moment for France as it was the first time a French team had won a test in Dunedin. To show their appreciation to French supporters at Carisbrook, the France players did a victory lap of the grounds. During their lap, a small number of fans in the terraces threw bottles onto the pitch with several France players dodging the airborne vessels to avoid being hit. This demonstration of disrespectful and arguably dangerous fan behaviour was appalling and embarrassing for rugby administrators, as well as the majority of other fans who had come to Dunedin for the test match, since:

> Few cities in the world embrace a test match as Dunedin does...Visitors to Dunedin, including national figures, have often lauded Dunedin as a test city with the most outstanding atmosphere and 'feel'. Not for nothing is Dunedin known as 'Test City' at international time.[36]

As a result of this incident, Dunedin's privilege of hosting future international rugby tests was temporarily jeopardized. Neil Sorensen, New Zealand Rugby Union's professional rugby manager, told the *Otago Daily Times* (Dunedin's daily broadsheet newspaper) that these bottle-throwing actions 'reflect very badly on our reputation as good hosts, and true rugby supporters, and on our national image internationally'.[37] Such a disgraceful occurrence serves to tarnish the highly regarded image of Dunedin as a 'Test City' with a robust core of staunch rugby fans, an image that is experienced locally, valued nationally and preserved globally. As the Otago Rugby Union website states:

> Rugby in Otago is more than just about the elite level of players or the national level of coaching. It is a game that is carried in the soul of Otago people and developed a culture that embraces the whole province and into which succeeding generations of Otago University students are inculcated. Otago graduates around the world retain the strong loyalty to Otago they developed as students.[38]

To this end, the association of the Speight's brand with the reputable place of Otago Rugby in Dunedin is unrivalled, inclusive of its strong links to the student culture of Dunedin, to which we now turn.

Speight's and Dunedin's student culture

> Dunedin is unquestionably a student city; it has a vibrant population of young people that give life to the otherwise older character. New Zealand's first university, the University of Otago (1869) is the second largest and unquestionably the finest in the country. Many students from throughout the country leave their homes to study at Otago University in Dunedin. This helps create a dynamic creative culture in the city that is represented in arts, music and events.[39]

This quote, taken from the Otago New Zealand Tourism Online Magazine and Tourist Directory website, clearly characterizes Dunedin as a student city that experiences a large migration of tertiary students during the academic terms. What this quote fails to speak to are the arguably frowned upon practices and traditional events that are notoriously associated with Dunedin's lively, yet frequently drunken and couch-burning, student culture. Here, we draw particular attention to three of these events (i.e., Flat Rescue, Cook-a-thon, and Undie 500) and how they inform the memories, histories and identities of Dunedin's student 'scarfie' lifestyle and a city struggling to forge a town-and-gown relationship.[40]

The first event we wish to highlight is the Speight's 'Flat Rescue', a relatively new competition for Dunedin's students. This event is strategically scheduled in February to correspond with the university's Orientation Week and the influx of students arriving to Dunedin to move into their accommodation for the academic year. Several city blocks of highly concentrated low-standard housing that surround the university are prime living locations for students. With a reputation for flats with mediocre living conditions, housing in this area has been described as Dunedin's student ghetto. The Speight's Flat Rescue event was promoted through local radio stations and proposed a challenge to those residing in the student ghetto. The students were charged with the task of decorating their flat with a Speight's theme, including the Otago Rugby colours of blue and gold, which, not surprisingly, are also the official University of Otago colours. In some cases, what is most alarming about this competition is the sheer amount of Speight's beer that some students consumed in order to decorate their flat with Speight's. Students creatively used Speight's products to make curtains and chandeliers from Speight's beer cans, wallpaper from Speight's stubbies cartons, and fireplace mantels from Speight's beer bottles, to name a few. With numerous flats in the student ghetto participating, the area soon adopted the name Speight's Village Enclave for a period of time. According to *D Scene*, Dunedin's free weekly magapaper, 'Speight's Brewery staff then drove around the campus region with some Highlanders [rugby] players handing out free alcohol' and judging the flats.[41] Leading the flat inspections were three beautiful, scantily clad, bosom-displaying young women. In 2008, the winning best-dressed student flat was home to six guys who modelled their flat to be a mock pub, complete with bar and patrons. The students' efforts and obvious drinking stamina were rewarded with the grand prize worth of 52 dozen of Speight's beer, a 12-pack for each week of the year.

Another 'invented tradition' held during Orientation Week is the Captain Cook Tavern's 'Cook-a-thon'.[42] Given its close proximity to the university, the establishment is one of Dunedin's infamous student pubs. More affably dubbed The Cook, the pub hosts the Cook-a-thon event as an all-day drinking affair where students dress in costumes and pay $25, which covers their entry, gives them a Cook-a-thon t-shirt, a jug of beer and three meals during the day. Kick-off for the Cook-a-thon officially begins at 10 a.m. when The Cook's doors open, but students are known to queue up outside the pub from as early as 8.30 a.m. to guarantee their entrance into the event. This posits a problem since the pub is located on one of Dunedin's busiest corners and the students, who typically pre-drink for the event, begin to cause mayhem and disorder while waiting for The Cook to open its doors. Recently, the Cook-a-thon has come under fire, criticized by Dunedin police and Otago University for being 'a day of binge-drinking leading to drunken disorder among students'.[43] Although The Cook is no longer a Speight's sponsored premises, it still retains memories for many distant Southern Men (and women).

Finally, we explore the 'Undie 500'. This is a weekend event where students from rival Canterbury University, which is located four hours north, purchase vehicles for under $500 and drive them on a pub crawl from Christchurch to Dunedin. The Undie 500 has gained notoriety in recent years with large numbers of students (approx. 600) congregating on Castle Street, one particular street in the student territory, burning couches, smashing beer and alcohol bottles and creating general boozy student bedlam. According to one concerned citizen, 'The student chaos seen in Dunedin doesn't exist elsewhere in New Zealand because no other city has students in such a concentrated small area.'[44] On the last two occasions, police dressed in riot gear and armed with pepper spray infiltrated the student ghetto to subdue and disperse the crowds during the Undie 500 weekend. The students responded by lighting fires and throwing bottles at police. 'The event has once again shown that when large numbers of young adults gather and drink to excess mass disorder is inevitable.'[45] We acknowledge that the Undie 500 is not a Speight's sponsored event, nor is the only alcoholic beverage being consumed a Speight's product. However, such events and incidents cannot and should not be considered in a detached manner from their specific contextual location. That is, there may be a connection between the historical development of both a national drinking culture,[46] and a more spatially specific Speight's drinking culture that articulates extreme consumption, sport and a student lifestyle that is manifest in new laddish behaviour.[47]

Collectively, these events (which are admittedly only a selection from many) serve as catalysts to a student culture heavily burdened with excessive alcohol consumption and harmful drinking traditions and practices.[48] Yet they are also profoundly entrenched with the nostalgia of Dunedin's 'scarfie' lifestyle, thus providing an experiential link between the past, present and the future. Moreover, in an increasingly commercialized world of consumption some parts of this experience are branded, with Speight's explicitly playing an influential role. In the next section, we explain how this branded experiential link may unfold through conceptualizing the city of Dunedin as a mnemonically defined *Speight's Space*, one that is aided by Speight's' promotional venture, the 'Southern Man' campaign. While the campaign is quite extensive and has evolved from sport sponsorship to include a theme song for radio commercials, wall posters and motorway billboards, we specifically focus on its most dominant promotional medium, television advertising.

Speight's 'Southern Man' promotional campaign

As we have suggested at the outset, the media has become a significant vehicle that shapes our sense of place and, in turn, how we relate to it.[49] According to Nicholson, 'for many of us, a perspective of geography, of place, of the relations between our immediate surroundings and the world, is conditioned primarily through films and television'.[50] To this we add a third form of media, that is, advertising, and beer advertising in particular. In this light, we draw on Strate's work, which explores beer advertisements as illustrations in the social construction of modern masculinity.

> The manifest function of beer advertising is to promote a particular brand, but collectively the commercials provide a clear and consistent image of the masculine role; in a sense, they constitute a guide for becoming a man, a rulebook for appropriate male behaviour, in short, a manual on masculinity.[51]

Starting from Strate's claim we assert that, collectively, the broad scope of Speight's promotional culture (its television advertisements, billboards, posters and events) represents a local or regional manual on masculinity. That is, a way in which to draw upon many of the globally dominant signs, symbols and practices of masculinity and either augmenting, localizing, and/or transforming them to suit local tastes, needs and markets.

The Speight's 'Southern Man' television campaign was created in response to several important dynamics concerning the reinvention of beer within the New Zealand marketplace which included: an overall shift in drinking practices; a change in New Zealand's alcohol advertising legislation for television; and, more specifically, the declining state of popularity in the Speight's brand.[52] In brief, the campaign features a version of white masculinity associated with high-country musterers in the geographical areas of Otago and Southland, effectively constructing a seemingly unapologetic local celebration of what it means to be a 'real' Southern Kiwi bloke. Additionally, the campaign's theme details a Southern Man identity that infers notions about the masculinizing practice of beer consumption, including what, where, when, how and with whom it should be consumed, as well as promoting the actual consumption of the beer itself to signify the manifestation of a hegemonic representation of a nostalgic, rural, explicitly white masculinity. Thus, Speight's beer has emerged as a medium for the masculinization of consumption and the consumption of masculinity.[53]

With the release of their first television advertisement in 1992, Speight's began its journey of creating a branded existence for its beer; one that signified loyalty, mateship and the transfer of knowledge through straight-talking, laconic, heterosexual, matter-of-fact, unemotional, bucolic Southern Man characters. Indeed, the strength of the 'Southern Man' series of advertisements is confirmed by its resilience considering the campaign spanned nearly a decade. In total, nine adverts were produced and aired on New Zealand television.[54] Within the context of this paper, one ad we draw particular attention to is 'Speight's Tour'. We choose this commercial because it is the only one in the campaign that is set in a real, tangible place: the Speight's Brewery. All other adverts were filmed either in an outdoor, rural landscape setting or a generic rural pub. Despite the high level of fictitiousness in the campaign, in that the two Southern Man characters are not necessarily real people, 'Speight's Tour' may dispel any notions of fantasy and instead offer the campaign and any nuances of its representation of hegemonic Southern Man masculinity a sense of fictionality, or fictional reality.

'Speight's Tour' advertisement

The opening scene for this 60-second spot is a brief filming of the exterior of the Speight's Brewery, in which we soon realize that the elder Southern Man (ESM) and his younger comrade (YSM) have taken a trip to Dunedin. The sound of a harmonica is heard in the background. The Brewery's exterior scene then fades quickly to a wooden sign that reads 'Brewery Tours', before setting the final scene for the remainder of the ad, which is the distillery room inside the Brewery. Here, a group of tourists congregate around one of the large copper vats of beer. Hidden from the scene, a male tour guide's (MTG) voice begins the commercial with the following declaration:

MTG: Well, that's that. Let's continue with the tour. Come on this way folks.[55]
(The male and female visitors on the Brewery tour slowly walk in single file past the

large copper vat and out of the room. The two Southern Men, distracted by the fact that they are standing in close proximity to a Speight's beer vat and thus staring in awe at it, remain in the distillery room.)

ESM: You're looking at the eighth wonder of the world, boy. And probably the ninth.
(ESM looks at the neighbouring copper vat.)

YSM: Reckon.

(The sound of a door closing and locking brings YSM back to reality and he saunters over to the door.)

ESM: *(as a soliloquy)* Times like this you feel humble about your own insignificance.
(YSM returns to where ESM is standing.)

YSM: Tour's gone. Door's locked. She don't open 'til Monday. We're trapped.

ESM: Some might say that boy, some might just say, thank you. *(He looks gratefully towards the heavens.)*

YSM: Suppose we better call for help.

(The two Southern Men slowly turn and look towards the locked door.)

ESM and YSM: *(in an unenthusiastic, unified whisper)* Help.

(The Southern Men resume their gaze at the copper vats.)

ESM: Don't know 'bout you, but all this yellin's left me fair parched.

(ESM turns and looks behind him. YSM follows his look, to a sign posted on the wall that reads 'Tasting Room' and a directional arrow pointing to their left.)

YSM: *(turns his head to look at ESM)* Shall we?

ESM: *(turns his head to look at YSM)* Good on ya, mate.

(The Southern Men begin to move in the direction of the Tasting Room.)

(The scene is now a selection of pints of different Speight's beers resting on a wooden bench top.)

Narrative Voiceover: Speight's. Pride of the South for over 125 years.

(The scene returns to the Brewery. The camera angle captures the rear view of the Southern Men walking away from the camera but towards the Tasting Room doorway.)

ESM: This could be the start of a whole new adventure, boy.

YSM: Reckon.

To ensure some continuity with the overall series of Speight's ads, 'Speight's Tour' focuses on the context and dialogue between the two Southern Men. As previously noted, a key difference in this ad is the relocation of our Southern Men into an urban, yet non-threatening, environment. To offset any concerns that our rural men of the land have become 'city slickers', their dialogue incorporates both their sly, dry humour and their unwavering commitment to mateship, drinking beer and, more specifically, loyalty to the Speight's brand. What is distinctive about this advertisement is that the Southern Men are filmed in a 'real place', the Speight's Brewery. The location of the ad in this authentic historical place gives the otherwise fictional campaign a realistic effect. This fictional reality, or fictionality, places the Southern Men in Dunedin and the Brewery in particular, a popular and iconic site for many students, tourists and Dunedinites alike. As such, the audience is privy to a unique historical moment: when the rural meets the urban, when the fictional (characters) explore a 'real' place but all within the comfortable context of masculinity signified by the Brewery and discourse about beer and its consumption. There is no attempt to transform the Southern Men into something they are not as was cleverly played out in another ad called 'Nightmare'; rather, they maintain their 'rugged, outdoor, hard-working folk hero' status,[56] reproducing the image of the white colonial frontiersman form of New Zealand masculinity. Notably, 'Speight's Tour' emerged just prior to when Lion Nathan, and the Speight's brand in particular, were seeking out new markets, both nationally and internationally. The local boys and their local beer were increasingly becoming global commodities. Therefore, the next phase of the Speight's advertising campaign is illustrative of the enduring importance of place and identity within the context of globalization.

Speight's goes global

When the Speight's advertising account changed agencies from MearesTaine to Publicis Mojo, the Southern Man characters disappeared and the novel campaign, 'The Great Beer Delivery' (GBD) transpired. The GBD proved to be the innovative idea necessary to inject the Speight's brand with energy and capture the media-savvy younger beer drinking market. As Sykes notes, although the values that form the foundation for the Speight's brand will remain constant, it is evident that the manner in which these values are expressed and communicated will change for future generations:

> While the 'Southern Man' ads had evolved from the brand's grounding in Southern values, the characters were in danger of becoming one dimensional... Speight's was engaging consumers with its one-way communication – the likes of print and TV ads – but there wasn't a lot of two-way, increasingly important in the mobile and digital age.[57]

A new marketing tagline: 'If you can't take your mate to the pub, take the pub to your mate', emerged as part of an epic media-saturated journey of a freighter boat. The boat (*Lida*), equipped with its own alehouse and stocked with the cherished Speight's beer, set sail from Dunedin, New Zealand and 70 days later docked in central London, United Kingdom.[58]

The journey began as a Speight's marketing gimmick that specifically targeted New Zealand ex-patriots living in the UK, through frequently visited UK websites. The adverts asked Kiwis living abroad to email the Brewery explaining why they missed Speight's.[59] From this, an endearing 'real life' human interest story developed about a Kiwi man living in the depths of London who longed for his favourite Speight's brew and his New Zealand-based mate's duty to help by delivering the beer. Assembling a crew of Southern Men to accompany the alehouse and transport Speight's half-way around the world proved to be a major undertaking. 'A recruitment drive was a key part of the campaign... By the time it closed [there were] 2009 applicants. Some 1300 were interviewed. They were whittled to 50, then ten attended a 'Speight's Camp' before the final four were selected.'[60] The one-hour documentary DVD, which screened on SKY TV and is available at retail outlets, traces the advent of the campaign and has charted new beer-marketing territory. The objective of the new promotional campaign was aimed at making 'Speight's more relevant to today's city drinkers while remaining true to the legendary Southern Man values of Generosity of Spirit, Mateship, and the Can-do attitude.'[61] The campaign was rendered so successful that the travelling alehouse shifted from London's Canary Wharf to a more permanent location above London's Temple underground station, where it was eventually replaced by a larger establishment, The Southerner.

Ultimately, the cultural intermediaries responsible for the GBD campaign accounted for the increasingly important mobile and digital age, using modern technology such as internet surveys, direct appeal to ex-pats overseas, underwriting documentaries and newspaper articles. By doing so, they also gained an aura of 'authenticity' for the beer, the brand and the campaign as it was covered on the national news programme. As Brian Sweeney, an advertising industry commentator, states:

> The greatest achievement of 'The Great Beer Delivery' was the way it broke out of paid-for media space and catapulted itself into the news... Authenticity is what consumers are

searching for and there are fewer stronger statements of authenticity than news media coverage.[62]

The GBD campaign demonstrates the growing, or at least enduring, popularity of the Speight's brand and the Brewery's intentions and strategies to launch the beer globally. To this end, the GBD is one example of how our local *Speight's Space* can fragment into satellite Speight's Places. That is, while Dunedin remains our original conception of a mnemonically defined *Speight's Space*, with all of its multiple meanings and significance, the advent of new technologies and the migration of people generates new Speight's Places. In this light, loyal Speight's consumers who leave Dunedin to inhabit other cities in New Zealand or abroad strive for ways to maintain their relationship to the South and a sense of identity. Arguably, the increasing delocalized consumption of Speight's enables them to retain the nostalgic values of the South, in effect safeguarding their memories of Dunedin's places, events and practices. The combination of these consumers' allegiances to the Speight's brand with the codes of masculinity embodied by the Southern Man identity are further articulated through a postmodern mix of nostalgia for a *Speight's Space* that is produced, represented and experienced through new technologies. As a consequence, we observe a parallel development between the emergence of an increasingly mobile market of consumers and the Speight's Brewery's ambitions to capitalize on the new global marketplace by providing a brand that serves as an anchor of meaning and identity. Stated another way, Speight's, for a number of strategic reasons, has shifted from a real commodity that is produced and consumed to a branded experience that is preserved through Speight's Places. Notably, although new Speight's experiences can be accessed in a range of ways, including virtually through the brand's website for 'Speight's TV', it remains dependent on tangible Speight's Places such as new Speight's alehouses throughout New Zealand and the UK.

There is perhaps no greater symbol of the intersection of Speight's places and spaces than the Southern Man sculpture that was donated by the Speight's Brewery to the Otago region as a millennium gift in 2000. The massive, 1200 kilogram, bronze statue of a high-country musterer on horseback is prominently displayed outside the main entrance/exit of Dunedin's International Airport. Here, the icon is both a message to all those arriving that they have landed in the Southern Man's city and a reminder to all those departing that they have encountered the spirit of the Speight's brand though a mnemonic *Speight's Space*. Indeed, this interpretation is largely subjective and far-fetched, but such a statue symbolizes that the legend and myth of the Southern Man remains a significant truism in the South. It is also privy to masking some of the realities of Speight's beer and its particular place amongst other brands within the broader space of the New Zealand beer marketplace and global beer cartels. For example, Speight's is but one of many brands operating under trans-Tasman parent company Lion Nathan. Moreover, Lion Nathan itself is a subsidiary of Kirin, a Japanese corporation that obtained total control of Lion Nathan and, by default, Speight's on 21 October 2009. Reminiscing about the good ol' days and also capturing the essence of the new global era of the beer industry, converted Southern Man Dene Mackenzie wrote: 'Speight's has gone from being a local brew to one that is made here but owned over there.'[63]

Conclusion

Speight's is not just a brewery or a brand but rather a particular form of identity that is constructed through a range of places, events, images and cultural practices, including the production and consumption of beer and the wider promotional culture in which it is located. As such, there is no real *Speight's Space* as traditionally conceived of in terms of a bounded geographic location. Yet, the Speight's brand, like all transnational corporate brands, emerged from and is arguably dependent on a particular local 'place'. To this extent our *Speight's Space* is similar to Michael Kimmel's notion of *Guyland: The Perilous World Where Boys Become Men*, which is not a place either but rather a space or 'new life stage' inhabited by males between boyhood and manhood.[64] According to Kimmel, Guyland is a place where 'they can re-create what they feel they've lost in reality – entitlement, control, unchallenged rule, and the untrammelled right to be gross, offensive, and politically incorrect'.[65] Arguably, the notion of a *Speight's Space*, with its advertising campaigns, branded social locations such as its alehouses and pubs, and sponsored sporting teams and fixtures provides men with places and events where they can express and perform their masculinity and, more importantly, where they can escape some of the constraints that they perceive as inhibiting that masculinity. Thus, when the world's civic elites argue for the necessity of new sports stadiums and franchises amidst fears that their city might become a backwater, perhaps they are also signalling deep-seated anxieties about the potential loss of a spatial 'holy trinity'.

In referring to the plausible interaction between globalization and masculinity, Kenway and colleagues note that:

> in altering places, globalization puts male (and other) identities and relationships under pressure *of* change and under pressure *to* change. Habit and history collide with such pressure as traditional expressions of masculinity confront more open, and sometimes more appealing or more threatening, identity possibilities.[66]

We argue that the global emergence of diverse manifestations of the 'holy trinity' – masculinity, sport and beer – is one response to what some have described as the contemporary crisis of masculinity.[67] Perhaps, what is most significant for those scholars and policymakers interested in issues related to gender, media and health is that Speight's is just one of literally thousands of local brands of beer that form part of a much wider, global network of 'holy trinities', all of which are dependent on particular places and spaces of both production and consumption.

Acknowledgements

We would like to thank the editors and reviewers for their careful reading of this paper and for their constructive comments.

Notes

[1] Flyvbjerg and Richardson, cited in Richardson and Jensen, 'Linking Discourse and Space', 7.
[2] Appadurai, 'Disjuncture and Difference'; Appadurai, *Modernity at Large*; Featherstone, *Global Culture*; Featherstone, *Undoing Culture*; Niezen, *A World Beyond Difference*; Robertson, *Globalization*; Tomlinson, *Globalization and Culture*.
[3] Sassen, *Losing Control?*, xxiii.
[4] Longhurst and Wilson, 'Heartland Wainuoimata', 215; cf., Daniels, 'Place and the Geographical Imagination'; Gregory, *Geographical Imaginations*.
[5] Wenner, 'In Search of the Sports Bar'; Wenner and Jackson, 'Sport, Beer, and Gender'.
[6] McCracken, 'Value of the Brand', 131.
[7] Dunedin is New Zealand's fifth largest city (approx. population of 120,000) and is located on the south-east coast of the South Island.
[8] Bell, *Inventing New Zealand*, 20.
[9] Burgess and Gold, 'Place, the Media and Popular Culture', 1.
[10] Kenway, Kraak and Hickey-Moody, *Masculinity Beyond the Metropolis*, 3.
[11] Wenner and Jackson, 'Sport, Beer, and Gender', 7.

[12] Edwards, *Cultures of Masculinity*, 1.

[13] Speight's website, www.speights.co.nz.

[14] C.f., Campbell, Law and Honeyfield, 'What it Means to Be A Man'; Gordon, *Speight's*; Law, 'Masculinity, Place, and Beer'. For a chronological account of the brewery's evolution and expansion readers are directed to the 'History' link on the Speight's website, www.speights.co.nz.

[15] Although keg beer is still brewed in Speight's bottling plant (for its stubbies) in Auckland, New Zealand and packaged Speight's (bottles and cans) beer is brewed in Auckland and Christchurch.

[16] Speight's website, http://speights.co.nz/Brewery-Tours.aspx.

[17] The six o'clock swill refers to a state regulation forcing pubs to close by 6 p.m. This deadline lead to men arriving quickly after work and drinking as much as possible before closing time.

[18] Campbell, Law and Honeyfield, 'What it Means to Be A Man'.

[19] Ibid., 175.

[20] Speight's website, http://speights.co.nz/Brewery-Tours.aspx.

[21] Ibid.

[22] City of Dunedin, *I am Dunedin*, 27.

[23] Wenner and Jackson, 'Sport, Beer, and Gender'.

[24] Phillips, *A Man's Country?*

[25] Campbell, Law and Honeyfield, 'What it Means to Be A Man', 180.

[26] Gordon, *Speight's*.

[27] Law, 'Masculinity, Place, and Beer', 24.

[28] Jackson, Gee and Scherer, 'Producing and Consuming Masculinity'.

[29] Jackson, Batty and Scherer, 'Transnational Sport Marketing'.

[30] Gordon, *Speight's*.

[31] City of Dunedin, *I am Dunedin*, 28.

[32] Otago Rugby Union website, http://www.orfu.co.nz/page.pasp?pageid=25.

[33] Bale, *Sports Geography*, 19.

[34] In 2009 the Dunedin City Council purchased Carisbrook from the Otago Rugby Union as part of the plan to build the new Forsyth-Bar stadium.

[35] Jackson, 'Beauty and the Beast'.

[36] Otago Rugby Union website, www.orfu.co.nz/page.pasp?pageid=32.

[37] Harvey, 'Rugby'.

[38] Otago Rugby Union website, www.orfu.co.nz/page.pasp?pageid=32.

[39] Otago New Zealand Tourism Online Magazine and Tourist Directory website, www.otago.co.nz/dunedin.htm.

[40] Jackson, Gee and Scherer, 'Producing and Consuming Masculinity'.

[41] *D Scene*, 'PHS Points Finger at City Council', 23 September 2009, 5.

[42] Hobsbawm and Ranger, *Invention of Tradition*.

[43] Sutton, 'Undie Fallout Continues', 4.

[44] Ibid., 4.

[45] *New Zealand Herald*, 'Undie 500'.

[46] Phillips, *A Man's Country?*.

[47] Hurley et al., 'Sportscafe Guide'; Whannel, 'Sport Stars'.

[48] In a memorandum to members of the University of Otago's Council on 5 October 2009, Professor and Vice-Chancellor David Skegg noted, 'One issue that has concerned me and many other members of the University is the advertising of alcohol on campus and the sponsorship of events by the alcohol industry. For example, Orientation Week has been sponsored by a liquor company for several years. Even before they arrived at Otago, new students in the past have received packages containing promotional material about alcohol products. When they arrive, students are greeted by banners promoting the brewery concerned. This year the liquor company paid provocatively clad women to dispense trays of free beer to students in flats. Is it any wonder that some students gain the impression that our "scarfie culture" is more about beer-drinking than the numerous attractions of New Zealand's leading university?'. While not mentioning the Speight's brand directly, he was clearly referring to the company with respect to Orientation promotions. The VC's memo highlights an increasing awareness of the potential links between advertising and drinking and the wider implications of media and promotional culture creating spaces of consumption.

[49] Burgess and Gold, 'Place, the Media and Popular Culture'.

[50] Nicholson, 'Images of Reality', 29.

51 Strate, 'Beer Commercials', 78.
52 Campbell, Law and Honeyfield, 'What it Means to Be A Man'.
53 Jackson, Gee and Scherer, 'Producing and Consuming Masculinity'.
54 Ibid., see page 193 for an overview of the entire campaign.
55 Although it is subtle the male tour guide has a Scottish accent which offers an interesting twist on the 'location' of Speight's. The Scottish brogue may have been used to help confirm Dunedin as the 'Edinburgh of the Southern hemisphere' (Dunedin is gaelic for Edinburgh) something that is a key signifier of the city complete with a prominent statue of Scottish Robbie Burns in the town centre.
56 Casswell and Zhang, 'Impact of Liking', 1211.
57 Sykes, 'Doing Legendary Things'.
58 Jackson, Gee and Scherer, 'Producing and Consuming Masculinity'.
59 Morris, 'How Speight's Crossed the World'. This is despite the fact that Speight's was already available in the chain of Walkabout pubs around London, UK. Morris reveals that 'the Walkabout is an Antipodean-themed pub chain with 49 venues across England, Scotland and Wales, including 11 in London, catering to masses of young New Zealand, Australian and South African travellers... And, in not one, but six, of the London Walkabouts, row upon row of Speight's bottles take pride of place inside a glass cabinet just behind the cash register.'
60 Sykes, 'Doing Legendary Things'.
61 Coloribus, 'Speight's Great Beer Delivery'. Retrieved 4 December 2008, from www.coloribus.com/paedia/prints/2008/06/10/201906.
62 Ibid.
63 Mackenzie, 'Ruling on Speight's'.
64 Kimmel, *Guyland*, 26.
65 Ibid., 160.
66 Kenway, Kraak and Hickey-Moody '*Masculinity Beyond the Metropolis*, 4–5.
67 Clare, *On Men*; Edwards, *Cultures of Masculinity*; Gee, 'Mediating Sport, Myth and Masculinity'.

References

Appadurai, A. 'Disjuncture and Difference in the Global Cultural Economy'. In *Global Culture: Nationalism, Globalization and Modernity*, edited by M. Featherstone, 295–310. London: Sage Publications, 1990.
Appadurai, A. *Modernity at Large: Cultural Dimensions of Globalization*. Minneapolis, MN: University of Minnesota Press, 1996.
Bale, J. *Sports Geography*. 2nd ed. London: Routledge, 2003.
Bell, C. *Inventing New Zealand: Everyday Myths of Pakeha Identity*. Auckland: Penguin, 1996.
Burgess, J., and J.R. Gold. 'Place, the Media and Popular Culture'. In *Geography, the Media and Popular Culture*, edited by J. Burgess and J.R. Gold, 1–32. London: Croom Helm, 1985.
Campbell, H., R. Law, and J. Honeyfield. '"What it Means to Be A Man": Hegemonic Masculinity and the Reinvention of Beer'. In *Masculinities in Aotearoa/New Zealand*, edited by R. Law, H. Campbell, and J. Dolan, 166–86. Palmerson North: The Dunmore Press, 1999.
Casswell, S., and J.F. Zhang. 'Impact of Liking for Advertising and Brand Allegiance on Drinking and Alcohol-related Aggression: A Longitudinal Study'. *Addiction* 93, (1998): 1209–17.
City of Dunedin. *I am Dunedin*. Dunedin City Council Production, 2005.
Clare, A. *On Men: Masculinity in Crisis*. London: Chatto & Windus, 2000.
Daniels, S. 'Place and the Geographical Imagination'. *Geography* 77, no. 4 (1992): 310–22.
Edwards, T. *Cultures of Masculinity*. New York: Routledge, 2006.
Featherstone, M. *Global Culture: Nationalism, Globalization, and Modernity*. London: Sage, 1990.
Featherstone, M. *Undoing Culture: Globalization, Postmodernism and Identity*. London: Sage, 1995.
Gee, S. 'Mediating Sport, Myth, and Masculinity: The National Hockey League's "Inside the Warrior" Advertising Campaign'. *Sociology of Sport Journal* 26, no. 4 (2009): 578–98.
Gordon, D. *Speight's: The Story of Dunedin's Historic Brewery*. Dunedin: Avon Publishers, 1993.
Gregory, D. *Geographical Imaginations*. Cambridge, MA: Blackwell, 1994.
Harvey, S. 'Rugby: Bottle Throwing Puts Tests in Doubt'. *Otago Daily Times* (Dunedin), 16 June 2009. http://www.odt.co.nz/sport/rugby/61291/rugby-bottle-throwing-puts-tests-doubt.

Hobsbawm, E., and T. Ranger. *The Invention of Tradition*. Cambridge: Cambridge University Press, 1983.

Hurley, B., M. Dickie, C. Hardman, N. Lardelli, and T. Bruce. 'The Sportscafe Guide to Kiwi Masculinity: Sports Comedy Shows and New Lad Culture in New Zealand'. In refereed proceedings of the SAA(NZ) Conference, The University of Waikato November 2006.

Jackson, S.J. 'Beauty and the Beast: A Critical Look at Sports Violence'. *Journal of Physical Education New Zealand* 26, no. 4 (1993): 9–13.

Jackson, S.J., R. Batty, and J. Scherer. 'Transnational Sport Marketing at the Global/Local Nexus: The Adidasification of the New Zealand All Blacks'. *International Journal of Sports Marketing and Sponsorship* 3, no. 2 (2001): 18–201.

Jackson, S., S. Gee, and J. Scherer. 'Producing and Consuming Masculinity: New Zealand's (Speight's) "Southern Man"'. In *Sport, Beer, and Gender: Promotional Culture and Contemporary Social Life*, edited by L. Wenner and S. Jackson, 181–201. Zurich: Peter Lang Publishers, 2009.

Kenway, J., A. Kraak, and A. Hickey-Moody. *Masculinity Beyond the Metropolis*. New York: Palgrave, 2006.

Kimmel, M. *Guyland: The Perilous World Where Boys Become Men*. New York: Harper Collins, 2008.

Law, R. 'Masculinity, Place, and Beer Advertising in New Zealand: The Southern Man Campaign'. *New Zealand Geographer* 53, no. 2 (1997): 22–8.

Longhurst, R., and C. Wilson. 'Heartland Wainuiomata: Rurality to Suburbs, Black Singlets to Naughty Lingerie'. In *Masculinities in Aotearoa/New Zealand*, edited by R. Law, H. Campbell, and J. Dolan, 215–28. Palmerston North: Dunmore Press, 1999.

Mackenzie, D. 'Ruling on Speight's Leaves Sad Aftertaste'. *Otago Daily Times*, (Dunedin), 9 October 2009. http://www.odt.co.nz/news/business/77283/ruling-speight039s-leaves-sad-aftertaste.

McCracken, G. 'The Value of the Brand: An Anthropological Perspective'. In *Brand Equity and Advertising*, edited by D.A. Aaker and A.L. Biel, 125–42. Hillside, NJ: Lawrence Erlbaum Associates, 1993.

Morris, C. 'How Speight's Crossed the World'. *Otago Daily Times* (Dunedin), 25 October 2008. http://www.otd.co.nz/news/business/28967/how-speight039s-crossed-world.

New Zealand Herald (Wellington). 'Undie 500: Rioting in Dunedin for Second Night'. 13 September 2009. http://www.nzherald.co.nz/nz/news/article.cfm?c_id=1&objectid=10596992.

Nicholson, D. 'Images of Reality'. *Geographical* 63, no. 4 (1991): 28–32.

Niezen, R. *A World Beyond Difference: Cultural Identity in the Age of Globalization*. Oxford: Blackwell, 2004.

Phillips, J., *A Man's Country? The Image of the Pakeha Male – A History*. Auckland: Penguin, 1996.

Richardson, T., and O.B. Jensen. 'Linking Discourse and Space: Towards a Cultural Sociology of Space in Analysing Spatial Policy Discourses'. *Urban Studies* 40, no. 1 (2003): 7–22.

Robertson, R. *Globalization: Social Theory and Global Culture*. London: Sage, 1992.

Sassen, S. *Losing Control? Sovereignty in an Age of Globalization*. New York: Columbia University Press, 1999.

Strate, L. 'Beer Commercials: A Manual on Masculinity'. In *Men, Masculinity and the Media*, edited by S. Craig, 78–92. London: Sage, 1992.

Sutton, M. 'Undie Fallout Continues'. *D Scene* (Dunedin), 23 September 2009.

Sykes, C. 'Doing Legendary Things'. *Unlimited*. Retrieved on 4 November 2008 from http://unlimited.co.nz/unlimited.nsf/default/91F3510837BB4B02CC257410001AF27.html.

Tomlinson, J. *Globalization and Culture*. Chicago: University of Chicago Press, 1999.

Wenner, L. 'In Search of the Sports Bar: Masculinity, Alcohol, Sports, and the Mediation of Public Space'. In *Sport and Postmodern Times*, edited by G. Rail, 301–32. New York: State University of New York Press, 1998.

Wenner, L.A., and S.J. Jackson. 'Sport, Beer, and Gender in Promotional Culture: On Dynamics of a Holy Trinity'. In *Sport, Beer, and Gender: Promotional Culture and Contemporary Social Life*, edited by L.A. Wenner and S.J. Jackson, 1–34. New York: Peter Lang, 2009.

Whannel, G. 'Sport Stars, Narrativization and Masculinities'. *Leisure Studies* 18 (1999): 249–65.

The football-fan community as a determinant stakeholder in value co-creation[1]

Patrizia Zagnoli and Elena Radicchi

Sport Management Laboratory, University of Florence, Italy

Fans are of central importance to sport-service production. Their passion, excitement and involvement are crucial for event implementation and value creation. This paper focuses on how a football-fan community engages in manifold interactions with its team, the local context and the network of actors as a whole. Within the theoretical framework of the *stakeholders* and the *network* approaches, a case study analysis and examination of ACF Fiorentina's season-ticket-holders database highlights a system of relationships where fans are able to influence the internal dynamics of the social network developed around the football club. In light of the empirical evidence emerging from the case studies and the database on supporters, we have proposed a first typology of fans' roles and strategic behaviours. Findings show not only the roles assumed by fans during the match in terms of identification and participation, but also underline the variety of ways in which fans behave as stakeholders of their own team. In terms of value co-creation, this research highlights the fan community as a salient stakeholder and not just a mere spectator grouping. As such, fans and supporters provide an important role by influencing choices and behaviours of the football club and other stakeholders.

Introduction

The new complexity of the sport sector has a strong impact on the implementation of sport products that nowadays are an expression of manifold subjects. Planning, production, distribution and communication of sports content involves numerous actors who participate in the implementation of sport with diversified roles and importance: sport organizations, athletes, institutions and local administrations, sponsors, media, etc. Fans and supporters are of course of central importance to sport-service production. The passion, excitement, involvement expressed by the audience has a crucial role for event implementation and value creation. Due to the importance of fans as 'co-producers' of the sport service, the hypothesis of this research is that a fan community is a salient stakeholder in the value co-creation process.

This research focuses on the fan community of a specific professional football club, *ACF Fiorentina* – the Florence, Italy, football club – a 'rich' example for identifying and analysing the manifold influences and interactions that fans can engage in with their team, the local context and the network of actors as a whole. The knowledge of this case study has profited from several investigations, research and theses carried out within the Master's Degree in Sport Management at the University of Florence. We started to monitor the football club and the relations with the local stakeholders in the year 2003 – after the club's failure and its 'rebirth' when the team went to an owner that, for the first time ever, was 'non Florentine' – up to the last 2009/2010 football season.

To develop this case study a quali-quantitative methodology was used. The analysis of the fan community starts with an examination of Fiorentina's season-ticket-holders database that highlights their socio-economic features.[2] One-to-one interviews and focus groups with fan-club representatives, the local chief of police, sport institutions, members of the football club (coach, managers, etc.) were also organized.[3] Further information was retrieved through the monitoring of sport magazines and national newspapers, and the site searching of the ACF Fiorentina official website, blogs and fan-club websites, in order to better explain data collected from interviews, focus groups and the database.

The complex context where fans move was studied by analysing different subjects with a specific interest in the football club. The mapping of actors who are more or less linked to the existence of Fiorentina was guided by the *stakeholder theory*. Nonetheless, this analytical tool does not seem to thoroughly explain all the relations developed within the sport sector. This approach is somewhat 'corporate-centred' and considers mainly the relationships activated by the 'focal organization' with its stakeholders.[4] It further aims to understand how a firm can create value through transactions and relations established with each stakeholder.

The present research takes a different focus. It analyses the relations within the sport network by focusing on a specific stakeholder, that in economic terms constitutes the demand for which the product or service is destined, in respect to the focal organization. The local fan community, Fiorentina's 'user', interacts with manifold actors such as the players and coach, owners, local citizens, institutions, media, sponsors and suppliers. By drawing on the theoretical tools of the *network analysis* it is possible to map the relations between the football club and its fans, as well as between fans and other stakeholders.[5] More particularly, it is possible to emphasize the special network of Fiorentina both in terms of internal dynamics as well as in regard to its connections with the external competitive football environment.

Even though the theoretical framework offered by stakeholder theory and the network analysis give us the analytical lens for exploring the system of relationships developed around the football club, these approaches have not offered specific analytical categories able to 'read' the peculiarities of a sport community until now. By not exhaustively highlighting the role of the fan community in the value creation process, these theories leave space for a *typological articulation* related both to the fans' behaviour in regard to the match, and to strategic behaviour adopted by the various subgroups of fans in the football sector.

Mapping stakeholders of a professional football club

The theoretical framework we decided to use to explore football-fan communities is referred to as the Service-Dominant (S-D) Logic approach.[6] One of the fundamental premises of this research recognizes a central role of networks and interactions in value creation. Many of the actors in sport, with their different roles and capabilities, *co-participate* in the sport service and create a 'constellation' of relations[7] that produce value by implementing the sport product.

Stakeholder theory[8] enables us to map the actors involved within the sport system. From the stakeholder's perspective a firm, or more generally a 'focal organization' (company, corporation, etc.), is at the centre of a network of stakeholders.[9] According to the definition proposed by Freeman that is: 'groups and individuals who can affect, or are affected by the strategic outcomes of a firm'.[10] Actors who are vital to the continued growth and survival of the organization can be grouped as *primary stakeholders* (e.g., customers, employees, manager, owners, suppliers, sponsors, local communities), while other groups that can affect or be affected by the focal organization, are called *secondary stakeholders* (e.g., competitors, media, government, consumer advocate groups, special interest groups).[11]

A case such as ACF Fiorentina football club gives us some interpretative insight into the system of stakeholders in regard to a professional football club. In recent years Fiorentina has undergone relevant changes in terms of ownership that for the first time ever is 'not Florentine'. This event has triggered a relationship process among the actors involved within the local system (fans, institutions, media, coach, top management, etc.) that enriches the empirical framework as shown in Figure 1.

Fiorentina, the only professional football club of Florence, is at the centre of a network of relationships with fans, spectators, players, coach, top management, media, sponsor, facilities managers, etc., who interact to implement the match end-product (see Figure 1). The football club is the actor around which many subjects and interests rotate. The team is the entity that satisfies the emotional need of fans. These fans are citizens and therefore the local and governmental institutions are involved in managing sport facilities, logistics, road conditions and liveable spaces that enable the team to carry out matches, for their direct and mediated enjoyment. In the following paragraphs we propose an interpretative and dynamic mapping of the main primary stakeholders that in different ways interact with the football club in Florence. The fulcrum of our analysis is therefore the fan community, which we will analyse both in socio-demographic and organizational terms.

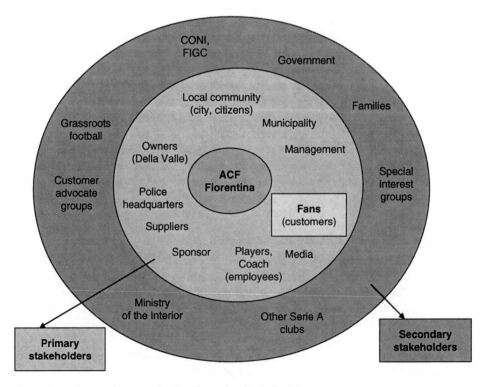

Figure 1.   A stakeholder map for the Fiorentina football club.
Note: Adapted from Freeman, Harrison and Wicks, *Managing for Stakeholders.*

Customers: the 'viola' fans

The *viola*[12] are fans, spectators, supporters of Fiorentina. These individuals can be considered as *customers* of the football team's product, whose emotional involvement is derived by attending the match. Subscribers and spectators of Fiorentina are a crucial support in producing the game and make it possible to deliver the sport event. They play a meaningful role in value creation since fans are the 'demand' and are able to drag friends, colleagues, family, etc. Fans are real activators of the potential demand. Fans, as direct consumers of the service offered by the sport club (matches), assume an important economic value since their satisfaction depends largely on football club revenues (tickets, merchandising, TV rights, etc.). In the case of Fiorentina, single and season ticket sales are an important source of income and of continuous growth,[13] being 10% of the total football club revenue. This datum is further reinforced by the average percentage of stadium[14] occupation, which in the season 2008/2009 amounted to 68%[15] in comparison to a national average of 59% of the total capacity. The ample live participation of fans is therefore one of the strengths of Fiorentina. This means the football club must offer services and apply technical policies (purchase and transfer of players, type of game, etc.) to be able to satisfy the fans' expectations and especially those of the season ticket holders who have the highest level of identification with the team.

Socio-demographic features of the 'viola' fans

Fiorentina fans can be considered a 'tribe' of people who share the same passion for the Florence football team. The concept of community used in this research is that of 'tribe' in the *anthropological* sense, rather than sociological or marketing sense.[16] The territorial bonds among city, fans and team in this case are particularly important. One anthropological definition of a tribe is a 'group of individuals united by a family bond and by the sharing of a territory'.[17] Following a sociological approach, Maffesoli uses the metaphor of the 'post-modern tribe' to point out 'micro-groups of people that share an affective drive'.[18] In the case of Fiorentina, this is a tribe of people who are passionate about a football team. Thus, while some historical football teams' fans, such as fans of Milan, Inter or Barcelona, are pluri-localized, viola fans are arguably a 'group of people geographically marked'[19].

The research on Fiorentina's season-ticket-holders database indicates a strong viola collective identity that underlines the relevant territorial origin of membership-ticket-holder fans.[20] Of these, 50% live in the city of Florence with a further 37% in the Florentine metropolitan area. Thus, this overall 87% of membership subscribers confirms the very strong territorial tie existing between the fans and the team (see Figure 2). This also implies that the stadium can easily be reached by many supporters using bicycles, scooters or even on foot, making it handy and immediate. The strong identification between Florence and its football team is confirmed by the high number of subscriptions purchased every year by Florentines. In the 2007–2008 season, there were 22,856 subscribers to ACF Fiorentina, a value pretty much confirmed as a trend for the last seasons, making Fiorentina one of the top five teams for maximum number of subscriptions sold.[21]

The bond between Florence and its football team has always been very strong. Even when the team downgraded to Division C2 following its bankruptcy in the 2001–2002 season, the number of supporters and membership-season-ticket holders remained the same as when it was in the First Division with about 17,000 subscribers. The collective viola identity emerges even in the current 'turbulent' football environment. Notwithstanding sporadic episodes of violence, increases in average ticket prices, alternative viewing choices for enjoying sports events (digital TV, internet, etc.) and the continuous change in the schedule of games, the 'active' participation of fans remains stable and relevant.

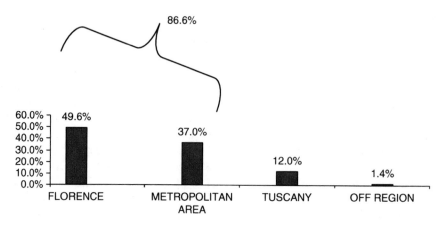

Figure 2.   The strong collective 'viola' identity.

Fans are predominantly male, aged between 25 and 44, have supported the 'Viola' for a long time, and can be divided into three socio-demographic profiles: the core fans, young people and seniors. Most of the *core group* (25–44 years) are male, live in Florence or in the metropolitan area and belong to the middle class. They have a high-school diploma and are white-collar workers. Many of these supporters choose a particular sector of the stadium (the Curva Fiesole).[22] This means not only 'watching' the match but engaging in the role of supporters who really incite their team. *Young people* (6–24 years) (students, apprentices, etc.) have a presence 'en masse' in the Curva Fiesole, the sector of the stadium with the liveliest fans who have a desire to join in and share the team's fortunes, emulate and admire the 'more expert' and better known supporters, and be part of the historical groups of the 'Curva' sector. *Seniors* (over 44 years), due to their mature age, tend to watch the game itself carefully rather than seek an active participation in supporting activities. They are more interested in comfort and safety, hence they are likely to occupy 'quiet' seats of the stadium like Maratona and Tribuna.

The socio-cultural level of fans is predominantly middle class[23] thus confirming that football is a mass sport. Nevertheless, the viola fans' social status seems to reflect the city's socially productive sector: workers, students, entrepreneurs, merchants, etc., who have an active role towards Fiorentina, considered by everyone as common 'property'. The structure of the fan community on the whole appears varied, encompassing those with very great or lesser degrees of 'fanaticism', those who enjoy going to bars[24] or a recreational facility, and who are affiliated with a fan club.

The dimensions and attributes of the viola fan community make it a remarkable phenomenon in the local context. On the occasion of every match the team can count on about 45,000 spectators between real and mass-media audience. The most relevant segment is the *membership subscribers* (around 23,000 in the season 2008/2009) who express their loyalty to the team through live participation in all home games and many of those out of town. There are about 9000 *live spectators* at home matches.[25] There are about 9000 *media spectators* who watch the matches on Sky television, the pay satellite TV station which broadcasts every Fiorentina game,[26] as well. Since 2007 the games are even broadcasted by the digital terrestrial TV[27] at half the price of Sky, and the estimated audience is around 8000 spectators. There are also many enthusiastic fans who do not go frequently to the stadium or watch the games on television, but who have an interest in the team's fortunes by reading newspapers and 'posters', and these numerically might involve a great part of the local population.

Even if they are not interested in football, they feel represented by the team and involved in its successes and failures. The fan's community is further amplified if we consider the grassroots football schools and young sectors connected to the team that constitute a sort of local 'breeding ground', not only for the next champions but also for growing fans. The Fiorentina team in Florence seems to be, therefore, the only 'event' able to mobilize, more or less simultaneously, the interest of tens of thousands of people, since fans share their passion with families, friends, colleagues, etc., making the team a meaningful expression of the city.

Fans organizational structure: the Viola Clubs

Analysing the manifold components that constitute the viola fan community, an ample group of 'organized' fans or members of the so-called 'Viola Club' emerges. As a whole, the structure of the supporters community appears as a variegated and composite network of micro-groups, a sort of 'tribal constellation'[28] (see Figure 3). Although there are some national and international fan clubs (i.e., Scandinavia, Malta, etc.), most of the population of Viola Clubs is rooted in the Florence metropolitan area, confirming the identity between the city and the fans.

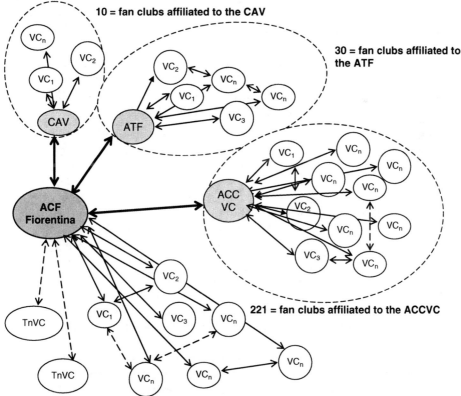

CAV = Collettivo Autonomo Viola;
ATF = Associazione Tifosi Fiorentini;
ACCVC = Associazione Centro Coordinamento Viola Club

Figure 3.   ACF Fiorentina fan community organisational structure.

Some Viola Clubs act autonomously. There are historical groups that for a long time have done their activities (single-ticket and season-ticket selling, websites, house organ dedicated to the supporters, etc.) without having higher coordination, such as the 'Settebello' founded in 1965. The *autonomous Viola Clubs* segment is quite small. The attitude of Fiorentina fans is therefore that of collaboration, or 'playing together' to achieve success and the continuity of the city team.

Many fan clubs of the Fiorentina are affiliated with associations that have an active supportive role in the football-club policies. The most important associations of Viola Clubs are the Centro Coordinamento Viola Club (ACCVC) which includes around 220 clubs, the Associazione Tifosi Fiorentini with 30 fan clubs and the Collettivo Autonomo Viola, which includes about 10 clubs specifically located on the Curva Fiesole. The size of Viola Clubs can vary from 20–30 people up to more than 500. If we hypothesize that the average number of fans enrolled within a single fan club is around 180–200 supporters, these create a community of fans affiliated to a Viola Club that accounts for about 50,000 people. Of these, a remarkable share are membership subscribers as well (23,000). The others are fans of Fiorentina who may not have a season ticket because they are not living in Tuscany, but they express their own attachment to the team through membership in a fan club, where they can share with others their enthusiasm for the Viola.

Fiorentina is aware of the importance of having good collaborative relationships with fan clubs. The representatives of the three main associations are often guests at official meetings, congresses, press conferences, operational groups for security,[29] to express points of view regarding decisions that concern the football club not only on technical terms, but also strategic and managerial (i.e., facilities management, training fields, out-of-town game management, etc.). Figure 3 shows the affiliation of each Viola Club to a higher organization, hence the connections among these actors are illustrated. The Viola Club associations have many activities for single fan clubs that can be grouped as follows:

- support of home game tickets and membership subscription selling;
- support of out-of-town game ticket selling and the organization of packages (ticket plus journey) for members who want to go to the match venue or even stay abroad for longer;
- organization and management of the typical supporters activities in the stadium, like banners, chants, drums, choreography, etc;
- support of new Viola Club start-up and growing implementation;
- management of the information and communication process towards the fans through the use both of new technologies (mobile phones,[30] websites) and traditional tools (i.e., magazines of the association of Viola Clubs);
- production and commercialization of 'non official' merchandising. Even though a good percentage of supporters buy Fiorentina material, only 30% of those fans purchase the official merchandise. The fans feel 'closer' to the gadgets (i.e., scarves, hats, hanging keys, etc.) offered by the Viola Club;[31]
- carrying out of convivial and 'social' activities in the area, such as the organization of parties, billiards and bowling tournaments, besides the management of five football fields and the athletic activities for children, with evident commitment to the local community.

Besides their coordination of a Viola Club, fan-club associations play a crucial role in the support of the team in addition to the mere sport itself as happened, for example, on the occasion of the failure of the football club. The rebirth of Fiorentina occurred thanks to the strong stimulus of local citizens[32] started by a small group of fans and supporters belonging to the main Viola Clubs, who became directly involved with the local institutions in the negotiations for the football club,[33] and pressured the appropriate institutions.[34] Despite the importance of the organizations of Viola fans, the number of supporters who are *not* members of a Viola Club is high. These participate in the team's activities by going to the stadium, following matches on TV, or staying informed about the sport results through the press.

The social network of ACF Fiorentina

Network analysis can be used to place the fan community within a network of relations where it operates using different strategies and adopting different policies.[35] The structure of ACF Fiorentina's network is characterized by a multi-directional set of relations (*polyadic network*).[36] In fact, one may observe the presence of a multiplicity of stakeholders (*nodes*) interacting with each other, such as, the team, the fans, the institutions, the media, the owners, etc. (see Figure 4), to contribute to providing the sports service.[37] Overall the network appears to be relatively 'dense'[38] since each stakeholder sets up interactions with all the other members of the community. Provision of the sports service implies the co-participation of multiple actors engaged in various ways in the organization of the sports event, which in the case of football takes place frequently.

Despite each team, and Fiorentina in the case in point, being the actor positioned *ab origine* at the core of the system (see Figure 4), the relational 'centrality'[39] of a stakeholder may be measured in terms of power, management of relations, specific importance within the network, etc.[40]

Using the concept of 'closeness', that is the extent to which one stakeholder is able to 'independently' activate connections with the other members of the network, we can define the fan community of Fiorentina as a central stakeholder.[41] As regards events keeping up the interest of fans in the club, such as the dynamics of player transfers, the introduction of the fan card, building of a new stadium etc., Fiorentina fans play an active role in the network, relating directly to the football-club owners and local institutions, and expressing their opinion both 'officially' (press releases, open letters, etc.) and 'diffusely' (intervening in the many local sports transmissions, blogs, online articles published on the net, etc.).

As regards interaction within the network, the fan community is particularly 'opinionated', putting pressure not only on the other stakeholders, such as local community institutions, but even in some cases considerably influencing the football club's strategic choices. But then the fan community strongly identifies with the team and, in the effort to maintain this identification, is open to dialogue and to collaboration, constantly pressing the owners to improve the team's technical competitive qualities. The ownership[42] and the management are thereby forced to assume a position in which it involves the fans and negotiates with them, asserting their role as protagonists of the city and therefore of its football, which in Florence is based on the strong ties between the football club, team of players, fans and institutions. A *virtuous circle* is thus created wherein, thanks to the collaboration of the various stakeholders, in part induced by relations of power, the entire local context pivots on the value created.

The case studied enables us to identify, as well as the variables used in literature to delineate a network (density, centrality, etc.), further dimensions which seem to influence the structure of the specific ACF Fiorentina system and the relations between the stakeholders who compose it. One variable which is decisive in structural terms is the *territory*, with the cultural aspects, values and principles which have, over time, instilled themselves

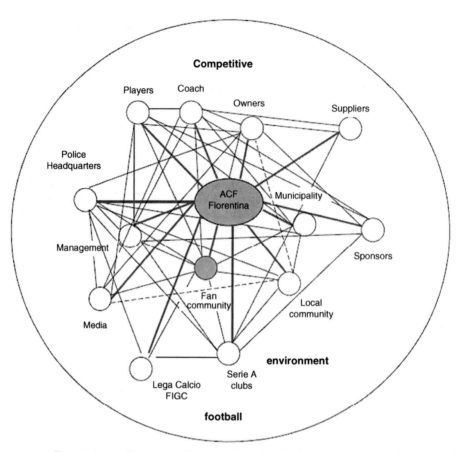

———— The continuous lines connecting the various stakeholders involved in the network show the existence of a collaborative relationship between the same. When the line is 'thicker' this means a stronger collaboration between two stakeholders.

— — The dotted lines show a lack of collaboration between the actors of the network.

Figure 4.   The social network of ACF Fiorentina.

in the people inhabiting a specific local context. The high level of interpenetration between the local environment, specific features of the territory and of civil society affects people's behaviour, delineating a largely atypical network structure compared to other networks of actors in the sports sector. For example, in terms of fans' behaviour, social exclusion and juvenile unease seem to be relatively limited phenomena at a regional level [43] so that the absence of forms of 'social deviation' throughout the territory may explain the almost total absence of violence among Fiorentina fans. The fans' tendency to continuously challenge the football club and institutions so as to 'fight' for something which they feel is theirs derives from the 'Florentine outlook' which 'enjoys a verbal scuffle and manifest dissent, which is diffident, suspicious, ever inclined to believe that someone wants to rip them off'[44] and therefore ready to 'shout' its opinion at anyone attempting to lay their hands on its heritage, whether the city itself, a monument or a football club.

On the sports side, a close connection emerges between Florence's social and economic features and the structure of the local football system. The situation of Fiorentina must be interpreted in the light of the Tuscan social-economic context, a region characterized by a dense network of medium-sized cities and which, compared to other Italian regions, has undergone a process of 'light industrialization' placing it in a 'peripheral' economic position.[45] Top-class clubs like Milan, Inter FC, Juventus, etc., are able to create top-performing teams not just because of the considerable financial resources provided by selling TV-rights but also because they are backed by large industrial groups that can afford to buy champion players and ensure organized and efficient technical management. In the case of Fiorentina, despite the owners being a business group at the higher end of the leather goods market, they are still a family firm, the expression of the economy of the *third Italy* characterized by the predominance of a system of small to medium-sized enterprises far from the process of economic development typical of historically industrialized regions such as Lombardy, Piedmont and Veneto.[46]

On one hand, the strictly 'local' nature of the supporters is a strong point, especially in moments of difficulty when they are able to mobilize the entire city, however on the other, this nature also reduces its 'appeal' to television networks. The game's local popularity make Fiorentina a 'minor' team in terms of audience: preventing it from negotiating consistent fees for broadcasting matches and denying it the significant resources needed to purchase top coached and players.[47] There is therefore a discrepancy between the perceived position of the club at a national and international level and its locally desired 'status'. Indeed the city would like to see its team among the top teams but comes up against a competitive, external environment dominated by the big teams with relative skills and resources. The continual gap between top-level competitive goals on one hand and strategic and economic restraints on the other affects the structure and relations within the network via the constant dialogue between fans, institutions, media and the football club which keeps the network of relations alive at a local level.

The dominant driving force in the Fiorentina network is the will to win. External competition triggers cooperative interaction of the various actors evident in the competitive commitment of the coach and players, economic investments by the owners, support of the team by fans, commitment of the institutions to ensuring the correct use of local facilities and logistic resources. In the last few years, subsequent to going bankrupt in 2002, an unusual situation has arisen in which the stakeholders have behaved according to a network logic, aimed at ensuring the success and continuity of the team. Despite the absence of star players, the cooperative boost of the coach, owners, sports director and management has led to important results being achieved. Each stakeholder therefore acts as part of a network with a strong local and sports identity in which each plays their role. The competitive strategy of Fiorentina over recent years has been to pursue ambitious goals (such as achieving classification in the Champions League) of an intermediate level in relation to the financial and economic resources available, valorizing to the utmost the resources of each individual stakeholder. This strategy has been adapted to external circumstances, shaping the football club's abilities to the competitive environment. Thus the distinctive capability of Fiorentina has been its ability to create a single project in which the owners, players, coach, fans and institutions collaborate.

The viola fan community sees the team as part of its cultural, historic and artistic heritage. Not only does it respect the team but it plays a role as central stakeholder helping to create value through commitment and social participation which seem, given the results achieved, to compensate for the technical performance discontinuity and scarcity of economic and financial resources.

Towards a typology of sports fans' roles and behaviour

In the light of the empirical evidence gathered we propose a first typology of fans' roles and strategies to add to current analysis classifying fans' behaviour with reference only to the sports event itself.[48] This paper analyses the fan community not only to show the roles assumed by fans at the stadium, but above all to underline the variety of ways in which fans behave as stakeholders of their own team.

To represent fans' roles and behaviour we built a simple matrix (see Figure 5) where on the ordinate axis we put the variable 'fans' level of identification with the team', while on the abscissa the 'type of participation in the event'. According to Sutton et al., fans' identification is defined as 'the personal commitment and emotional involvement people have with a sports organization' and can be highly varied in degree: from low levels of participation (*low*) when the fan does not feel 'part' of the club but is more interested in satisfying a need for entertainment, to an intense (*high*) level in which *soccer identity* subtends a *common social identity* that expresses the fan's affiliation to a sports club and/or to a specific local context.[49]

Fan participation in the event can be direct or indirect. Real or *live spectators* are those who directly watch in the match, while *indirect spectators* enjoy the game through free-view television, digital, satellite and terrestrial television, radio, the internet and mobile phones. Sometimes the choice between direct or mediated participation seems correlated to numerous variable factors that are, in nature, *organizational* (change in schedule of games), *social* (friends and family's influence), *economic* (increase in average ticket prices), *distributive* (ever-increasing 'virtual' choices for enjoying sports events), *technical-sportive* (match location, team combination, refereeing), and related to *safety* and *security* (episodes of violence occurring inside and outside stadiums. Such factors can influence fans' choices to attend sports events. Moreover fans themselves, in turn, modify their participation by adopting broadly diversified behaviour depending on the intensity of identification and the 'importance' of the match, apart from the various participation options, compatibility with the timing of games, sport facilities and other commitments (work, family, etc.) (see Figure 5).

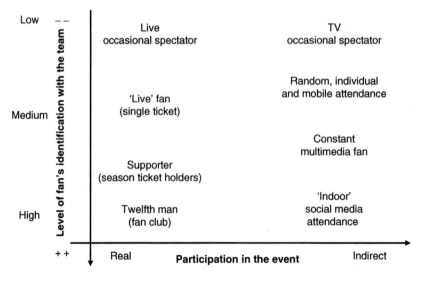

Figure 5.   Fans' roles.

In terms of direct participation, *live occasional spectators* 'consume' sport as with any other type of entertainment such as movies, music concerts, etc. In this group we can also include those people who go to the stadium sporadically to capture the 'aesthetic' dimension of the event, the atmosphere and the 'neat play' on the field.

For the *live fan*, participation in the event is not continuous, but motivated by the importance and the 'drama' of each match. Live fans do not buy a season ticket. Their choice is guided each time in part depending on the 'social' dimension: going to the stadium is a moment of aggregation with other people, friends, family, a way of having a good time together. The *supporter* is not just a spectator, but 'participates' in the event continuously, by purchasing his season ticket to the home games. Despite following each match with excitement the supporter is not an active member of the fan club, even though he/she feels highly motivated and part of the team.

The 'twelfth man', as the term suggests is an essential support to the game and the success of the team as much as the players and coach are. The actions performed by fans during the game (ritual chants, songs, banner waving, etc.) motivate the team and 'intimidate' the other side and thus to an extent, fans' emotions, passions and moods can influence the result of the match. The twelfth man seems to actively and passionately follow every match, both home and away, in national championships and international tournaments. Fans truly believe they must 'participate' in the game to 'help the team win'.[50] What strengthens and distinguishes the role of the twelfth man compared to that of the supporters is the importance he gives to rituals (which he spends a great deal of his time in) and in planning the celebratory routines, the wording to put on the banners, the songs to be chanted, and the coordination of the fan clubs. During pre-match days, fans meet up to discuss their 'scenographic' strategies and keep themselves up-to-date with the line-ups of their own team and the opponents', as well as downloading online statistics on players' performance.

In terms of indirect participation, the growing use of new technologies is largely responsible for the reduction of live spectators. Opportunities offered by the new media have modified fans' behaviour in relation to how they enjoy a game which for years characterized the sports culture rooted in our country.

Occasional TV spectators are those who watch the most important matches both at national and international level (Champions League finals, European and World football championships, etc.) on television. In this case the level of identification with a single team is quite low. What influences the type of participation is the passion for sport. Even when they do not have a 'favourite team', the competitive spirit of football makes them 'take sides'. Spectators' motivation to be a fan of a club can be influenced by multiple intangible factors such as the popularity of a football player, the fame of a club or the passion for a specific jersey or other tangible aspects, such as the country of origin of the teams competing on the pitch, the participation of star players and the refereeing.

Within the segment *random, individual and mobile attendance* we have classified sports fans that 'sporadically' follow football, mainly but not exclusively through web sites and mobile phones. Having a general interest for sport, they do not limit themselves to attending matches of a single team but, for example, download onto their laptops and/or phones the most thrilling highlights. Fans included in this category often combine viewing the match with 'live betting' services, where betting on the event is streamed on websites or mobile phones. With the new media, traditional 'passive' participation in a football match is enriched by additional contents which can be enjoyed wherever the spectator is, by maximizing his level of entertainment as being a football (content) and new media (tools) expert.

Constant multimedia fans create virtual communities of people with whom to share their passion for the same team. These fans usually attend matches on pay-TV or through websites that offer live football services. Through multimedia match attendance, fans are not only able to follow their own team, but can even have real-time exchanges of information with other fans, strengthening their own 'ties' with the team. Despite there being no direct participation, the use of new media can increase the fans' voice and the flow of information and comments, increasing the level of attention paid to the team.

The *indoor social media attendance* segment includes fans who *usually* meet up in small groups in public places like cafes, fans' clubs, etc., or in friends' and families' houses for championship and Champions League matches and very often recreate a sort of 'stadium atmosphere'. Although they express a high sense of identification with the team, this group of fans prefers to attend the match by buying a seasonal membership card to a digital or satellite television network, mainly on account of the increasing cost of live matches, the continuous schedule changes, the 'distance' from the venue, etc.

The typology of roles proposed does not set out to be exhaustive, but provides some interpretative indications of the multiple combinations of fans' behaviour in the light of empirical evidence. The representation of roles is not static. The positions (fans' role classification) assumed by fans are closely related to the strategies of the football club both in technical and managerial terms, the role played by the owners, the competitive position of the team, the calendar of events, the media channels on which the sport content is provided (matches, interviews with players and coaches, dedicated channels, etc.), and to social and personal relationships (family, social class, income, etc.). Since *success* is what drives the popularity of a football club, a winning team can generally guarantee greater attendance in terms of fans and spectators. Fan loyalty is in fact a variable 'depending' first and foremost, on the success of a team.

Being included in important championships, achieving victories on the field, together with popularity, history, legend and the international flavour acquired over time by a team, are the prime factors influencing fans' involvement. Nevertheless, the construction of a continuous club-supporters relationship aimed at preserving a certain level of fan loyalty and avoiding lower levels of identification and participation, is developed though the ability of each individual football club to undertake new sports-technical challenges and to set up initiatives able to involve the fans. These initiatives might include tangibles such as the modern management of football venues, an exciting team performance, appealing merchandising, the organization of collateral events, and the offer of additional services (call centre, services online for the fans such as games and chat, info services on mobile phones, etc.).

Strategic postures of fans as a stakeholder

In concluding this paper the need emerged to explore and offer a possible classification of strategies adopted by fans as stakeholders of a football club. Figure 6 was built by counterposing the fans' *inclination to cooperate* with their *inclination to be a threat* to the football club and for the network as a whole. The analytical framework used here is drawn from the theoretical tools proposed by Freeman et al., to outline the strategic behaviour of a firm's stakeholders.[51] The variables in Freeman's model – 'relative cooperative potential' and 'relative competitive threat' – can be applied to the fan community to delineate a first typology of fans' 'strategic postures' and outline the different ways in which the latter are able to influence the decisions of the football club. The graphic representation of Figure 6 highlights a continuum of strategic behaviour: from maximum cooperation (*partner*) to dysfunctional behaviour.

Partners have very high cooperative potential, but at the same time may have great control over the football club's decisions and can therefore shape its strategic outcomes. Partner fans

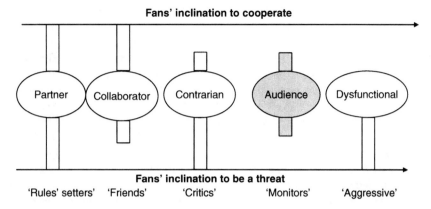

Figure 6.   Strategic postures of fans as a stakeholder.
Note: Adapted from Freeman, Harrison and Wicks, *Managing for Stakeholders*.

can be defined as 'rule setters' and may be particularly opinionated and able to voice their concerns towards the football club. This can be done not only through open letters to the football-club chairman and owners, press releases, speeches on local radio and TV (traditional media), blogs and websites (new media), or sit-ins involving the entire local community, but also through direct contact with the football club's top management, coach and local institutions. Partners are generally an inner circle of fans who do not 'speak' as individuals, but rather it is the fan club which interacts with the other stakeholders (football club, media, local government, etc.). Apart from their official duties of coordinating fans, supporting the team and assisting the football club in managing ticket sales, fan clubs have over the years moved away from being almost 'piloted' by the owners – since it was the club itself which elected the official representatives and chairmen of the fan clubs[52] – to assuming an independent role not only towards the football club, but also towards other stakeholders such as the municipal government and related institutions. Partners' strategic behaviour is therefore distinguished by a high level of freedom of opinion and action toward the football club, but also by their inclination to be 'propositively open'. At the same time, the football club acts towards the partners in a spirit of dialogue and negotiation, involving them in its strategic choices. For example, it usually invites them to official meetings and local and national conferences where other stakeholders (e.g., local government, local police, etc.) take part.

The group defined *collaborator* is characterized by a high level of cooperation and a relatively low threat potential. As with partners, the activities performed by this segment of fans assume a 'collective' dimension; it is not the single fan who acts, but rather the association coordinating the fan clubs. The strategic behaviour of the collaborators aims to find 'friendship and dialogue with the football club, thinking of football merely as an exciting sports event'.[53] Their aim is to keep in contact with, and coordinate, each fan club's activities, to maintain direct relationships with football clubs and local institutions, and restore the human side to the match-event; for example, by seeking moments of encounter with the opponents' supporters through the organization of convivial meetings, twin fan clubs, exchanges of team flags and jerseys, etc. Collaborators are an active but moderate part of the fan community. They play an important role in the success of the event in terms of safety and security. The friendly attitude of the fans towards their opponents' supporters[54] can help football clubs, local government and the institutions responsible for public order to manage public safety, welcoming away-fans and controlling the areas around the stadium.

In stark contrast, our model poses *contrarians* as a strong threat to the football club, while having very limited collaboration potential. The contrarians' strategic behaviour enables fans to continually influence the football club's choices responding specifically to an action or a decision of the latter, by spreading counter arguments, refusals, criticisms, etc. This is a rather dangerous strategy for the football club, since this segment of fans does not seem willing to negotiate and collaborate. At the same time, the football club cannot 'ignore them' since they may have a strong influence on achieving competitive goals. If the contrarians do not approve of the football club's decisions, they are openly 'critical' and tend not to activate relationships with other stakeholders, but rather express their own opinions through the new media, such as, blogs, social networks and fans' websites. The threat deriving from this kind of behaviour is amplified by use of the new media: digital technologies contribute to *viral spreading*[55] a general complaint due to the tendency of the fan community to share their emotions and experiences with friends, relatives, colleagues, etc.,online, which in some cases may even influence the social and sports atmosphere.

The *audience* are fans who are characterized by having contextually low cooperation and threat levels. This group does not specifically express its position, whether supportive or critical, towards the football club; the audience does not make its point through the media or the fan clubs, as happens with partners and collaborators. Nevertheless, their strategy is not 'neutral' since this stakeholder is an important asset for a football club: by not going to the stadium or not purchasing a pay-TV subscription, they can considerably influence the football club's revenues both in terms of single-ticket and season-ticket sales, and in terms of the audience on television networks. The variation in number of 'indirect' consumers can influence the value of a match's broadcasting rights thus decreasing this segment of revenues. Fans included within the audience react in an indirect way to the choices of the football club, for example, as regards the team line-up and its technical level, the purchase and/or transfer of players, increases in the average prices of tickets and season tickets, etc. Nevertheless, the audience's behaviour is able to negatively influence the number of spectators of the team.

The *dysfunctional*[56] group appear to have a very high threat level and non-existent attitude to collaboration. For these people, the football event is merely an occasion to yell out their anger, frustration and personal dissatisfaction through oral and physical abuse of power, destructive fury and violence towards things and people. Their aggressive behaviour and their violent gestures are scarcely related to the results of the match. Violence is mainly the result of a long process starting in the mind of the individual before the event. It is usually an expression of the social unease of the individual.[57] In fact, aggressive behaviour occurs outside the sports context (the stadium) as well, for example near train stations, bus stops, subways, and takes the form of out-and-out criminal actions (devastation of cars, trains, buses and damage to shops, etc.). The aggressiveness is not only a threat to the football club, but also disrupts the value created by generating negative feedback affecting the entire network of stakeholders (fans, institutions, media, local citizens, etc.).

Conclusions

A number of articles have been written about the football-fan phenomenon both in the popular press and in academic papers, but not much systematic research has been found related to the role of a football-fan community as regards the way it behaves as stakeholder of its own team. This paper aimed to increase our understanding of the concept of value co-creation in the football sector. Therefore our main research question was: *how can a football-fan community participate in value co-creation?*

To answer to this question we referred to the empirical case of ACF Fiorentina, by studying the interaction among all the actors involved within the local social network and trying to highlight the central role of the fan community. Although we are aware of the limits of single case study research, the case of Fiorentina can nevertheless be considered a kind of active and dynamic 'laboratory' from where we tried to draw a first classification of fans' roles and strategic behaviours.

The empirical research illustrated a variety of fans' roles connected to the intensity of the identification with the team and to the type of participation in the event (direct or mediated). The typological articulation of fans' roles goes from a live occasional participation where sport is consumed as with any other type of entertainment (movies, music concerts, etc.) to a continuous participation with the submission of a season membership (*supporter*). The highest level of participation corresponds to the twelfth man, a component as essential to the game as the players and coach. In terms of indirect participation, new media modify fans' behaviour in relation to how they enjoy a football game. Different roles emerged depending on the media channels (TV, mobile phones, internet) through which the game is enjoyed; which, in turn, is closely related to several variables (e.g., the calendar and the location of the matches, the behaviour of friends and relatives with whom to watch the game, etc.).

In terms of strategies adopted by a fan community as a stakeholder of a football team, this paper develops a first classification of *strategic postures* that have been built by matching the 'inclination to cooperate' with the 'threat potential' of the fans. Building on Freeman's work, the empirical case highlights a variety of strategic behaviours that move along a continuum. On one extreme side there are *partners*; this group of fans have a great cooperative potential, but at the same time they are particularly opinionated and often they can considerably influence the football club's strategic choices. Nevertheless partners are propositively open to dialogue and negotiation. On the other extreme we found fans that have a very high level of threat to the club (*dysfunctional*) and their aggressiveness disrupts the value created for the social network. In the middle of the continuum we have identified three other strategic positions of fans. *Collaborators* are an active but moderate part of the fan community. They play an important role, especially on the sport side of the team, by helping the club to maintain a safe and secure environment. *Contrarians* are fans that can pose a strong threat to the football club since they do not want to collaborate. If contrarians do not approve of the club's decisions, they are openly critical and tend not to activate relationships with other stakeholders. The *audience* are fans with contextually low cooperation and threat levels. They do not specifically express their position, whether supportive or critical. Nevertheless, their strategy is not neutral since by not going to the stadium or not purchasing a pay-TV subscription, they can considerably influence the football club's revenues.

The typological articulation of roles and strategic postures proposed here is not exhaustive and therefore does not exclude the exploration of additional fan behaviours through further research. However, the empirical evidence of Fiorentina illustrates the viola fans' specificity as stakeholder of their team. In a global football environment where 'productive resources' like players and coaches come from different countries and not within their team's local context, and where football ownership is often the expression of foreign investors, fans frequently develop 'emotional relations' with top international teams (e.g., Manchester United, Inter, Barcelona, etc.). Indeed, the media broadcasting of football matches and the process of global branding pursued by several clubs have favoured the growth of worldwide supporters' communities.

Against these currents, the Fiorentina football club is an example where the strong local identity between the fans and the club is still persistent, irrespective of the fact that other stakeholders, like players, the coach and the owner are 'non Florentine'. The territorial identity between the team and the fan community is an intangible asset that is crucial to the continued growth and survival of the club. Indeed Fiorentina's fans are repositories of the history and the Viola cultural continuity. They play a role that goes beyond that of the twelfth man: fans do not only support the team by following every match, but through the fan clubs they can speak their voice, they interact with the football club and other stakeholders (owner, coach, local institutions, etc.), and they are involved in its strategic choices. The viola fans play a leading role within the social network of Fiorentina by helping to create value through commitment, collaboration and social participation, which seems to compensate for the continuous evolutions and changes of the technical results, the players, the owners and the coach. The very strong territorial tie existing between the fans and the local context, the attachment to the 'viola jersey' in itself, and the high level of identification with the city and the team make the viola supporters a key determinant stakeholder for the value creation process within the Fiorentina's social network.

Notes

[1] Although the authors have shared their research work, Patrizia Zagnoli has written: Introduction; Mapping stakeholders of a professional club; Towards a typology of sports fans' roles and behaviours. Elena Radicchi has written: Customers: the 'Viola' fans; Socio-demographic features of the 'viola' fans; Fans organizational structure: the Viola Clubs; The social network of ACF Fiorentina; Strategic postures of fans as a stakeholder; Conclusions.

[2] See Zagnoli et al., 'L'identità collettiva viola'.

[3] Associazione Centro Coordinamento Viola Club, Associazione Tifosi Fiorentina, Collettivo Autonomo Viola.

[4] Freeman, Harrison and Wicks, *Managing for Stakeholders*; Harrison, Bosse and Phillips, 'Managing for Stakeholders'; Rowley, 'Moving Beyond Dyadic Ties'.

[5] For network analysis compare Burt, 'Range'; Freeman, White and Romney, *Research Methods*; Håkansson and Snehota, 'Analysing Business Relationships'; Gummesson, *Marketing Relazionale*; Mitchell, Agle and Wood, 'Toward a Theory'; Rowley, 'Moving Beyond Dyadic Ties'; Salvini, *Analisi delle reti sociali*; Scott, *Social Network Analysis*; Wasserman and Faust, *Social Network Analysis*.

[6] Lusch and Vargo, 'Service-dominant Logic'; Lusch and Vargo, *Service-dominant Logic of Marketing*.

[7] Normann and Ramirez, *Le strategie interattive di impresa*.

[8] Freeman, *Strategic Management*; Harrison et al., *Managing for stakeholders*.

[9] Harrison, Bosse and Phillips, 'Managing for Stakeholders'.

[10] Freeman, *Strategic Management*, 25.

[11] Freeman, *Strategic Management*; Harrison Bosse and Phillips, 'Managing for Stakeholders'.

[12] The term 'viola' means 'violet', i.e., a bluish-purple colour, and this is the colour of 'la Fiorentina's' jerseys, hence the fans team formal name *viola*.

[13] The season tickets sales for the ACF Fiorentina rose from more than six million euro in 2007/2008 to eight million euro in 2008/2009. Source: Poesio, 'Poveri, ma belli', 10–11.

[14] The stadium where the Fiorentina plays its home games is named 'Artemio Franchi'.

[15] See Lega Calcio, *Analisi del trend*.

[16] Muniz and O'Guinn, 'Brand Community'.

[17] Sitz and Amine, 'Consommation at groups de consommateurs', 3.

[18] Maffesoli, *Le temps des tribus*, 18.

[19] Zagnoli et al., 'L'identità collettiva viola'.

[20] Ibid.

[21] See Lega Calcio, *Analisi del trend*.

[22] Curva Fiesole is the place to be for chants, songs, drums and non-stop team support; thus it is the area in the stadium where most young people are found.

[23] The number of subscribers that hold a university degree is lower than that with a high-school diploma and a middle-school certificate.

[24] The place where traditionally young and senior Fiorentina's supporters meet up to discuss matches results, technical aspects of the team, players performance, etc., is the 'Bar Marisa', which is located near the stadium Artemio Franchi.

[25] Average number of live spending spectators for each match. Source: Lega Calcio, *Analisi del trend*.

[26] Average number of Sky spectators for each match. Source: Lega Calcio, *Analisi del trend*.

[27] Mediaset Premium broadcasts Champions League matches, while Dahlia TV offers a full package with all the Fiorentina home and away games.

[28] Cova, 'Community and Consumption'.

[29] The Operational Group for Security includes representatives of the police headquarters, local municipality, fire department, health service, besides representatives of the guest team and local fan clubs.

[30] For example, the ACCVC, one of the most well organized supporters associations, has implemented an SMS service to communicate in real time with all the Viola Club Chairmen. This service enables each club to be up-to-date on changes of instructions, new services and general meetings of the Association.

[31] Some fan clubs have registered a trademark – the *Indiano* – expression of the Curva Fiesole clubs, to be placed on their merchandise. In this case the Viola Club seem to provide for the football club deficit, by offering products and gadgets that satisfy the particular needs of fans, first and foremost, with regard to the price.

[32] During the months before the football club's failure, through the local press and other media, fans succeeded in informing the whole city about the financial crash Fiorentina was heading for. They also organized initiatives aimed at increasing the level of protest, such as the famous torchlight procession of April 2001 in the streets of the city centre which involved over 30,000 fans, or the boycotting of season tickets subscription, and so on.

[33] After bankruptcy hit the former owner Cecchi Gori, on 1 August 2002, AC Fiorentina also failed. The same day, in the light of several initiatives, demonstrations, and sit-ins by the supporters and local citizens during the previous weeks, the Mayor and the Sport Councillor of Florence, following the FIGC resolution allowing 'expression' of a team representing the city, founded a new football club: Fiorentina 1926-Florentia Srl, with the Mayor as president. In the following days the football club was transferred to a new owner, the business man Diego Della Valle.

[34] *Lawsuits* contemplated by some representatives of Viola Clubs have been central in expressing their disagreement with the decisions made by the Florentine Court, the FIGC and the Lega Calcio. Those acts were aimed at speaking out against a 'sick' football system widespread among many professional teams which were not penalized as Fiorentina was.

[35] Håkansson and Snehota, 'Analysing Business Relationships'; Gummesson, *Marketing Relazionale*; Mitchell, Agle and Wood, 'Toward a Theory'; Scott, *Social Network Analysis*; Wasserman and Faust, *Social Network Analysis*.

[36] Freeman, White and Romney, *Research Methods*.

[37] The graphic representation of the network is the result of qualitative analysis without the use of specific statistical software. The connections between focal organizations and stakeholders were developed by interpreting the results of interviews and discussion groups.

[38] Network density is the *extent to which all actors in the network are connected*. It describes the general level of linkage among members and measures the ratio of the number of ties that exists in the network to the number of possible ties, if each network member were tied to every other member (Scott, *Social Network Analysis*).

[39] Network centrality refers to an individual actor's position in the network relative to others. Centrality measures the extent to which communication within a network passes through an actor. Network centrality refers to power obtained through the network's structure (Rowley, 'Moving Beyond Dyadic Ties').

[40] Burt, 'Range'.

[41] On concept of 'closeness', see Rowley, 'Moving Beyond Dyadic Ties'.

[42] Following the failure of the football club and its rebirth in 2002, the team went to the well known Italian entrepreneur Della Valle, for the first time ever a 'non Florentine' owner. Although not Florentine, the new owner won support for his operational, technical and business choices. He started a process of creating collaborative relationships in the city, among supporters, institutions and the football team.

[43] Istat, *Indagine Multiscopo sulle famiglie 'Aspetti della vita quotidiana'*.

[44] Taken from the blog of a Fiorentina fan. See http://blog.libero.it/archiaraviola/5735501.html.

[45] Becattini, *Lo sviluppo economico della Toscana*.

[46] Bagnasco, *Tre Italie*.

[47] By way of comparison, the signing budget of a team such as Inter FC, considered among the top international and national clubs is about 150 million euro a year and coach Mourinho's salary is about eight million euro net per season. In the case of Fiorentina, the annual signing budget is about 35 million euro and the coach Prandelli earns a net salary of slightly under two million euro. See http://www.legacalcio.it.

[48] Harada, Saito and Hirose, 'Segmentation of Sports Fans'; Hunt, Bristol and Bashaw, 'A Conceptual Approach'; Kozanli and Samiei, 'Segmenting the Football Audience'; Tapp and Clowes, 'From Carefree Casuals'.

[49] Sutton, McDonald and Milne, 'Creating and Fostering', 15; Finn and Giulianotti, 'Scottish Fans'.

[50] As an example consider some banners written by the Fiorentina fans for the Champions League match Fiorentina–Liverpool, 29 October 2009: *'Our faith is your strength'*, *'Fedelissimi'*, *'A unique city, a never ending love'*.

[51] Freeman, Harrison and Wicks, *Managing for Stakeholders*.

[52] In Italy, the control of the fan club by the football club was justified by the relevant economic support given to the former, which very often in return entailed the possibility for the owners to name the majority of fan clubs' representatives and chairmen. See Papa and Panico, *Storia sociale del calcio in Italia*.

[53] See Sancassani, *La voce dei tifosi*.

[54] For example, for the Champions League match Fiorentina–Liverpool (29 September 2009), some fans from the Collettivo Autonomo Viola launched a twin fan club initiative with the English supporters, called the 'Reds' after the colour of the team's jerseys, welcoming them before the match outside the stadium, exchanging flags and jerseys and expressing their friendship through chants and banners such as 'Reds, your name is a legend'.

[55] Wilson, 'Six Simple Principles'.

[56] Hunt, Bristol and Bashaw, 'A Conceptual Approach'.

[57] Elias and Dunning, *Quest for Excitement*.

References

Bagnasco, A. *Tre Italie. La problematica territoriale dello sviluppo italiano*. Bologna: Il Mulino, 1977.

Becattini, G. *Lo sviluppo economico della Toscana, con particolare riguardo all'industrializzazione leggera*. Firenze: IRPET, 1975.

Burt, R.S. 'Range'. In *Applied Network Analysis. A Methodological Introduction*, edited by R.S. Burt and M.J. Minor, 176–194. Beverly Hills: Sage, 1983.

Cova, B. 'Community and Consumption. Toward a Definition of the Linking Value of Products or Services'. *European Journal of Marketing* 31, no. 3 (1997): 297–316.

Elias, N., and E. Dunning. *Quest for Excitement. Sport and Leisure in the Civilization Process*. Oxford: Basil Blackwell, 1989.

Finn, G.P.T., and R. Giulianotti. 'Scottish Fans, not English Hooligans! Scots, Scottishness, and Scottish Football'. In *Popular Culture. Production and Consumption*, edited by C.L. Harrington and D.D. Bielby, 314–27. Oxford: Blackwell Publishing, 2001.

Freeman, E.R. *Strategic Management: A Stakeholder Approach*. Boston, MA: Pitman, 1984.

Freeman, R.E., J.S. Harrison, and A.C. Wicks. *Managing for Stakeholders: Survival, Reputation, and Success*. New Haven and London: Yale University Press, 2007.

Freeman, L.C., D.R. White, and A.K. Romney, eds. *Research Methods in Social Network Analysis*. Fairfax, VA: George Mason University Press, 1992.

Gummesson, E. *Marketing Relazionale*. Milano: Hoepli, 2006.

Håkansson, H., and I. Snehota. 'Analyzing Business Relationships'. In *Understanding Business Markets*, edited by D. Ford, 151–75. London: The Dryden Press, 1995.

Harada, M., R. Saito, and M. Hirose. 'Segmentation of Sports Fans Using the Experiential Value Scale'. Conference Proceedings, 17th Annual European Sport management Conference EASM, Amsterdam, 16–19 September 2009.

Harrison, J.S., D.A. Bosse, and R.A. Phillips. 'Managing for Stakeholders, Stakeholder Utility Functions and Competitive Advantage'. Working Paper, University of Richmond, VA, February 2009.

Hunt, K.A., T. Bristol, and R.E. Bashaw. 'A Conceptual Approach to Classifying Sport Fans'. *Journal of Services Marketing* 13, no. 6 (1999): 439–52.

Istat. *Indagine Multiscopo sulle famiglie 'Aspetti della vita quotidiana'*. Roma: Istat, 2008.

Kozanli, A., and M. Samiei. 'Segmenting the Football Audience. A Market Study Based on Live Attendance'. Master Thesis, Stockholm University School of Business, 2007.

Lega Calcio. *Analisi del trend degli spettatori allo stadio e degli ascolti televisivi della Serie A TIM e della Serie B TIM*, 30 May 2009.

Lusch, R.F., and S.L. Vargo. 'Service-dominant Logic: Reactions, Reflections and Refinements'. *Marketing Theory* 6, no. 3 (2006): 281–8.

Lusch, R.F., and S.L. Vargo, eds. *The Service-dominant Logic of Marketing: Dialog, Debate, and Directions*. Armonk, NY: ME Sharpe, 2006.

Maffesoli, M. *Le temps des tribus, le decline de l'individualisme dans les sociétérs postmodernes*. Paris: La Table Ronde, 1988.

Mitchell, R.K., B.R. Agle, and D.J. Wood. 'Toward a Theory of Stakeholder Identification and Salience: Defining the Principles of Who and What Really Counts'. *Academy of Management Review* 22, no. 4 (1997): 853–86.

Muniz, A.M., and T.C. O'Guinn. 'Brand Community'. *Journal of Consumer Research* 27 (March 2001): 412–32.

Normann, R., and R. Ramirez. *Le strategie interattive di impresa*. Milano: Etas Libri, 1995.

Papa, P., and G. Panico. *Storia sociale del calcio in Italia*. Bologna: Il Mulino, 1993.

Poesio, E. 'Poveri, ma belli'. *Corriere della Sera*, 3 July 2009.

Rowley, T.J. 'Moving Beyond Dyadic Ties: A Network Theory of Stakeholder Influences Author(s)'. *The Academy of Management Review* 22, no. 4 (October, 1997): 887–910.

Salvini, A., ed. *Analisi delle reti sociali: teorie, metodi, applicazioni*. Milano: Franco Angeli, 2007.

Sancassani, M. *La voce dei tifosi*, Italian Federation of Football Club supporters, June 2009.

Scott, J. *Social Network Analysis: A Handbook*. London: Sage, 2000.

Sitz, L., and A. Amine. 'Consommation at groups de consommateurs, de la tribu postmoderne aux communautés de marque: Pour une clarification des concepts'. Colloque 'Societè et Consommation', Rouen, 11–12 March 2004.

Sutton, W.A., M.A. McDonald, and G.R. Milne. 'Creating and Fostering Fan Identification in Professional Sports'. *Sport Marketing Quarterly* 6, no. 1 (1997): 15–22.

Tapp, A., and J. Clowes. 'From Carefree Casuals to Professional Wanderers: Segmentation Possibilities for Football Supporters'. *European Journal of Marketing* 36, no. 11–12 (2002): 1248–69.

Wasserman, S., and K. Faust. *Social Network Analysis: Methods and Applications*. New York: Cambridge University Press, 1994.

Wilson, R. 'The Six Simple Principles of Viral Marketing'. *The Web Marketing Today*, no. 70, 2000.

Zagnoli, P., D. Fanti, E. Radicchi, and E. Lamanna. 'L'identità collettiva viola: Analisi socio-economica degli abbonati della ACF Fiorentina (2003–2004)'. Università di Firenze, Giugno, 2004.

Get into the 'Groove': travelling Otago's super-region

John E. Hughson[a] and G.Z. Kohe[b]

[a]International Football Institute, University of Central Lancashire, UK; [b]Institute of Sport and Exercise Science, University of Worcester, Worcester, UK

This essay sets out the plan for *Groove*, a tourist experience connecting the destinations of Dunedin and Queenstown in New Zealand's South Island, Otago region. Inspiration is drawn from the inter-urban planning ideas of the English architect Will Alsop for the development of a 'super region' to maximize the public benefit from a potential, but as yet unrealized, coordinated tourism strategy. We argue the case for academics to take up an initiatory role as 'public intellectuals', in this case by promoting a tourism experience rather than merely being responsive critics to the plans proposed by government and private enterprise interest groups. Within the argument we advance a position of 'postmodern boosterism', which locates us as the 'soft drivers' of a plan involving tourism development intended for the public good. We make our proposal not so much in the expectation that it will be taken up as an actual blueprint sometime soon, but in the hope that it moves an imaginative tourism idea a little closer to the planner's table.

Introduction

In November 2007 an opinion piece written by the lead author of this essay was published in the major newspaper in circulation in southern New Zealand, the *Otago Daily Times*.[1] The opinion piece advocated the development of a common tourism identity to be named *Groove*, stretching between the eastern and western destination points of the South Island's Otago province. The piece was critical of what was referred to as a missed opportunity to maximize the tourism possibilities of the Otago region, by a promotional failure to present a unified tourist experience between Dunedin and Queenstown. This is to suggest that such an experience exists to some extent at present and that the experience should be greatly enhanced via investment, development and marketing. The opinion piece promoted the idea of a 'super region', drawing inspiration from the 'super city' concept advanced by the English architect and radical urban-planner Will Alsop.

The spirit of boosterism evoked in the opinion piece is reflected upon and elaborated in the present essay. An original position on boosterism – *postmodern boosterism* – is explicitly advanced. Our notion of postmodern boosterism promulgates an urban, suburban or regional strategy somewhat ironically, in the knowledge that it is unlikely to ever be put into full effect. However, postmodern boosterism suggests putting a daring idea into the public realm in a manner that will spark debate, enliven thought about creative possibilities and hopefully have at least some degree of transference into the lived and visited environment. Such is our hope for Otago's *Groove*. The essay commences with an outline of our postmodern boosterist position, is followed by a discussion of Alsop's inspiration and then the specific case for *Groove* is set out. Buoyed by postmodern optimism, and although considering cons and obstacles, we are largely disinterested in inevitable naysaying and our case remains focused on the merits of *Groove's* possibility.

Postmodern boosterism and soft driving

Boosterism is a term approached with some trepidation within urban planning and related academe. Indeed, a distinction can be drawn between what is mostly referred to as 'civic boosterism', as the activity followed by boosters, including politicians, business people and those with vested interest in urban growth or particular event promotion, and 'civic boosterism' used in reference to a loose academic school of thought.[2] The 'civic boosterism school' is critical of civic boosterism in practice because the latter is assumed to elicit the compliance of the citizenry via the dissemination of hyperbole, talking up proposals for particular developments or projects. From a critical academic perspective such boosterism is regarded as a form of 'hegemonic power' wielded in the quest for consensual support from the citizenry.[3] Even more rudimentarily, civic boosterism in action is criticized by the 'civic boosterism school' for playing a binary power game, one level of discourse concentrated on positive promotion, running alongside another designed to discredit groups or personages potentially opposed to the development agenda or to keep oppositional possibilities from coming into public discussion in the first place.[4]

Such linear-directional characterizations of power, developed within the sociological study of organizations from the 1950s, predominated in one version or another into the 1970s. The three levels of power identified by Lukes in the relevant sociological and related literature[5] – the mechanical model of one-way decision-making,[6] the 'two-faces of power' involving prevention of alternative decisions[7] and the exercise of power via consensual sway[8] – may all be regarded as relevant to boosterism in practice, depending on the prevailing mode of power. By the 1980s, analyses of power based on the notion of hegemony – developed in the social sciences in the 1970s in adaptation from the 1920/30s writings of the Italian activist Antonio Gramsci – put focus on the ability of those in positions of power to strongly influence public opinion by consensual means, especially through manipulation of the mass media.[9] The hegemony model provided neo-Marxist and related 'critical' academics with a persuasive means to challenge agendas in a variety of areas involving organizational and institutional activity, including urban and regional planning.[10] This theory of power, as with the preceding sociological theorizations, recognizes power as a zero-sum game in which the interests of some benefit to the foreclosure of the interests of others.

However, by the end of the 1980s an alternative position on power providing a more open-ended view emerged via Michel Foucault. From the social philosophy of Foucault we understand that power does not always operate repressively, nor does it always operate according to unilateral or bilateral ends. Power tends to work through a complex interplay:

> It is never localised here or there, never in anybody's hand, never appropriated as a commodity or piece of wealth. Power is employed and exercised through a net-like organisation. And not only do individuals circulate between its threads; they are always in the position of simultaneously undergoing and exercising this power.[11]

From Foucault's perspective, power is not simply held and wielded. It ebbs and flows and a variety of outcomes are possible. Social agents, more usually regarded within sociological theorizing as subject to overarching power, are not stationed in such a way as to prevent their interest pursuit, i.e., they are not merely positioned at the mercy of *in* power social agents. Furthermore, the Foucaldian position does not assume the existence of a self-interested power elite; agents may act from positions of well defined and exclusionary interest, or they may not.

Such an interpretation of power allows for a reconsideration of boosterism beyond the familiar analyses of 'civic boosterism'. The usage of the word civic within this terminological construct has implied that boosterism is led by town hall mandarins or those within private enterprise who have succeeded in having their interests prevail within public development agendas. A circulatory view of power affords not only a more layered understanding of how these *hard drivers* of boosterism operate, but also the role of *soft drivers* within some boosterist schemes. By soft drivers we mean agents – either individuals or groupings – that are pro-boosterism but not in a way that fully aligns them with officially sanctioned or corporately devised boosterist plans. Soft drivers will establish relationships as necessary to have their boosterist plans put into public forums and onto planning tables, but their alliances to hard drivers will be organizationally arms-length and fraught. Furthermore, we regard soft-driven boosterism to be genuinely mindful of the public interest, whereas hard-driven boosterism may or may not deliberately have such sympathy. Soft-driven boosterism will work according to certain ambitions but will not have tightly defined ends. In this way soft-driven boosterism is postmodern as it acknowledges and even embraces an uncertainty in outcome, remaining confident that positive public returns will be enjoyed while planning is conducted in a multisided context of goodwill.

The inspiration of Alsop's *SuperCity*

Will Alsop's plan for the UK 'super city' presents an interesting example of soft-driven boosterism. Alsop's grand plan was revealed in the appropriately named television series *SuperCity*, which screened on Britain's Channel 4 in 2003. The series presented plans for three linear super cities to be named 'Coast to Coast' (from Liverpool on the north-west coast to Hull in the east), 'Diagonale' (from Birmingham in the Midlands, across the top of London to Southend-on-Sea) and 'Wave' (along the south-east coast from Hastings to Poole). The 'Coast to Coast' SuperCity was further displayed in an exhibition at the Urbis Gallery, Manchester in 2005. A blurb gave advertisement to the exhibition as follows:

> Imagine a future in which the vast M62 corridor is a singular entity, a huge coast to coast 'SuperCity', 80 miles long and 15 miles wide. Here city limits are blurred, its inhabitants live in Liverpool, shop in Leeds and go clubbing in Manchester. Using the latest forms of advanced transportation, SuperCity residents could wake up by the Mersey and commute to an office overlooking the Humber. Air travel from a central hub puts the world on our doorstep. What impact will this have on the traditional definition of a city and the people who work, rest and play in this radical new landscape?

The Urbis exhibition elicited polarized responses. Those who disliked it tended to concentrate criticism on either Alsop's building designs, or his geo-demographic plan for 'Coast to Coast'. Alsop's architecture has been described alternatively, as late-modernist, postmodernist and post-postmodernist.[12] But, whichever category applies, his building design has certainly brought controversy. Perhaps mostly so his design for a 'fourth Grace' building – affectionately and rather playfully named 'Cloud' – to be built on Liverpool's World Heritage listed waterfront. Alsop's commission was hotly debated in the public forum and was eventually dropped ahead of Liverpool's conferment as the European City of Culture in 2008.[13] The buildings Alsop imagined and imaged for 'Coast to Coast' – multi-coloured and oddly shaped – would undoubtedly not appeal to the architecturally conservative-minded but then neither have his known finished works, such as the major-award-winning Peckham Library in south-east London.[14] The designs for 'Coast to Coast' remained true to Alsop's long-stated intention that buildings should inspire fun and enjoyment.[15]

Alsop's seemingly growth-based urban/regional plan also drew criticism from visitors to the 'Coast to Coast' exhibition.[16] Although Alsop has a track record of environmental concern and active involvement in organic architectural design,[17] his claims for the sustainability of the 'super city' failed to placate concern that he was proposing a new 'megalopolis'. Pejorative usage of the term megalopolis dates back to the American urban historian Lewis Mumford.[18] According to Mumford, megalopolis describes a stage of decline in which the city has become overgrown, bloated and an ecological burden to its surrounding region. A number of international cities across time are declared by Mumford to have undergone a megalopolis stage. The first megalopolis he cites is Alexandria of the third century BC and the latest, to his time of writing, New York in the early twentieth century. He especially blamed technological change for causing cities to overstretch their limits. From the 1950s, Mumford believed that mass private ownership of the automobile and the related expansion of road networks had devastated the outer urban environment and beyond.[19]

Alsop explicitly promotes the importance of motor-transport to the extent of declaring motorways the 'lifeblood of the *SuperCity*'. He would appear here to be at odds with Mumford, although Alsop's plan carries the qualifier that traffic should be reduced as much as possible to bus coaches carrying passengers along the thorough-way of the 'super city'. The main function for automobiles would be to carry commuters along tributary roads to creatively designed park-and-ride facilities whereby they would join buses for the majority of their journey. Alsop's plan may be seen as trying to get the best out of systems that are currently in place and in this way he may be regarded as anti-megalopolis. By trying to maximize the living, work and recreation possibilities along an established corridor Alsop also envisions the organic-like regrowth of towns and villages outwith – a hope shared by the Tuscan village admirer Mumford.

We recognize Alsop as a soft-driving boosterist. As an architect he would assumedly stand to benefit should his 'super city' plan be enacted upon and should he gain commission to design buildings along its corridor. But, importantly, Alsop's plan is at heart public spirited and not primarily targeted at self-interest. Despite quipping in one of the Channel 4 television programmes that his own architectural designs should hold sway, Alsop has a strong record of public consultation.[20] The importance of discussion with members of the local citizenry, including children, remained apparent in the *SuperCity* programmes. Alsop the soft driver may also be regarded as a 'public intellectual'. As Bairner suggests in a recent essay, public intellectualism is not usually considered in connection with public activism, but in regard to academics drawing on their expertise to comment within the public realm on certain issues of currency.[21] Such intellectualism is responsive whether or not made in support or criticism of particular public agendas. But need 'public intellectualism' necessarily be confined to the responsive mode? In this essay we assume the contrary position that public intellectualism may also be initiatory. Accordingly, we regard Alsop's – Alsop has held visiting appointments at a number of universities in different countries – *SuperCity* plan as a form of initiatory public intellectualism. We conclude the essay by reflexively regarding our proposal for *Groove* by the same term. Before this we set out the case for *Groove*.

Groove: on the road to an Otago 'super region'

Dunedin: Groove *gateway or the town time forgot?*

A key difference between Alsop's plan for the *SuperCity* and ours for *Groove* is that the former is focused on residence, the latter on visitation. While both plans have respective implication for residency and tourism, the common theme is the interest in maximizing the benefit of cross-regional connectivity underpinned by a currently missing 'integrated rural tourism' strategy.[22] We imagine the *Groove* tourist experience commencing in Dunedin, heading south on Highway 1 before turning west at Milton onto Highway 8 and travelling on to Queenstown. The *Groove* journey will be approximately 280 kilometres in total, variance depending on whether or not interesting diversionary points such as Clyde, Arrowtown and Wanaka are included in the visit.

It seems not unreasonable to suggest that the jewel in the crown of *Groove* is Queenstown, described within its own tourist information as 'New Zealand's premier visitor destination'. Queenstown is well known for adventure tourism, including jet-boating, and for extreme sports such as snowboarding. Queenstown is also a popular place for bungee jumping since the 'invention' of that activity in the 1980s by New Zealander A.J. Hackett. Dunedin on the other hand is the grand city of New Zealand's south, an architectural treasure of the early colonial period.[23] The leading protagonists were largely Presbyterian Scottish settlers who left a distinct flavour on many civic sites. However, as indicated by the commencing part of the aforementioned opinion piece in the *Otago Daily Times*, Dunedin faces considerable hurdles to improve its tourism image:

> In a recent conversation a wealthy and well-travelled Australian friend told me that he regards Queenstown as the most beautiful place in the world. He has visited Queenstown on many occasions, mainly for skiing holidays in the winter. To my disappointment, if not surprise, my friend added that he has never visited Dunedin . . . The immense popularity of Queenstown as a tourist destination is both undeniable and understandable. It is a place of immediately recognisable natural beauty and known for its excellent nearby ski-fields. Dunedin, although being set within a location of coastal beauty, does not feature prominently within the tourist imagination. The reputation of its weather, as bleak and highly changeable, does not help. Dunedin also receives mixed reviews in well-known guidebooks such as *Lonely Planet*, being described as historically significant yet rundown.[24]

Obviously enough, the opinion piece was intended to make a case for Dunedin lifting its status as a tourist destination, by establishing and benefiting from a coordinated connection to the thriving destination that is Queenstown. It was noted that there is currently little promotion in place for Dunedin and Queenstown to be regarded as related parts of a tourist experience. A trip to the tourist information centre in Dunedin's Octagon supports this claim. Pamphlets regarding places to visit in Dunedin and surrounds are stored in shelves on the opposite side of the entrance door to those pamphlets for Queenstown and other towns along the roadway. The *Dunedin Visitor Strategy 2008* (from hereon referred to in reference as DVS) is looked at below in terms of how it addresses this perceived problem. Of course, whether or not Dunedin necessarily benefits from an enhanced tourist profile in connection to Queenstown might be disputed. However, given the almost total decline of Dunedin as a centre of trade and finance, tourism undoubtedly exists as an industry of key promise into the city's future. Furthermore, the development of regionally focused tourist strategies is in keeping with trends elsewhere, especially Australia.[25]

Our proposal intends to put *Groove* on the table as an imaginative idea for how Otago's regional tourism potential might be better realized. Obvious enough at this point, we have chosen to concentrate much of the discussion on the location we see as the most problematic to our proposal – Dunedin. This is not meant to detract from the undoubted benefits of Dunedin, especially the historical significance of its architecture. Dunedin does well to maximize its distinct 'cultural capital' in tourism,[26] but this can continue to be done with a broadened outlook to a regional identity. In short, we believe that Dunedin needs to move beyond its rather entrenched civic identity. This identity, unhelpfully in our view and as suggested above, tends to set Dunedin apart from the greater Otago region. The civic identity has much to do with Dunedin's origins as New Zealand's first post-white-settlement city and as home to the country's oldest university and churches – its historical uniqueness has promoted a form of symbolic isolationism. Relatedly, the remnants of an old-white establishment structure responsible for giving Dunedin an air of civic aloofness still tend to exist, affecting public decision-making on tourism and other urban/regional issues.

The Dunedin Visitor Strategy 2008

In July 2008 the DVS was released by the Dunedin City Council (DCC) in conjunction with Tourism Dunedin (a charitable trust funded by the DCC) and Dunedin HOST (a representative organization for 'local tourism operators'). The DVS mentioned the need to make 'additional investment in marketing alliances' with 'other regions', including Queenstown, but no intention was declared as to how this might be done as a unified strategy. Indeed, the overall impression given was of Queenstown as a rival for the tourist dollar. In our view, a visitor strategy for Dunedin should embrace not a spirit of competition with Queenstown, but a spirit of partnership. The more established rivalry for Dunedin comes from Christchurch. The Australian friend mentioned in the quote above has used Christchurch over a number of years for his point of arrival *en route* to Queenstown. His case is common and Dunedin planners appear not to be proactive in attempting to lure Australian and other overseas tourists entering New Zealand from Australia to Dunedin as a first stop destination. The especial difficulty posed for Dunedin by the existing situation with international air links is discussed further below.

In January 2009 both authors had opportunity to meet with two DCC officials responsible for the implementation of the DVS. Our promptings regarding the prospect of a connected tourism strategy with Queenstown were met with responses prioritizing the need for Dunedin to focus on its distinctness as a tourism location – 'we need to get our own house in order' – prior to any possible plan for cross-regional liaison. A senior DCC official described Otago as a 'difficult beast' and this being largely because Dunedin and Queenstown are 'as different as Venus and Mars' – tourist destinations of very different type with rather different customer markets. Thus regarded, Dunedin's attraction is mainly cerebrally based, Queenstown's physically based. But this viewpoint relies on an assumption that the tourist interested in the tranquillity of visiting historical buildings in Dunedin will not be interested in the action leisure pursuits of Queenstown. This seems a rather limited vision. Apart from possibly underestimating the diversity of interests that an individual tourist may have it fails to acknowledge that the wildlife of the Dunedin peninsula may also be of interest to the nature lover who visits Queenstown. It also fails to acknowledge that the thriving café culture of Dunedin may be of interest to the Queenstown enthusiast, and that travelling families may find something for every member in the range of possibilities offered jointly by Dunedin and Queenstown.

The propensity for silo-like thinking as indicated by the DVS, and its subsequent explanation, appears to reflect the reactive rather than proactive process that coincides with the involvement of a range of government stakeholders in New Zealand tourism.[27] The problem is compounded by the particular central-to-local governmental power structure that holds sway in New Zealand. Governmental authority extends from the centre directly to the district level with regional council bodies existing in a rather secondary liaison capacity. Leberman and Mason's study of tourism in Manawatu on the North Island shows how regional issues can stay off the planning table when decision-making is concentrated with local government[28] and Lovelock and Boyd's study of the Catlins coastal and hinterland region on the South Island shows how cooperative planning is thwarted when two local authorities with jurisdiction over a particular area have different ideas about its tourism promotion and development.[29]

The local governmental bodies of key pertinence to the present discussion are, respectively, the DCC and the Queenstown Lakes District Council. The relevant regional authority, the Otago Regional Council – as per the point on governmental authority made above – is regarded as something of a toothless tiger. Our *Groove* idea would likely be best served by the regional council eventually becoming the prevailing pan-regional decision-making body with the authority of the district councils being relegated to secondary importance. This would involve a fairly radical overhauling of the present political system but a change of institutional arrangement that may well provide a dynamism seemingly lacking in the current centre-to-locality structure.

Overall, the DVS consolidates our view regarding the inability of civic bureaucrats to envision any sort of creative long-term trajectories for their city within a grander regional cultural-tourism project. The DVS expresses an aim, to be developed over the next seven years, for Dunedin to be successfully promoted as a 'premier regional tourism destination for *all* visitors'.[30] The thrust of the strategy is to capitalize on the city's key draw cards, viz., its wilderness, heritage, culture, hospitality and education. The DVS represents the DCC's concerted and calculated attempt to carve out a considerable slice of New Zealand's lucrative tourist market. Tourist expenditure is worth \$18.6 million, and contributes around 9% to the national GDP. In Dunedin, the visitor industry accounts for 6.5% of the employment sector, and generates around \$211 million in value-added income (around 5.2% of the city's GDP).[31] While the DCC appears optimistic about the future growth of the tourism industry, the DVC indicates awareness that Dunedin has not followed the growth experienced in other national centres, particularly in regards to international visitors. For example, while international visitor arrivals to New Zealand have doubled for each of the past three decades, this has not translated into significant growth in the number of international tourists to Dunedin. Domestic travel to Dunedin has shown some increase, but there has also been a recorded decline in domestic overnight stays.

In attempt to address this decline the DVS emphasizes the need for future projects to attract free independent travellers (FITs) as opposed to other tourist groups. The former refer to visitors who have the freedom (essentially, the time and money) to stay longer in and around the city, as opposed to other tourists who may only pass through very briefly *en route* to elsewhere or come as part of a prearranged/pre-packaged holiday group whose experiences have been already tailored for them. In our view this privileging of free independent travelling tourism over other forms is misguided and based on a dubious conceptual dichotomy between visitors and tourists. Furthermore, as another New Zealand, South Island focused study indicates, FITs have a propensity to fickleness as their decisions are made and remade at last minute, from the point of one destination to the next.[32] And nor is the package-tour experience necessarily as predetermined as its stereotype would suggest. Tucker's ethnographic study of a package tour in New Zealand revealed a considerable degree of negotiation between the tourists and operators, the former's responses she describes as exhibiting 'performative resistance'.[33]

While the distinction between visitors and tourists can be made sense of within the logic of the DVS, from our perspective, in proposition of *Groove*, the distinction is unnecessary and unhelpful. We are more inclined to see the experience working in this way: *Groove* welcomes travellers to begin their journey at either terminus. Ultimately, *Groove* is not interested in the tourist or visitor profile but in offering a variety of encounters that provide a multi-dimensional experience to those that navigate its pathways and surrounds. As such, the plan is more inclined to favour 'destination marketing' than tourist profiling.[34]

Getting to Groove: *the problem of air travel*

The future of international and domestic air travel to and from Dunedin, and also Queenstown, presents a major concern to our *Groove* project. Much of the fluctuation in tourism to Dunedin (national and international) in recent years can be attributed to the inconsistencies in airline operations, flight schedules and variable fare structures. Not only so in regard to the city's main provider, Air New Zealand, but also its competitors, primarily Qantas, and the emergent budget airlines Jetstar and Pacific Blue, that fly into and out of other New Zealand destinations. Although, the availability and capacity of flights to and from Dunedin has improved considerably over the years, direct international flights to Australia are still highly seasonal and expensive. A particularly difficult issue within the air travel context of *Groove* is the relationship between Dunedin and Queenstown. While opposing the very idea of rivalry between the two locations, it must be recognized that the expanding air traffic coming into Queenstown from New Zealand centres, Christchurch, Auckland and Wellington, and Australia represents the biggest challenge to our *Groove* concept and to incoming Dunedin visitor travel more immediately.

To both authors, the most surprising aspect of our discussion with DCC representatives was the lack of concern shown about the escalation in air travel to Queenstown and the relative decline in direct flights between Dunedin and Australian cities. An increase in flights to Australia has been spurred by the newer budget airline companies providing competition to the established international carriers. Dunedin had previously faced competition for Otago-bound air travellers coming into Christchurch and taking motor transport along Highways 6 and 8, via the splendorous Mt Cook and the Mackenzie Country and on to Queenstown. But now the additional, if not surpassing, threat is posed by direct flight to Queenstown. The DCC ambivalence to this development was again based on the view that Dunedin and Queenstown draw different travelling clientele. From our perspective this is myopic and a resultant lackadaisical attitude is potentially harmful to Dunedin as a visitor destination. Admittedly, addressing what we see as a problem in this regard is a difficult task. Whether or not, and as to how, competitive advantage for flights to and from Dunedin International Airport can be maximized is beyond the scope of this essay and the expertise of its authors. But as an indirect yet equal shareholder of Dunedin International Airport Limited (a publicly unlisted company) it can be assumed that the DCC can be a key and proactive player in this process, disinclination notwithstanding.

A regionally focused tourism plan such as *Groove* would be able to impact favourably on air travel to Dunedin. Coming back to an earlier point and contrary to the related DVS recommendations, this can be either by way of advertising *Groove* to visitors as a 'packaged' experience or to FITs who would arrive and then find their own way around the region. According to this plan, there need be no rivalry between Queenstown and Dunedin for air services. Indeed, the aim would be to have in place a total compatibility of service – particularly in regard to Australian destinations – so that the traveller can arrive at one end of *Groove* and depart from the other. The choice of arrival and departure points would obviously enough depend on a person's itinerary, with the possibility of planned attendance of a set event being in some cases the determinant. In this regard, sport has the potential to become a key factor.

Sporting Groove

Groove will benefit from a regional brand embedded within a convincing and significant cultural identity. New Zealand is somewhat justifiably known as a 'sport mad' country, national pride accruing over the years from New Zealand's not inconsiderable achievements in international sporting arenas and domains. Whatever criticisms might be levelled at the country's jingoistic sporting mentality, it is difficult to deny the impact that New Zealand's participation in global sporting cultures has had on national and local tourism, as evidenced in the recent rugby tournaments which have been used as a platform to promote the Tourism Board's '100% Pure' New Zealand branding. While not to the same extent as other main centres, Dunedin has basked in some of the tourism benefits from the infrequent international and national sporting fixtures. Sporting tourism also holds promise for Queenstown.

Accordingly, opportunity exists for *Groove* to enhance its cohesive identity via the promotion of sport. Within a future plan, we envisage Queenstown becoming a centre of cricket in New Zealand. Queenstown's no. 1 cricket ground has already hosted one-day internationals and has the potential of being upgraded to an international test-match facility. In short, Queenstown would become the southern home of cricket in New Zealand – permanent home to the State Championship team the Otago Volts and a regular test-match location for the New Zealand Black Caps. Connected to the cricket ground is the Queenstown Events Centre. From March 2009 an aquatic centre has become part of the complex, fuelling the not fanciful pretension of the development of a 'sports centre of excellence'. The Queenstown Events Centre has already emerged as a facility that can attract sport-related functions of the highest calibre. In April 2009 the Oceania National Olympic Committee held its annual meeting in Queenstown with Jacques Rogge, International Olympic Committee President, and Sebastian Coe, Chair of the Organising Committee for the London Olympic Games, in attendance.

While Queenstown would become the home of cricket, Dunedin would continue, and be enhanced, as the home of rugby. The profile of the Otago team in the National Provincial Championship is well established and an international sports profile has been brought to southern New Zealand by the Highlanders in the Super 14s competition that brings leading New Zealand rugby teams together into competition with teams of similar status in Australia and South Africa. The Highlanders 'unite' three rugby regions – Otago, North Otago and Southland – under the one banner. Within our planned 'super region' the Highlanders would become the 'Southern Groove' – a rugby team representative of the south of the South Island, both physically and symbolically located at the coastal gateway of the South's key destination – viz., Dunedin in *Groove*. This ambition for the enhancement of rugby in Dunedin must be matched by the delivery of a stadium of international standard.

Heated public debate in Dunedin has waged over the last few years over the proposed building of a 'multi-purpose' stadium in the rundown end of the city's University district.[35] Various points have been made against the building of the stadium, three negativities stand out: (1) the stadium should not be built at additional taxpayer expense; (2) the stadium will become a 'white elephant' as there is not enough rugby played in Dunedin to warrant the building of a large scale stadium; (3) Dunedin already has an adequate rugby venue at the existing Carisbrook Stadium towards the city's southern end. Whether or not and the extent to which taxpayer money should fund a stadium is a moot point, but those in support of the plan emphasize that the stadium would be used for more than rugby and be a major social forum for various events on the civic calendar.

This consideration also has relevance in counter to the second above objection. Less contentious, in our view, is the third objection. The existing Carisbrook stadium is clearly on the outer margins of suitability for international sporting events of any kind and without a new stadium or at the very least significant upgrading of Carisbrook, Dunedin would lose international sporting status altogether.

At the time of writing, the building of the new stadium is under construction, its opening planned to coincide with the 2011 Rugby World Cup to be played in New Zealand. The stadium, designed by the well known stadium specialists Populous (formerly HOK Sports), is to be completed by the New Zealand firm Warren and Mahoney. The stadium is to carry the name of its main commercial backer Forsyth Barr (an investment banking firm) but agreement has been reached with the International Rugby Board (IRB) that during the World Cup the stadium will be de-branded and referred to simply as the Dunedin or Otago Stadium. Dunedin – whether at the new stadium or the existing Carisbrook – is scheduled to host three 'pool' matches during the World Cup. The finals matches are to be played in Auckland, Christchurch and Wellington. Had Dunedin had a stadium of the kind currently being built at the time of the World Cup planning, it is arguable that the city may have enjoyed a fixture of higher profile than has been allotted by the IRB.

The stadium is to receive approximately 10 million dollars (NZD) in funding from the University of Otago, which will have teaching and other facilities within the stadium complex. It will fit into an overall regeneration of the university precinct and is to be located upon what will be known as University Plaza. The plan, as announced by the University of Otago's vice-chancellor, is for the stadium to be incorporated into an 'important campus hub where students and citizens can mix'.[36] More than simply overcoming the traditional town-and-gown rivalry this plan has the ambition of extending or recreating the urban leisure centre of Dunedin to stretch from the new stadium on the harbour to and along the length of Dunedin's current high street. In her chapter in *Will Alsop's SuperCity* volume, Peake claims that sports stadiums have the potential to take on an 'iconic' status within cities, but to do so – unlike most football stadiums in the UK – require a presence either in or in close proximity to the urban heart.[37] The new Dunedin stadium is being built with a view to offering this potential.

The plan for *Groove* to become the base for southern sport teams with a national or international profile extends to netball. A similar arrangement can be put into place for netball as that for rugby. In 2008, a new elite southern hemisphere competition, the ANZ Championship, was established for teams from New Zealand and Australia. The super-league required the amalgamation of the pre-existing teams within the New Zealand National Bank Cup league. In southern New Zealand this resulted in the unification of the Otago Rebels and the outstanding Southern Sting to form the Southern Steele. While at the current time the team is largely based in Invercargill, we suggest that the team 'relocate' to *Groove* and be re-branded as Southern *Groove* – Netball. The team would play some games in Invercargill, given the popularity of the sport in that town, but its headquarters, along with Southern *Groove* – Rugby, would be at the new sport stadium in Dunedin. To have *Groove* sport teams located in Dunedin would, of course, not only benefit the city's economy and regional profile, but the relocation would be advantageous for trajectories of the main *Groove*; specifically, the State Highway 1 link between Dunedin and Invercargill (approximately 200 kilometres apart). Related economic spin-off benefits could be had by smaller centres such as Balclutha and Gore, which currently suffer the brunt of economic downturn. The physical and economic relationship between Dunedin and Invercargill is currently sustained largely on agricultural trade and associated traffic, but in the *Groove* extension plan the link takes on a new significance as a feeder route for our southern cultural travellers.

Diverse Groove

Of course, there is a long road between Dunedin and Queenstown and *Groove* must have key points of excitement and interest along the way. Such locations as Lawrence, Alexandra and Cromwell must assume a secondary prominence within the 'super region' and in turn reap the benefits that association with *Groove* affords. Given the non-existence of a rail system across Otago, Highway 8 from the Milton turn-off serves as *Groove's* land transport route. Given this circumstance, bus coach services are our preferred system of travel and we envisage a *Groove* tour package involving coach travel as a key part of the promotion. However, as suggested by Becken further development in coach touring in New Zealand requires mindfulness of limitation to environmental damage.[38] Accordingly, we want *Groove* auto-bus travel to be involved in a broader planning framework for environmentally efficient coach touring on the South Island.

Whether travelling by organized coach or in private vehicle, the visitor will use the aforementioned towns as short-stop points so a good standard of cuisine and beverage availability is paramount. There is some indication of current preparedness in this regard. Both researchers have travelled *Groove* on a number of occasions and enjoyed meals of good standard that should find favour with visitors. Notable in this regard is Lawrence, approximately 90 kilometres from Dunedin. Given its proximity to the *Groove* gateway, Lawrence is well placed as either a first or final stop rest and refreshment point. It presently offers five locations for sit-down meals – four cafés and a hotel restaurant – which are positioned on Highway 8. Even with the development of *Groove* this provision is possibly adequate in number, although greater diversity in the range of cuisine would not go amiss. The importance of cuisine to *Groove* is matched, if not surpassed, by that of wine. The Central Otago region is now internationally renowned for wine production with over 30 wineries in existence. Unsurprisingly, then, wine tourism and promotion in the area is already strong, with some wineries joined on a wine-tour schedule, which offers tasting to connoisseurs and dilettantes alike. Many of these wineries have also established relationships with local restaurants and bistros to promote their products. For *Groove*, the intention would be to support the growth of the regional wine industry and to give wine tours prominence within the promotion of the overall tourism experience.

Existing points of interest in towns along *Groove* should receive prominence within coordinated advertising. An example is the impressive local history museum in Lawrence. As the birthplace of New Zealand's gold-mining rush Lawrence is a place of especial interest and its museum contains a number of rare artefacts. With some additional investment the museum could be developed in a way to appeal to not only the gold-mining history enthusiast but a more general audience. We also believe the *Groove* journey would be greatly enhanced by the commissioning of 'public art'. Antony Gormley's 'Angel of the North' near Gateshead and the recent 'Dream', designed by Barcelona sculptor Jaume Plensa in conjunction with local residents and workers, located on a filled mining site near St Helens, Merseyside, offer outstanding examples from the UK of how art projects can become key points of identity while fitting in with the natural landscape.

In New Zealand businessman and philanthropist Alan Gibbs has shown the potential for such projects on his 1000-acre property 'The Farm' north of Auckland.[39] Gibbs, obviously at enormous personal cost, has commissioned a number of well known contemporary artists and sculptors to visit 'The Farm' and prepare permanent large-scale outdoor artworks for installation on the property. Importantly, the blending of art and landscape is crucial to Gibbs who remains at all times aware of environmental conservation and restoration where necessary. Although his example is one of private art rather than public art, Gibbs could offer useful advice on how projects might be commissioned for *Groove*. Art interventions along *Groove* need not be limited to permanent or semi-permanent commissioned work. Lovelock uses the term 'tourist-created attractions' to describe roadside interventions made by tourists themselves, such as a 'shoe fence, a bra fence and rock art'.[40] These artistic interventions, to some extent, turn the concept of tourism on its head from consumption to production experience. However, as long as the intervention remains intact other tourists may also 'consume' them as they pass by. In the spirit of Alsop, we see *Groove* as a fun experience and would thus welcome 'creative tourism' along its thoroughfare.

Despite the difficulty of determining sustainable tourism,[41] genuine green ambitions for projects such as *Groove* remain paramount. In this regard we envisage the development of a large-scale visitor site along the lines of the Eden Project in Cornwall. Featuring a dazzling array of plant life housed in futuristic-looking conservation domes, the Eden Project has proven an immensely popular green attraction.[42] Such a facility would help to further promote the eco-friendly reputation of the Otago region[43] and add to the diversity of the *Groove* experience. A committee of environmental experts would be given the brief to determine the location of *Green Groove* at an appropriate place in proximity to Highway 8. An environmental leisure image for *Groove* has already been established by the Otago Rail Trail (ORT), a gravel track for cycling, walking and horse-riding set on a former rail line. The town of Alexandra provides *Groove's* point of intersection with the ORT and from here tourists have the option of making the relatively short eight kilometre journey from Alexandra to Clyde, the more adventurous can take the 144 kilometre journey from Alexandra to Middlemarch north of Dunedin. As well as providing an environmentally friendly leisure experience the ORT has provided an economic boost to the Central Otago Region.[44] Incorporation into the *Groove* plan should serve to enhance this benefit.

The environmental outlook for *Groove* involves respect for land and the other natural elements. Related to this respect is the need for planning to involve consultation with the indigenous Māori people of the area.[45] The Ngai Tahu iwi (tribe), the indigenous people for most of the South Island are involved in a number of tourism ventures and we would hope for their related involvement in the design and implementation of *Groove*. As novel as we regard *Groove* to be, the template does interestingly mirror ancient trading routes between the South Island's east and west coast lakes districts. Hopefully, in consultation with Ngai Tahu, *Groove* could be developed in a way that promotes regional Māori heritage and identity.[46] Should Māori wish to have distinct cultural and arts sites developed within *Groove*, then this should be prioritized within planning. It is our intention that our soft-boosterist and publicly spirited approach to tourism planning be favourable to the Māori worldview.

Groove: a project in 'public intellectualism'

The case for *Groove* has been presented in terms of initiatory public intellectualism, outlined earlier in the essay. The initiatory approach is somewhat unusual for academics as they are inclined to work responsively by critiquing policy agendas and proposals from either government, the private sector or a mixture of both. By putting forward the idea for *Groove* our intention has been to enunciate a plan that may influence the actual development of a unified tourist strategy for Otago into the future. We are under no illusion of our essay being the blueprint for a plan that will be enacted any time soon. A previous submission was made by the lead author to the DCC in answer to an open call to the public in advance of the DVS. The published DVS gives no indication that the recommendations of this submission were taken into consideration by its formulators.

However, rejection on one occasion does not serve as a deterrent to the perseverant and the present authors may well take the *Groove* idea forward in another public forum with renewed vigour. Admittedly, our plan raises a good many challenges should it come to implementation, but in the spirit of postmodern boosterism, *à la* Alsop, this is not in itself problematic. The purpose is to generate the public debate and have the details regarding funding, sponsorship, planning and development, and maintenance thrashed out once the proposal moves onto the table for serious consideration. As articulators with a non-vested interest, public intellectuals (including but not exclusively academics) are well placed to initiate and soft-drive tourist development proposals that are daring and intended to be publicly beneficial. We regard this as a key claim in general (i.e., beyond the proposed project) for the type of interventionism advocated in this essay. Accordingly, we put forward the *Groove* idea in sincerity that it may eventually prove inspirational to actual outcomes, but also as encouragement to academics with an interest in tourism planning to have a proactive and original voice.

Notes

[1] J. Hughson, 'Getting into the Groove', opinion piece, *Otago Daily Times*, 17 November 2007.
[2] Waitt, 'The Olympic Spirit'.
[3] Ibid., 249.
[4] Short, 'Urban Imagineers'.
[5] Lukes, *Power*.
[6] Dahl, 'Concept of Power'.
[7] Bachrach and Baratz, 'Two Faces of Power'.
[8] Gramsci, 'Selections'.
[9] Harris, *From Class Struggle*.
[10] Thornley, *Urban Planning Under Thatcherism*.
[11] Foucault, *Power/Knowledge*.
[12] J. Glancey, 'Run Away to the Circus', *The Guardian*, 13 December 2004; Rattenbury, Bevan and Long, *Architects Today*; S. Rose, 'Cladding: The Comeback', *The Guardian*, 16 May 2005.
[13] D. Ward, 'Liverpool Scraps Plans for Cloud', *The Guardian*, 20 July 2004.
[14] L. Barber, 'Firm Foundations', an interview with Will Alsop, *The Observer*, 8 April 2007.
[15] Alsop, 'Towards an Architecture'.
[16] Hughson, 'Supercity or Megalopolis'.
[17] Powell, *Will Alsop 1990–2000*, 162–5.
[18] Mumford, *Culture of Cities*.
[19] Miller, *Lewis Mumford*, 478–85.
[20] L. Barber, 'Firm Foundations', an interview with Will Alsop, *The Observer*, 8 April 2007.
[21] Bairner, 'Sport, Intellectuals'.
[22] Petrou et al., 'Resources and Activities Complementarities'.
[23] Wright, *Old South*.
[24] J. Hughson, 'Getting into the Groove', opinion piece, *Otago Daily Times*, 17 November 2007.
[25] Pforr, 'Realignment of Regional Tourism'.
[26] Apostolakis and Jaffry, 'Effect of Cultural Capital'.
[27] Hall, *Tourism Planning*, 176.
[28] Leberman, and Mason, 'Planning for Recreation'.
[29] Lovelock and Boyd, 'Impediments'.
[30] *Dunedin Visitor Strategy*, i (emphasis added).
[31] Ibid., 1.
[32] Stuart, Pearce and Weaver, 'Tourism Distribution Channels'.

[33] Tucker, 'Performing'.
[34] Pike, *Destination Marketing*; Baker and Cameron, 'Critical Success Factors'.
[35] Sam and Scherer, 'Fitting a Square Stadium'.
[36] *Otago Daily Times*, 26 August 2009.
[37] Peake, 'Smashing Icons'.
[38] Becken, 'Towards Sustainable Tourism Transport'.
[39] Garrett, 'Alan Gibbs'.
[40] Lovelock, 'Tourist-created Attractions'.
[41] Moscardo, 'Sustainable Tourism Innovation'; Farsari, Butler and Prastacos, 'Sustainable Tourism Policy'.
[42] *The Independent*, 18 December 2001.
[43] Dickey and Higham, 'A Spatial Analysis'.
[44] *Otago Daily Times*, 17 June 2009.
[45] Barnett, 'Manaakitanga'.
[46] Ryan, 'Māori and Tourism'.

References

Alsop, W. 'Towards an Architecture of Practical Delight'. In *Theories and Manifestos of Contemporary Architecture*, 2nd ed., edited by C. Jencks and K. Kropf, 298–300. Chichester, West Sussex: Wiley Academy, 2006.

Apostolakis, A., and S. Jaffry. 'The Effect of Cultural Capital on the Probability to Visit Cultural Heritage Attractions'. *International Journal of Tourism Policy* 1, no. 1 (2007): 17–32.

Bachrach, P., and M.S. Baratz. 'Two Faces of Power'. *American Political Science Review* 56 (1962): 947–52.

Bairner, A. 'Sport, Intellectuals and Public Sociology'. *International Review for the Sociology of Sport* 44, no. 2–3 (2009): 115–30.

Baker, M.J., and E. Cameron. 'Critical Success Factors in Destination Marketing'. *Tourism and Hospitality Research* 8 (2008): 79–97.

Barnett, S. 'Manaakitanga: Māori Hospitality – A Case Study of Māori Hospitality Providers'. *Tourism Management* 22, no. 1 (2001): 83–92.

Becken, S. 'Towards Sustainable Tourism Transport: An Analysis of Coach Tourism in New Zealand'. *Tourism Geographies* 7, no. 1 (2005): 23–42.

Dahl, R. 'The Concept of Power'. *Behavioural Science* 2 (1957): 201–15.

Dickey, A., and J.E.S. Higham. 'A Spatial Analysis of Commercial Ecotourism Businesses in New Zealand: A *c* 1999 Benchmarking Exercise Using GIS'. *Tourism Geographies* 7, no. 4 (2005): 373–88.

Dunedin Visitor Strategy: 2008–2015. Dunedin: Dunedin City Council, Tourism Dunedin & Dunedin HOST, 2008.

Farsari, Y., R. Butler, and P. Prastacos. 'Sustainable Tourism Policy for Mediterranean Destinations: Issues and Interrelationships'. *International Journal of Tourism Policy* 1, no. 1 (2007): 58–78.

Foucault, M. *Power/Knowledge: Selected Interviews and Other Writings, 1972–77*, edited by C. Gordon. Brighton: Harvester, 1980.

Garrett, R. 'Alan Gibbs: Collector Profile'. *Art World* 12 (August/September 2009): 124–9.

Gramsci, A. *Selections from the Prison Notebooks of Antonio Gramsci*, edited by Q. Hoare and G.N. Smith. London: Lawrence & Wishart, 1971.

Hall, Michael C. *Tourism Planning: Policies, Processes and Relationships*. 2nd ed. Philadelphia: Trans-Atlantic Publications, 2008.

Harris, D. *From Class Struggle to the Politics of Pleasure: The Effects of Gramscianism on Cultural Studies*. London: Routledge, 1992.

Hughson, J. 'Supercity or Megalopolis: Will Alsop's vision and the place of sport'. Paper presented to the 'Sport in the City: Cultural Connections' Symposium, School of Physical Education, University of Otago, Dunedin, New Zealand, 4 November 2007.

Leberman, S.I., and P. Mason. 'Planning for Recreation and Tourism at the Local Level: Applied Research in the Manawatu Region of New Zealand'. *Tourism Geographies* 4, no. 1 (2002): 3–21.

Lovelock, B. 'Tourist-created Attractions: The Emergence of a Unique Form of Tourist Attraction in Southern New Zealand'. *Tourism Geographies* 6, no. 4 (2004): 410–33.

Lovelock, B., and S. Boyd. 'Impediments to a Cross-border Collaborative Model of Destination Management in the Catlins, New Zealand'. *Tourism Geographies* 8, no. 2 (2006): 143–61.

Lukes, S. *Power: A Radical View*. London: Macmillan, 1974.

Miller, D.L. *Lewis Mumford: A Life*. Pittsburgh: University of Pittsburgh Press, 1989.

Moscardo, G. 'Sustainable Tourism Innovation: Challenging Basic Assumptions'. *Tourism and Hospitality Research* 8 (2008): 4–13.

Mumford, L. *The Culture of Cities*. London: Martin Secker & Warburg, 1938.

Peake, L. 'Smashing Icons'. In *Will Alsop's SuperCity*, edited by James Hulme, 39–49. Manchester: Urbis, 2005.

Petrou, A., E.F. Pantziou, E. Dimara, and D. Skuras. 'Resources and Activities Complementarities: The Role of Business Networks in the Provision of Integrated Rural Tourism'. *Tourism Geographies* 9, no. 4 (2007): 421–40.

Pforr, C. 'Realignment of Regional Tourism: The Case of Western Australia'. *International Journal of Tourism Policy* 1, no. 1 (2007): 33–44.

Pike, S. *Destination Marketing: An Integrated Marketing Communication Approach*. Oxford: Elsevier, 2008.

Powell, K. *Will Alsop 1990–2000*. London: Laurence King, 2002.

Rattenbury, K., R. Bevan, and K. Long. *Architects Today*. London: Laurence King, 2004.

Ryan, C. 'Māori and Tourism: A Relationship of History, Constitution and Rites'. *Journal of Sustainable Tourism* 5, no. 4 (1998): 257–78.

Sam, M., and J. Scherer. 'Fitting a Square Stadium into a Round Hole: A Case of Deliberation and Procrastination Politics'. *Sport in Society* 13, no. 10 (2010): 1434–1444.

Short, J.R. 'Urban Imagineers: Boosterism and the Representation of Cities'. In *The Urban Growth Machine*, edited by A. Jonas and D. Wilson, 37–54. Albany, NY: State University of New York Press, 1999.

Stuart, P., D. Pearce, and A. Weaver. 'Tourism Distribution Channels in Peripheral Regions: The Case of Southland, New Zealand'. *Tourism Geographies* 7, no. 3 (2005): 235–56.

Thornley, A. *Urban Planning Under Thatcherism: The Challenge of the Market*. London: Routledge, 1991.

Tucker, H. 'Performing a Young People's Package Tour of New Zealand: Negotiating Appropriate Performances of Place'. *Tourism Geographies* 9, no. 2 (2007): 139–59.

Waitt, G. 'The Olympic Spirit and Civic Boosterism: The Sydney 2000 Olympics'. *Tourism Geographies* 3, no. 3 (2001): 249–78.

Wright, M. *Old South: Life and Times in the Nineteenth-century Mainland*. Auckland: Penguin, 2009.

Index

ACF Fiorentina 116–126, 131–132 *see also* fans: age of fans 120; Centro Coordinamento Viola Club (ACCVC) 122; football club politics 122; local identity strength 125, 131–132; "minor" team, as 125; "non-Florentine" owner 116–117; satellite television, and 120–121; social network of 123–125; strategies of 131; "viola" fans 119–123; Viola Clubs 121–123

Alsop, Will: *Supercity* 138–139

America 7–30 *see also* stadiums: American National Baseball Hall of Fame 85–86; Baseball Hall of Fame 90–91; leisure expendable income, impact of 7–8; urban identity of 7–8; Washington DC 11; World War II, and 8

boosterism 136–139: Alsop's Super City 138–139; "civic boosterism" 138; postmodern boosterism 137–139; public consultation 139; soft driving, and 137–138

Britain 22–41: differences from North America 31; economy, and 26–8; European Sport Charter 23; events, sporting 29–30; Home Office 25; London 2012 Olympic Games 33–35 *see also* London 2012 Olympic Games; Manchester, and 22; model of sport regeneration 24; New Labour 25; Percy, on 23; Policy Action Team 32–33; regeneration through sport 22–25 *see also* economic regeneration; Single Regeneration Budget 25; Sport England 26

Carisbrook Stadium 45–50, 53–66, 105: blackmail 58–59; cost of 60; Carisbrook Working Party (CWP) 45–48, 64; Dunedin, and 56; "House of Pain" 104; local activities groups 65–66; New Media, and 53–66 *see also* New Media; Our Stadium 61–64; pro-stadium websites 59–62; Special Consultative Procedures (SCPs) 45; Southern Man *see* Southern Man ; test

matches, and 54; "The House of Pain" 62–63

Chicago: "Beirut by the lake" reputation 11; Bears, The 13–14; corporate search for profit 14; Cubs, The 16–17 *see also* Cubs, The; culture-driven urban identity, and 18–19; Navy Pier 12–13; New West Side 17–18"old" stadiums 14; public work programme, projects of 12–13; Soldier Field 18–19; South Armour Square 15–16; stadium locations, MLB 13; stadium locations, NFL; 12; stadiums, and 11–14; Tribune Company, The 16–17; White Sox, The 14–16, 17–18 *see also* White Sox, The

cities 1–6: expectations of 1; irrationality of development 3; positive developments of 2; sports management, and 5

Cubs, The 16–17: community meetings on 17; lights, impact of 16–17Tribune Company, The 16–17; Wrigley Field 16

Daley, Richard M.: public expenditure, and 18–19

Davies, Larissa E.: urban policy initiatives, on 3

deliberation and procrastination 42–51: autonomy or accountability 47–48; Carisbrook debate 43–44; Carisbrook Stadium 45–50 *see also* Carisbrook Stadium; democratic local politics, impact on 49–50; Dunedin ,New Zealand, and 43; length of development 60–61; neoliberal imperative 51; policies or bureaucracies 46–47; "public interest" 48–50; stadiums, and 42–43; studying the process 44; transparency 49–50

Dunedin 139–147 *see also* Groove: Carisbrook stadium, and 56; deliberation and procrastination and, 43; Dunedin City Council 55, 89; internet technologies, and 3; new media, and 57–58 *see also* new media; New Zealand Sports Hall of Fame 82, 88–93 *see also* New Zealand Sports